Cultural Studies in the Interregnum

Edited by Robert F. Carley, Anne Donlon,
Beenash Jafri, Laura J. Kwak,
Eero Laine, SAJ, and Chris Alen Sula

Cultural Studies in the Interregnum

TEMPLE UNIVERSITY PRESS
Philadelphia • Rome • Tokyo

TEMPLE UNIVERSITY PRESS
Philadelphia, Pennsylvania 19122
tupress.temple.edu

Copyright © 2025 by Temple University—Of The Commonwealth System
  of Higher Education
All rights reserved
Published 2025

Library of Congress Cataloging-in-Publication Data
Names: Carley, Robert F., 1973– editor. | Donlon, Anne, editor. | Jafri,
  Beenash, editor. | Kwak, Laura J., 1984– editor. | Laine, Eero, 1981–
  editor. | SAJ, 1986– editor. | Sula, Chris Alen, 1982– editor.
Title: Cultural studies in the interregnum / edited by Robert F. Carley,
  Anne Donlon, Beenash Jafri, Laura J. Kwak, Eero Laine, SAJ, and Chris Alen
  Sula.
Description: Philadelphia : Temple University Press, 2025. | Includes
  bibliographical references and index. | Summary: "This book interrogates
  and refigures possibilities for activist-intellectual work during times
  of social transformation"— Provided by publisher.
Identifiers: LCCN 2024054252 (print) | LCCN 2024054253 (ebook) | ISBN
  9781439924365 (cloth) | ISBN 9781439924372 (paperback) | ISBN
  9781439924389 (pdf)
Subjects: LCSH: Culture—Study and teaching—21st century. | Social
  change—21st century. | Social movements—21st century. | Social
  values—21st century.
Classification: LCC HM623 .C8635 2025 (print) | LCC HM623 (ebook) | DDC
  303.48/4—dc23/eng/20250120
LC record available at https://lccn.loc.gov/2024054252
LC ebook record available at https://lccn.loc.gov/2024054253

The manufacturer's authorized representative in the EU for product safety is
Temple University Rome, Via di San Sebastianello, 16, 00187 Rome RM, Italy
(https://rome.temple.edu/).
tempress@temple.edu

9 8 7 6 5 4 3 2 1

Contents

Defining the Interregnum

Introduction: Cultural Studies in the Interregnum   3
Robert F. Carley, Anne Donlon, Beenash Jafri, Laura J. Kwak, Eero Laine, SAJ, and Chris Alen Sula

1. What Break?   20
   Chris Hall

2. Black and Indigenous Feminist Notes on the Interregnum: A Conversation with Alexis Pauline Gumbs and Leanne Betasamosake Simpson   32
   Alexis Pauline Gumbs and Leanne Betasamosake Simpson with Beenash Jafri

3. A Reformation of a Communist Kind: Class Struggle after the "End of History"   43
   Manu Karuka

Temporality and the Interregnum

4. "Freedom is Near!!!": Insurgent Punctuations in Chester Himes's *Plan B*   57
   Yumi Pak

5. Police-Time 69
   Tia Trafford
6. Blackness and Disability Justice in Pandemic Times: A Conversation with Therí A. Pickens and Sami Schalk 81
   Therí A. Pickens and Sami Schalk with SAJ

Spaces of the Interregnum

7. Decolonizing Gender: Reading Interregnum in the Colonial Disruption of Matriliny 95
   Anna Karthika
8. Banana Republicans and the Capitol Riot 107
   Jorge E. Cuéllar
9. Mobile Privatization and the COVID-19 Pandemic: Charting the Interregnum 120
   Andrew Ó Baoill and Brian Dolber

Perils of the Interregnum

10. Reforming White Supremacy: The Comparative Grammars of Counterextremism 137
    Najwa Mayer
11. The Sea Birds, Still: Spirit Work and Structural Adjustment 156
    James Bliss
12. The Interregnum of Care and the Rearticulation of Hegemonic Safe Space 171
    Sean Johnson Andrews
13. Co-opting Liberation Technology 183
    John R. Decker

Tactics for the Interregnum

14. Afro-Asian Solidarity in the Interregnum: Revisiting Cold War Politics in *Da 5 Bloods* and *Lovecraft Country* 199
    Evyn Lê Espiritu Gandhi and Rachel Haejin Lim

15. NdN Popular Culture: Musings on Cultural Appropriation 212
    Kyle Mays
16. Kanaka Maoli Radical Resurgence: Walking the ʻĀina, Past, Present, and Future 222
    Mary Tuti Baker, Candace Fujikane, and C. M. Kaliko Baker

Contributors 237
Index 241

Cultural Studies in the Interregnum

Defining the Interregnum

Introduction

Cultural Studies in the Interregnum

Robert F. Carley, Anne Donlon, Beenash Jafri,
Laura J. Kwak, Eero Laine, SAJ, and Chris Alen Sula

> The old is dying and the new cannot [yet] be born.
>
> —Antonio Gramsci[1]

> But worlds end all the time.
>
> —C. Riley Snorton[2]

This volume advances a strategic, perhaps speculative argument: that we are in the midst of an *interregnum*—that is, that we are in a time between world orders. Antonio Gramsci, with our addition, and C. Riley Snorton provide two vital ways of conceiving of that in-betweenness that will resonate throughout this volume. Taken together, these quotations articulate a sense of entrenchment in the face of significant collapse that also evokes the enormous potential in the mundanity of such shifts: this is the *midst* of social change. Signs of such change abound: from public conversations debating the end of neoliberalism and shifting geopolitical powers; to mass movements for Black lives and abolition, and global Indigenous resurgence against land expropriation; to the expanding judicial and extrajudicial violences against trans people and reproductive justice, such as in the United States; to transnational complicity with—and resistance against—Israel's continued assault on Gaza and Palestine; to the waning and waxing of the COVID-19 pandemic; to transformations in colonial reach, such as Barbados's official exit from the British monarchy and the United States' retreat from Afghanistan. In staking this claim, the volume seeks to both define today's interregnum and some of its historical precedents and to ask what might lie ahead beyond a return to business as usual. The book itself is thus a political gambit of naming this time of economic, ecological, relational, and subjective disruption not just as a crisis but as a space between, the ground on which to view and shape new horizons both liberatory and horrific. The multifaceted chapters and examples pose arguments that, when taken together, offer an articulation of the stakes of thinking with and in an interregnum.

Cultural studies' material interrogation of culture has a history shaped by its involvement with postwar labor struggles, decolonization, new social movements, alter- and antiglobalization struggles, and contemporary uprisings against austerity, white supremacy, and impending environmental disaster. With focus on the relationships between system and person, field and habitus, and totalities and subjects, cultural studies employs a robust historical materialism that seeks to chart and even change systems as they are lived. By thinking through the interregnum, we can position cultural studies to confront the shifting guise of power and create a model for collective scholarship in precarious times.

In the In-Between

If this is the end of the world, it is not going how pop culture imagined it. The people who are fighting back, fleeing, or adapting to the catastrophes of this moment are overwhelmingly disabled, poor, non-Western, Black and Indigenous people, and other people of color, not the white or white-adjacent, conventionally attractive, able-bodied actor types represented in many Western cultural depictions of apocalypse and its aftermath. And no amount of postapocalyptic media prepared us for the vast swathes of people fighting *on the side of* the apocalypse, actively organizing or passively being organized for an ongoing onslaught of ruination patterned to keep a select elite distant from the worst of it. There are no zombies or aliens, no lab-created virus, no single evil mastermind. Inept as it is, the U.S. government has not fallen, and prisons and police are, in many places, better equipped and supported than ever. And yet each death at the hands of the police and the state, every community ruined from climate disasters, and the organized abandonment shaping the COVID-19 pandemic *is* the end of the world, again and again and again.

However, perhaps this is not *the* end of the world. Perhaps the world has already ended, many times over: it might just depend on who you are speaking to. As the scholar Cutcha Risling Baldy (Hupa, Yurok, Karuk) points out, Indigenous peoples have survived multiple forms of apocalypse; the Ohlone/Coastanoan-Esselen writer Deborah Miranda, for instance, describes the California mission system as "the end of the world."[3] The world has seen many ends and many beginnings. Aimé Césaire eagerly sought, as "the only thing in the world/ Worth beginning[,]/ The End of the world of course."[4]

One major consideration in Césaire's enthusiasm is the world's anti-Black configuration. As Frank Wilderson has articulated, "the structure of the entire world's semantic field—regardless of cultural and national discrepancies... is sutured by anti-Black solidarity."[5] While work in this tradition of what has come to be known as Afro-pessimism posits the end of the world as necessary for the end of anti-Blackness, the disproportionate premature deaths and burden of this "ending" being carried by Black people continue to demonstrate that ends of the world are not *necessarily* patterned to end anti-Blackness. On the one hand, this period is marked by a thousand different fronts, both named and not named as "Black," by which power, resources, community, and imagination are being reorganized by and for Black diasporic peoples. This is both not new to this period and always new; such fronts are often hacked down by racial capitalism before they can take root in antagonistic soil, and yet they still powerfully proliferate.[6] On the other hand, this period is also marked by a perpetuation and expansion of all kinds of patterns and structures of anti-Blackness. We long for and fight for the end of anti-Blackness but find it impossible to claim *this* necropolitical devastation of Black people as the form that this called-for end takes.

Rather than sacrificing the *now* to the past or the future, Christina Sharpe considers what is made during the changing continuity of the afterlives of slavery; this is "wake work... a mode of inhabiting *and* rupturing this episteme with our known lived and un/imaginable lives."[7] It is in the present doing that the future is shaped, that the world can be ruptured, again and again and again. Thinking against teleologies of transition as arrival, Hil Malatino has similarly posited interregnum as "the crucial and transformative moments between past and future... a kind of nowness that shuttles transversally between different imaginaries of pasts and futures and remains malleable and differentially molded by these imaginaries."[8] Malatino's understanding of the interregnum, like Sharpe's, gives weight and power to the now as moveable and moving, shapeable and shaping. Although they decline to address the term specifically, Leah Lakshmi Piepzna-Samarasinha populates the section of *The Future Is Disabled* on the interregnum with "The Stories that Keep Us Alive," positioning the interregnum as defined by the radically open potential and work of living.[9]

These Indigenous, Black, trans, and crip understandings of epistemology, ideology, and praxis adjust and enhance Antonio Gramsci's conceptualization of the interregnum. Gramsci closely relates the interregnum to the concept of conjuncture, which refers to both a particular moment and a particular coming together of various actors. Interregnum is a specific flavor of political/historical crises, one that Gramsci specifies more precisely as the failure of "politics as usual" to solve a crisis of legitimacy. That is, Gramsci illustrates that an interregnum is not merely a conjunctural point of no return or a crisis without a clear resolution. Rather, it is a breakdown in, and a possibility for change in, the order of meaning making itself. As adrienne maree brown has it, "There are a million paths into the future."[10] An interregnum is a temporal locus for the power to transform how we collectively think and imagine, a period when symbolic power relations both become most evident as material and become most possible to alter.

The interregnum is thus defined by in-betweenness, by interposed endings and beginnings, by process, by praxis, by the present. The interregnum as we theorize it is thus focused particularly on what is made possible in the interstices, in this moment of uncertainty and unpredictability. As Malatino draws out, "the meaning of the interregnum shifts if we refuse to place emphasis on what was and what might be, and instead focus on the pause, the interim, as a moment of foment, generation, complexity, and fervor, rife with unexpected partnerships, chance events, and connections fortuitous and less so—a space of looseness and possibility, not yet overcoded and fixed in meaning, signification, or representative economy."[11]

The stance of this volume is that the concept of interregnum and the methods and conversations of cultural studies provide a way to work through the various analyses, strategies, and possibilities that this moment calls for. An interregnum is necessarily a time of uncertainty—the "million paths" are not clear or even yet evident. By gathering a range of positions on interregna—past and present—this volume grapples with the precariousness of what is underway and what is to come. The present is both in and of history and therefore inherits material patterns of power exchange and influence that shape and determine its outcomes. Building from the understanding of temporality Sharpe describes in *In the Wake*, we define interregnal thinkers and actors as those whose understandings and world-shaping powers are situated in the present, shaped inevitably by the ongoing past, and productive of the in-process future.

And yet future outcomes remain uncertain, leaving the "possibility [and necessity] of creating a new culture."[12] The volume also grapples with the language we use to describe the moment. Although it most prominently employs interregnum, how does interregnum relate conceptually to adjacent terms like *apocalypse, the end of the world, crisis, crisis of legitimacy,* or *conjuncture*? Not all of the volume authors are in agreement here. The chapters respond to questions raised by the premise of an interregnum in divergent ways, and it is the position of this editorial collective that such disagreement and tension must necessarily be brought to the fore so that we might reckon with it. These acts of thinking through and grappling with the moment offer great potential for understanding, confronting, and transforming our collective horizon of possibility.

Futuring Work

The otherwise is already underway in everyday practice now. We think, for example, of the Anishinaabe Seventh Fire Prophecy, which states:

> New People will emerge to resurrect the Anishinaabe Nation and culture. Additionally, they will have to choose between two paths; one that is green and inviting, the other that is black and charred. In the prophecy, they choose neither and instead turn around to reclaim the wisdom of those before them, and live a traditional Anishinaabe way of life. If they choose the correct road, it will light the Eighth and final Fire, resulting in a life of peace and brotherhood among Turtle Island's (Earth's) people.[13]

We think, too, of the late disability justice activist Stacey Park Milbern, who understood living as building to be key, intergenerational, world-transformational practice and encouraged us to see the legacies that have brought us to this point as connections with ancestors that can enable us to "demand and entice the world to change."[14] Malatino also posits "a t4t praxis of love" as a potential "blueprint . . . for getting by in the interregnum, which may end up being the only time we have."[15] And Piepzna-Samarasinha notes that crips "create the future *all the time*. . . . We have to fight to have a future, always, in a world trying to kill us, which means daily struggles to survive, create joy and organize."[16] In these deadly conditions, these interregnal praxes offer ways of being in the in-between.

In her speculative novel *July's People*, set in a South Africa where apartheid ends through civil war, Nadine Gordimer uses the concept of interregnum as a framing device in precisely this way, to examine the "morbid symptoms" of the novel's present.[17] More recently, Dartmouth College's 2021 public consortium on the "White Interregnum," along with the collaborative essays on "Interregnum" included in the December 2021 issue of *Social Text*, speaks to the provocative potential of interregnum as an organizing frame. We cannot say with certainty what is to come, but an interregnum—a time of the in-between—is a moment both for pause and reflection, and for generating and powering alternate futures. Black and Indigenous scholars and artists have been making crucial interventions that analyze and imagine what is possible beyond the constraints of current systems and discourses. We heed the prophet Lauren Olamina's words in Octavia Butler's *Parable of the Sower*: "All that you touch / You Change. / All that you Change / Changes you."[18] We ponder the Driftpile Cree poet-scholar Billy-Ray Belcourt's reminder that "decolonization is apocalyptic: entire worlds have hardened around patterns of thinking, forms of sociality, and state-building practices that unevenly distribute life. Decolonization therefore pushes us to live, however precariously, at the juncture of the then and the next."[19]

This is futuring work, the continuous, ongoing building of the liberatory future through the now, a futurity that is the antithesis of racial capitalism, ableism, cis-heterosexism, and imperialism—it is not only that these forms cannot imagine liberatory futures for us; it is that they are designed against such futures. The "work" in "futuring work" (as in "wake work") is key for its emphasis on presence and doing. This is a particular orientation to the past, the present, the future, one in which the present active verb is what separates the interregnum from utopic or dystopic prophecies. As Angela Davis has famously described it, "You have to act as if it were possible to radically transform the world. And you have to do it all the time."[20] The *act* of speculation, the building that which might be, is in the now.

Artists and organizers craft the future work that should lead us through this moment and demonstrate the essentialness of creativity and imagination. Walidah Imarisha coins the term "visionary fiction . . . to distinguish science fiction that has relevance toward building new, freer worlds from the mainstream strain of science fiction."[21] Imarisha sees the space they have gathered for the short stories in the volume *Octavia's Brood: Science Fiction Stories from Social Justice Movements* as "vital for any process of decolonization, because the decolonization of the imagination is the most dangerous and subversive form there is: for it is where all other forms of decolonization are born."[22] Similarly, Indigenous writing and activism is futuring work, says Lawrence W. Gross: "Along with many other Native American peoples, the Anishinaabe have seen the end of our world."[23] Cutcha Risling Baldy likens this to living on after the zombie apocalypse in the TV show *The Walking Dead*.[24] And yet the Anishinaabe scholar Gerald Vizenor articulates "Native survivance" as "an active sense of presence"; this is also futuring work, building through "the continuation of stories"[25] despite these ends of the world.

Black Futures, edited by Kimberly Drew and Jenna Wortham, explores the expansive potential of this ideological work, understanding its collection of cultural objects as something that cannot be comprehensively defined or contained. The editors note, "Blackness is infinite—a single book cannot attempt to contain the multitudes and multiverse. This is just one manifestation of a project that spans millennia . . . a series of guideposts for current and future generations who may be curious about what our generation has been creating during time defined by social, cultural, economic, and ecological revolution."[26] They go on, reflecting a material vision of history unbounded and unrestricted by the failure of the racial capitalist state and its faltering legitimacy narratives: "There is no past, present, or future, nor is there a beginning, middle, or end." They see their work as exceeding temporal and geographic linearity, in a way that serves as "an invitation to create

Black futures alongside" them, an invitation we take up as the potential of interregnal thinking, both positing and constituting Black futures making.[27]

Black futuring work also shapes the science fiction writing of N. K. Jemisin, who, in *The Broken Earth* trilogy, considers apocalypse as ongoing and cycling disaster in a way that does not equate "repeated" with "inevitable."[28] In an interview about the series, Jemisin considers how race-, ability-, and class-based demarcation and hierarchization distinguish those who experience apocalyptic transformation *during* an apocalypse from those who are *already* living it. The resulting shift necessitates a world-breaking view: "You need to change the entire goddamn world... when you begin to understand the scope of forces arrayed against a concept like Black equality."[29] In this formation, apocalypse is not the end of hope. The status quo is the end of hope, and the ongoing, interregnal apocalypse is the answer.

Situating hope in the messiness of transformation, futuring work has been powerfully practiced in recent decades by abolitionist organizers. Summarizing abolition under one definition is difficult, but we might say that it aims to transform through "one million experiments"[30] practices (and the structures around them) that are foundational to society and relationality: how we consider and address safety, wellness, and harm. In *Beyond Survival: Strategies and Stories from the Transformative Justice Movement*, the editors Ejeris Dixon and Leah Lakshmi Piepzna-Samarasinha offer proliferating views of such potential futures in progress, "some of the million different ways 'not 911' can look."[31] From a locus of both disability justice thinking and abolitionist feminist thinking, they gather a collection of examples from those who practice transformative justice. In the foreword to that text, Alexis Pauline Gumbs considers the collection, "a journey beyond what we can imagine right now," and notes "there is no way to beyond but through.... Imagine that a more ethical and loving world can emerge in the middle of the worst muck of racialized, ableist heterocapital."[32] Beyond simplistic utopia, the futuring work they document is hard, messy, real, and already in progress. As Angela Davis, Gina Dent, Erica Meiners, and Beth Richie point out in *Abolition. Feminism. Now.* about futuring work—such as the creation of abolition feminism or the transformative justice work collected and exemplified in *Beyond Survival*—it is "far from utopian, this world is ready at hand, already underway."[33]

Giving stage time and a spotlight to the practice of the "already underway" future, Sins Invalid's *We Love Like Barnacles: Crip Lives in Climate Crisis* (2020) envisions and enacts disabled lives throughout ecological disasters.[34] Indeed, Sins Invalid's foundational work on the principles of disability justice identify it as a praxis of the in-between no matter the current crisis, something that specifically spans past and future: "Disability Justice is not yet a broad based popular movement [but] ... a vision and practice of what is yet-to-be, a map that we create with our ancestors and our great-grandchildren onward."[35] Similarly enacting disabled futuring work, Alice Wong, Jen White-Johnson, and Aimi Hamraie's Society of Disabled Oracles project collects disabled knowledge and practices as prophetic, future-shaping wisdom.[36] Discussing their book *The Future Is Disabled*, Piepzna-Samarasinha celebrates this crip power: "As disabled people we dream a lot of wild shit into existence that the powers that be and ablest reality could never imagine, and we do it out of our places of being written off as 'crazy' or 'asking for too much'—like, yeah, we are Mad / neurodivergent and yeah, we are asking for everything, including shit the abled world doesn't even know exists.... We're told that we can expect nothing, or barely more than nothing, and we counter that by saying we want more than everything."[37] This futuring work, like abolitionist futuring work, is not just about imagination and vision but also about everyday practices in the now that feed rather than stifle that imagination: those of us who are left out of or violently removed from social infrastructure are always already crafting the world we need in order to survive.

To be in the midst of interregnum means to be in a period rife with the potential to transform the world as we know it in liberatory ways, while at the same time state and other powerful actors struggle to foreclose such transformation. As evidenced by debates and conversations within Indigenous, critical disability, and Black studies in particular, decolonization, crip, and abolitionist frames—and the attendant futurities they open up—are current avant-gardes of this interregnal struggle. Artists, organizers, and writers in these traditions theorize and craft the interregnal work that should lead us through this in-between and demonstrate the essentialness of creativity and imagination of an otherwise that is resolutely *not* a return to the status quo.

Crisis in/of Legitimacy

In an interregnum, articulations across multiple social struggles occurring on different fronts are entirely cut off *from legitimate political expression*. Avenues of association, communication, collaboration, trust, and conflict among the people and between the people and the relatively sturdy edifice of a democratic polity no longer function. The routes that would be available to unestablished militants, intellectuals, activists, and others seeking a world beyond established patterns of compromise and reform are cut off. Existing legitimacies waver and, without adaptation and the lifeblood of social support that accompanies it, crumble to institutional relics. Meanwhile, social struggles have social support but no avenues for which their appropriateness can be recognized and result in social change. Revolutionary work is simultaneously somehow socially inconceivable and entirely in the hands of the groups and movements that constitute the politics of the present.

Legitimacy is the result of a dialectic between both mass (although by no means necessarily majority) and institutional recognition. There are numerous potential masses (which peoples grant the recognition) and structures (which existing bureaucracies and institutions grant recognition, from court and elections to industries, families, and media) at play in such an equation, and legitimacy and recognition can happen at various scales. Additionally, successful acceptance is not always necessary for a movement, struggle, expression, or idea to have legitimate political expression; legitimacy and the recognition that grants it can range from recurrent denial to celebrated embrace, encompassing adaptation, interpolation, debate, and refutation along the way. Avenues for legitimate political expression can take a wide variety of forms, and which avenue might be desired and granted depends on the historically specific interplay between society, masses, and institutions at the time of the struggle.

Certainly a significant factor in the current interregnum is how the social has been winnowed for five hundred years down to the barest exploitative hierarchization, from the world-digesting attempts of white supremacist colonialist violence to the past half century's wringing of the forms of media, art, science, and other social structures into purely economic tools. In part, the use of the concept of the interregnum in this volume signifies the culmination (and crisis) of neoliberal ideology and its effects. Neoliberalism here is a historically specific form of racial capitalism; the culmination of neoliberalism as/in crisis is *not* synonymous with the crisis of the entire operating logic of racial capitalism, which exceeds the neoliberal period. This relationship accounts for why the current moment—which this volume attempts to capture—is simultaneously (1) a "break" in the capacity of the status quo to operate, and (2) a relentless, uninterrupted, (un)accelerated maintenance of the status quo.

Even if capitalism's capacity to legitimate itself continues to crumble, its production of and capitalization on differential distributions of premature death continues its roaring monotony.[38] These two pieces constitute each other, so the strength of one maintains the strength of the whole. *Yet these two pieces constitute each other,* so a break in one is also a break in the whole. The shifting groundwork for resistance and transformation, the possibility of what can be made with the break, is what is most compelling about seeing this period as an interregnum. Though *interregnums* are crises and broad in scope, at the same time they are radically contextual and experiential. If, as Franz Fanon notes, the interregnum is marked both by opacity and the inevitability of acting,[39] then theorizing the current moment as a process of history tests uncertain possibilities and demands a future.

Of course, it is not enough to simply declare an interregnum. An interregnum implies the maturation and collective recognition of crises as fundamental limits but with no clear, legitimated leading edge for how to address limitations. We employ interregnum here as a framing device and a tactical term that explores such crises broadly, with room for individual contributors to maneuver and yet with enough specific reference to the political context and conditions that signal an *interregnal* conjuncture. We believe that Gramsci's twin description of an interregnum is at work today. In interregnums, Gramsci notes (1) a "framing" crisis lasting for decades, to which politics has failed to respond in the long term, and resultantly, (2) the accumulation of crises and, with the lack of a significant political response, the appearance of "morbid phenomena of the most varied kinds."[40] We may think of the current framing crisis as existing at least since the economic and fiscal crisis of 2008, itself perhaps initiated by events that marked the turn of the millennium. The crises that have accumulated as a result of this failure to generate and legitimate effective political response are broad; we might consider the acute rise of forms of authoritarian populism around the world; the appearance and re-appearance of fascist, white-nationalist, and virulent expressions of residual right-wing politics; and the state-backed corporate struggle to expand profit through the COVID-19 pandemic so far. The inability of contemporary politics to frame an affirmative and new horizon outside of authoritarian populism or a renewal of neoliberalism speaks to the uncertainty and danger of interregnal times, as well as the possibilities of otherwise answers.

The interregnum is the result of the accumulative process of material relations disarticulated, over time, from the social norms held in place, more broadly, by the polity (or through the hegemony of the state-civil-society relation). As a result, the legitimation struggle that culminates in an interregnum cannot be addressed through the politics that inaugurated it. The morbid phenomena that demarcate an interregnum refer to indications of "the slow death of the old regime and the indeterminate status of the political projects which aimed to replace it."[41] Gramsci notes that although there is a palpable maturation of social contradictions in an interregnum, there is, at the same time, a proportional political repression of the ability to both express those conditions and act on them. The contradictions that press themselves into ever more urgent evidence in an interregnum are, in broad terms, material (economic and embodied) but are reflected in the baldness of social contradictions associated with violence and erasure: settler colonialism, genocide, slavery, imperialism, militarism, gender and sexual violence, and class exploitation. In this period as in any other, struggles from the marginalized and oppressed may establish a leading and, even possibly, a coordinating position across different movements, but political opportunities for any such thought and action leaders become more scarce, and resistance to these movements becomes more fierce.

Crises may be settled politically and not result in an interregnum. An example that illustrates the difference between the concepts of interregnum and crisis is Clinton's crime bill as a legitimated restoration of "order." The crime bill came in response to the Reagan administration's policies: eviscerating health and social services designed to alleviate poverty and replacing them with a federally funded block grant structure to reduce funding for them. Reaganism built crises that were furthered by both subsequent administrations. Socially charged as an outlet for centrist political discontent, the Clinton regime responded within the racial capitalist legitimation framework of neoliberal policies by hardening the neoliberal state's policing role. Policing was legitimated as the ideological "solution" to the material crises of the period, while such ideology was made material through the redirection of resources to policing and prisons; both political parties, across first the Reagan presidency and then the Clinton presidency, extended the crisis, but in the latter instance did so in the name of "solving" the relationship between state and society. Unlike in this example, an interregnum signals the insufficiency of governance as it pertains to the relationship between state and society.

Cultural Studies in the Interregnum

Stuart Hall, reflecting on the emergence of neoliberalism, specifies the dynamic that Gramsci describes wherein the descent into a crisis can give rise to the mobilization of oppositional groups. In doing so, he notes that understanding these crises and the ways that groups struggle to meet them is at the core of contemporary cultural studies. In conversation with Black feminist intersectionality theory and cultural interventions,[42] Hall states, "Such an understanding... rejects reductionism in favor of an understanding of complexity in unity or unity through complexity."[43] This attention, Hall argues, is intimately material, "not merely a local problem of organizing but the theoretical problem of the noncorrespondence of the mode of production and the necessary relative autonomy of different political and ideological formations."[44] This complex, changing, and multifaceted interplay between the social and the structural "is the site of the emergence of cultural studies."[45]

As a form of inquiry, cultural studies is distinctively positioned to attend to history in process, to address both the organizing patterns of culture (such as in art, media, production, labor, finance, politics, affiliations, social movements, and norms) and the lived experience of those patterns ("structures of feeling").[46] We name cultural studies here as a formation with multiple intellectual and activist genealogies that emerge from both the United Kingdom (for example, the Birmingham Centre for Cultural Studies) and the United States (through interdisciplinary scholarship predominantly by women of color and queer people that forms a significant intellectual foundation of spheres such as gender and critical race and ethnic studies, and that has shaped recent decades of American studies), as well as other locations and theoretical traditions that may be less cited but are no less important.[47] Across these distinct genealogies, we see a shared project of engaging and mobilizing culture as a site through and from which structural violence is enacted but also critiqued, disrupted, and transformed.

Cultural Studies in the Interregnum features sixteen chapters organized into five sections. Across these, contributors deploy a range of cultural studies methods to think through, with, and beyond the interregnum. The three chapters in the first section, "Defining the Interregnum," raise urgent provocations around what it might mean to dwell in the interregnum. Chris Hall questions whether there is a constitutive "break" through which we set the parameters for the interregnum, urging us to inhabit the break in between to reckon with the continuities of violence across the past and present. Leanne Betasamosake Simpson (Michi Saagiig Nishnaabeg) and Alexis Pauline Gumbs, in conversation with Beenash Jafri, engage the insights of Black and Indigenous feminist theory, art, and activism to present alternate genealogies and reflections on how we might understand the in-between and its potential. Manu Karuka's deft analysis calls out the liberal complicities of cultural critique and calls for the recentering of class struggle as essential for revolutionary struggle in the interregnum.

Contributors to section two, "Temporality and the Interregnum," draw on Black literature, theory, and activism to trouble normative constructions of time. Yumi Pak turns to the wisdom of the novelist Chester Himes—particularly his conceptualization of absurdity—to argue that the linear temporal framework of the interregnum "privileges an epistemological standpoint of liberalism over all others and simultaneously forecloses the possibilities of different modes of resistance." Tia Trafford considers the persistence of anti-Black violence across time in a case study of policing and the 1993 stabbing death of Stephen Lawrence in London. In conversation with SAJ, the Black disability scholar activists Therí Pickens and Sami Schalk point to redefinitions of periodicity, speed, and apocalypse, exploring the challenges and promises of solidarity temporalities.

In section three, "Spaces of the Interregnum," authors turn to the analytics of geography and space to examine the uneven framing and contextualization of the in-between across disparate locations. Chapters by Anna Karthika and Jorge Cuéllar decenter Europe and the United States in their turns to the Global South. Karthika examines how the introduction of colonial modernity in Kerala required the abolition of matriliny that remains incomplete and unfinished, thus inaugurating an interregnum that persists into the present. Cuéllar's critical genealogy of the term *banana republic* reveals how the term diagnoses the extent of U.S. political disarray and hypocrisy, particularly in the wake of the January 6, 2021, U.S. Capitol riots. The third chapter in this section, by Brian Dolber and Andrew O'Baoill, charts the mobile privatization of space and argues for a renewal of the public commons as essential to this interregnal moment.

Sections four and five are future oriented. Chapters in the fourth section, "Perils of the Interregnum," pose questions about the differential ends and possibilities of interregnal struggle. Najwa Mayer problematizes the deployment of analogy in liberal/progressive criticisms of the January 6 capitol riots, pointing out that speculations on how responses to the riots would have varied had insurgents been Black and/or Muslim fail to understand that event as historically and contextually produced and mediated. James Bliss traces the Black feminist critique Toni Cade Bambara develops across her novels *The Sea Birds Are Still Alive* and *The Salt Eaters*—a critique that not only names the continuities of racial capitalism's violence across time but offers ways of healing through inhabiting an in-betweenness. Sean Johnson Andrews's essay reveals how care and safety are not universal goods: social transformation will necessarily generate feelings of unsafety, discomfort, and vulnerability for those with power and privilege, he contends. John R. Decker's essay troubles the critical promise of social media as an organizing tool, pointing to their co-optations by corporations, governments, and antidemocratic groups.

In section five, "Tactics for the Interregnum," contributors write to and from social movements, meditating on possibilities for transformation. Evyn Lê Espiritu Gandhi and Rachel Lim's essay asks what the potentially radical imaginaries of the film *Da 5 Bloods* and television show *Lovecraft Country* might teach us about how to work through our current interregnal moment. Kyle Mays (Saginaw Anishinaabe) questions the utility of critiques of cultural appropriation as he argues for building Indigenous popular cultures not invested in a colonial politics of representation. Finally, C. M. Kaliko Baker (Kanaka Maoli), Mary Tuti Baker (Kanaka Maoli), and Candace Fujikane engage in a lively conversation reflecting on Kanaka Maoli resurgence in Hawai'i—specifically, the relationships of mutual respect and radical reciprocity that Native Hawaiians and settlers have been forging in the struggle against colonial conquest and capitalist expropriation.

Taken together, these contributions understand cultural studies as a key discipline and set of methodologies to explore this in-between of an interregnum because the groups and movements that constitute the politics of the present are cultural workers. While this term includes those involved in the cultural industries (recognized novelists, painters, actors, etc.), it also exceeds it, just as culture making is a significantly more expansive and nebulous practice than the boundaries by which capitalism is able to profit from it. A recently popularized term that might be useful for reframing cultural workers is *front-line workers*: those most at risk of exposure to COVID-19 were also those engaged in the face-to-face, messy, intimate, dangerous work of building relationality from an unsafe distance. Much more than a profession or aspiration, culture building is a social practice at the front lines, engaged in by activists, laborers, care-workers, and makers as much as by artists and creatives.

ACKNOWLEDGMENTS

The editors and co-authors would like to thank each other, the contributors, and the team at Temple University Press, as well as Leila Easa, John McMahon, Makeda Tadesse, and our anonymous reviewers.

NOTES

1. Gramsci, *Prison Notebooks*, 33; notebook 3 §34, with an addition by the editors of this volume.
2. Snorton, *Black on Both Sides*, 198.
3. Baldy, "Z Nation"; and Miranda, *Bad Indians*, 1.
4. Césaire, *Collected Poetry*, 27.
5. Wilderson, *Red, White & Black*, 58.
6. Kelley, *Freedom Dreams*.
7. Sharpe, *In the Wake*, 18; emphasis in original.
8. Malatino, "Future Fatigue," 644.
9. Piepzna-Samarasinha, *Future Is Disabled*, 175–240.
10. brown, *Emergent Strategy*, 8. We are thinking about this coupled with the future-building work of One Million Experiments (1ME) (https://millionexperiments.com/). See also Bordino, *Interregnum*.
11. Malatino, "Future Fatigue," 644.
12. Gramsci, *Prison Notebooks*, 33; insertion in original.
13. McCoy, "Seventh Fire Prophecy."
14. Milbern, "On the Ancestral Plane."
15. Malatino, "Future Fatigue," 657.
16. Piepzna-Samarasinha, *Future Is Disabled*, 28–29.
17. Gordimer, *July's People*.
18. Butler, *Parable of the Sower*, 11.
19. Belcourt and Roberts, "Making Friends."
20. Davis, lecture at Southern Illinois University, Carbondale, February 13, 2014.
21. Imarisha and brown, *Octavia's Brood*, 4.
22. Imarisha and brown, 4.
23. Gross, "Comic Vision," 436–459.
24. Baldy, "On Telling Native People."
25. Vizenor, *Survivance*, 1.
26. Drew and Wortham, *Black Futures*, xiii.
27. Drew and Wortham, xiii.

28. Jemisin, "Apocalypse," 467–478.
29. Jemisin, 476.
30. The 1ME project cocreated by Mariame Kaba is a website and podcast documenting and evidencing community safety projects. "Liberation is the work and the work is liberation. There is no one answer to how we get free—there are one million." One Million Experiments, About page, https://millionexperiments.com/about.
31. Dixon and Piepzna-Samarasinha, *Beyond Survival*, 9.
32. Dixon and Piepzna-Samarasinha, 2.
33. Davis et al., *Abolition*, 131.
34. Sins Invalid, *We Love Like Barnacles*.
35. Sins Invalid, *Skin, Tooth, and Bone*, 26–27.
36. Wong, Hamraie, and White-Johnson, Society of Disabled Oracles.
37. Neilson and Piepzna-Samarasinha, "'World Has Been Cripped.'"
38. Gilmore, *Golden Gulag*, 28.
39. "Each generation must discover its mission, fulfill it or betray it, in relative opacity." Fanon, *Wretched of the Earth*, 145.
40. Gramsci, *Prison Notebooks*, 33. See also Achcar, "Morbid Symptoms," 379–387. Achcar notes that although this has traditionally been translated as "morbid symptoms," the Italian phrase *fenomeni morbosi* is more accurately understood as "morbid phenomena."
41. Montgomery, "Earth Interregnum."
42. Johnson and Joseph, "Black Cultural Studies," 833–839.
43. Hall, *Cultural Studies*, 185.
44. Hall, 185.
45. Hall, 185.
46. Williams, *Culture and Society*.
47. For example, see Kamugisha, "On the Idea," 43–57; and Keenan and Kadi-Hanifi, "Epistemological Moor-ing," 855–870.

BIBLIOGRAPHY

Achcar, Gilbert. "Morbid Symptoms: What Did Gramsci Really Mean?" *Notebooks: The Journal for Studies on Power* 1, no. 2 (2022): 379–387.

Baldy, Cutcha Risling. "On Telling Native People to Just 'Get Over It' or Why I Teach about the *Walking Dead* in My Native Studies Classes . . . *Spoiler Alert!*" *Sometimes Writer-Blogger Cutcha Risling Baldy*, December 11, 2013. http://www.cutcharislingbaldy.com/blog/on-telling-native-people-to-just-get-over-it-or-why-i-teach-about-the-walking-dead-in-my-native-studies-classes-spoiler-alert.

———. "*Z Nation* Was the First Post-Apocalyptic Zombie TV Show to Feature Native Americans and It Was Bad . . . Bad . . . Really Bad . . . I'm Sure There Was Something Redeeming . . . Eddie Spears Is Cute." *Sometimes Writer-Blogger Cutcha Risling Baldy*, November 18, 2015. http://www.cutcharislingbaldy.com/blog/z-nation-was-the-first-post-apocalyptic-zombie-tv-show-to-feature-native-americans-and-it-was-bad-bad-really-bad-im-sure-there-was-something-redeeming-eddie-spears-is-cute.

Belcourt, Billy-Ray, and Maura Roberts. "Making Friends for the End of the World: A Conversation." *GUTS Magazine*, May 23, 2016. https://gutsmagazine.ca/making-friends/.

Bordoni, Carlo. *Interregnum: Beyond Liquid Modernity*. New York: Columbia University Press, 2016.

brown, adrienne maree. *Emergent Strategy: Shaping Change, Changing Worlds.* Chico, CA: AK Press, 2017.
Butler, Octavia. *Parable of the Sower.* New York: Warner Books, 1993.
Césaire, Aimé. *Aimé Césaire, the Collected Poetry.* Translated by Clayton Eshleman and Annette Smith. Berkeley: University of California Press, 1983.
Davis, Angela. Lecture at Southern Illinois University, Carbondale. February 13, 2014.
Davis, Angela Y., Gina Dent, Erica R. Meiners, and Beth E. Richie. *Abolition. Feminism. Now.* Chicago: Haymarket Books, 2022.
Dixon, Ejeris, and Leah Lakshmi Piepzna-Samarasinha. *Beyond Survival: Strategies and Stories from the Transformative Justice Movement.* Chico, CA: AK Press, 2020.
Drew, Kimberly, and Jenna Wortham, eds. *Black Futures.* New York: One World, 2020.
Fanon, Franz. *The Wretched of the Earth.* Translated by Richard Philcox. New York: Grove, 2004.
Gilmore, Ruth Wilson. *Golden Gulag: Prisons, Surplus, Crisis, and Opposition in Globalizing California.* Berkeley: University of California Press, 2007.
Gordimer, Nadine. *July's People.* New York: Penguin Books, 1981.
Gramsci, Antonio. *The Prison Notebooks: Volume I–III.* Translated by Joseph A. Buttigeig. New York: Columbia University Press, 2011.
Gross, Lawrence. "The Comic Vision of Anishinaabe Culture and Religion." *AIQ* 26, no. 3 (2002): 436–459.
Hall, Stuart. *Cultural Studies 1983: A Theoretical History.* Edited by Jennifer Daryl Slack and Lawrene Grossberg. Durham, NC: Duke University Press, 2016.
Imarisha, Walidah, and adrienne maree brown, eds. *Octavia's Brood: Science Fiction Stories from Social Justice Movements.* Oakland, CA: AK Press, 2015.
Jemisin, N. K. "An Apocalypse Is a Relative Thing: An Interview with N. K. Jemisin." Interview by Jessica Hurley. *ASAP/Journal* 3, no. 3 (2018): 467–478.
Johnson, Marcus, and Ralina L. Joseph. "Black Cultural Studies Is Intersectionality." *International Journal of Cultural Studies* 23, no. 6 (2020): 833–839.
Kamugisha, Aaron. "On the Idea of a Caribbean Cultural Studies." *Small Axe* 17, no. 2 (2013): 43–57.
Keenan, John, and Karima Kadi-Hanifi. "Epistemological Moor-ing: Re-positioning Foucault, Bourdieu, and Derrida Theory to Its North Africa Origins." *Teaching in Higher Education* 26, no. 6 (2021): 855–870.
Kelley, Robin D. G. *Freedom Dreams: The Black Radical Imagination.* Boston: Beacon, 2002.
Malatino, Hil. "Future Fatigue: Trans Intimacies and Trans Presents (or How to Survive the Interregnum)." *TSQ: Trans Studies Quarterly* 6, no. 4 (2019): 635–658.
McCoy, Lindsay. "The Seventh Fire Prophecy." https://www.the7thfireprophecy.org.
Milbern, Stacey Park. "On the Ancestral Plane." Disability Visibility Project, March 10, 2019. https://disabilityvisibilityproject.com/2019/03/10/on-the-ancestral-plane-crip-hand-me-downs-and-the-legacy-of-our-movements/.
Miranda, Deborah. *Bad Indians: A Tribal Memoir.* Berkeley, CA: Heydey, 2013.
Montgomery, Jesse. "Earth Interregnum." *A-Line: A Journal of Progressive Thought* 2, no. 3 (2020). https://alinejournal.com/politics/earth-interregnum/.
Neilson, Sarah, and Leah Lakshmi Piepzna-Samarasinha. "*The Future Is Disabled* Envisions a Time 'Where the World Has Been Cripped.'" *them*, October 20, 2022. https://www.them.us/story/leah-lakshmi-piepzna-samarasinha-the-future-is-disabled-interview.

Piepzna-Samarasinha, Leah Lakshmi. *The Future Is Disabled: Prophecies, Love Notes, and Mourning Songs*. Vancouver: Arsenal Pulp, 2022.

Sharpe, Christina. *In the Wake: On Blackness and Being*. Durham, NC: Duke University Press, 2016.

Sins Invalid. *Skin, Tooth, and Bone: The Basis of Our Movement Is Our People*. 2nd ed. Berkeley, CA: Sins Invalid, 2019.

———. *We Love Like Barnacles: Crip Lives in Climate Chaos*. 2020. https://www.sinsinvalid.org/we-love-like-barnacles.

Snorton, C. Riley. *Black on Both Sides: A Racial History of Trans Identity*. Minneapolis: University of Minnesota Press, 2017.

Vizenor, Gerald. *Survivance: Narratives of Native Presence*. Lincoln: University of Nebraska Press, 2008.

Wilderson, Frank B., III. *Red, White & Black: Cinema and the Structure of US Antagonisms*. Durham, NC: Duke University Press, 2010.

Williams, Raymond. *Culture and Society*. New York: Columbia University Press, 1983.

Wong, Alice, Aimi Hamraie, and Jen White-Johnson. Society of Disabled Oracles. https://societyofdisabledoracles.com/.

1

What Break?

Chris Hall

What interregnum? What break? Surely there has been, of late, little respite from the crush of pandemic fear and death, from the racist violence of the state, from incessant consumption, from the desperate labor of daily life support, from the devastation of climate collapse. The barest of breaks that can be carved out of this edifice turn out to be nothing of the kind, injunctions to enjoy and relax and unplug that cannot be excised from the forces that render them necessary and even possible. The result is the omnipresent, unflappable, sovereign "order" of crisis capitalism with which we have become acutely acquainted in the past decades. If this crisis of crises adds up to some kind of possibility, some kind of much-needed ga(s)p of fresh air that might clear political space for something else . . . Well, what something?

We should not delude ourselves: if by "interregnum" we mean some total break, then we are not in an interregnum. The much-hyped rejection of Trumpism in the 2020 U.S. presidential election, the hope of structural changes in response to the catastrophes of the COVID pandemic, and the ever more fantastical specter of "normalcy"—all of these optimistic promises of literal and ideological regime change largely have ended up signaling little more than the further entrenchment of the neoliberal status quo. As Mike Davis, deeply skeptical about any hopefulness remaining in the Gramscian interregnal framework for thinking contemporary crisis, wrote in March 2022: "That assumes that something new will be or could be born. I doubt it."[1] We cannot simply break the neoliberal order, and it cannot be *simply* broken.

And yet, if we cannot just shut off politics as usual and replace it, we are, unavoidably, *in its break*.[2] It breaks us and breaks over us, and in breaking—not snapping or failing but *roiling*—it seethes and foams and creates pockets for breath and play. In this chapter, then, I move to think interregnum in this kind of break of the sovereign Western state, in its interregnal *un*sovereignty. What might *an other politics*, an *other* interregnum, look like, amid such a cacophony?

If the questions to ask are to remain those of the interregnum, they must be the questions of what is between sovereignty, what is in the interstices of sovereignty itself. And what is this sovereignty today, the hegemonic tendrils of which encircle the globe, since it cannot any longer be simply the sovereignty of monarchs? If the interregnum owes its history to the need to name what takes place between reigns, then it always presupposes a reign to come and centers an "inter" that must indelibly link that reign with the previous; regnal legitimacy depends upon this. This would be as much the case (though in different ways) for a transition of kingship, for a transition of contemporary global governance, for the transitions of aesthetic and critical traditions. As Fred Moten writes, however, apropos Amiri Baraka, attending to the interstices of an assumed order might reveal not inevitability but delicious contingency; in such a break, "syncopation, performance, and ... anarchic organization" might be overheard.[3] If forms of resistance have so far been ineffective or counterproductive, and notions of replacement seem either unworkable or cyclical, there remains another possibility: not against or through but *into*. This would be a matter for not only cultural theorizing but for political theory,[4] for artistic and social and personal and political testimony[5]—how to go *in*. This essay pursues the path, suggested in the volume's introduction, of an interregnum of the between, in what will turn out to be a rereading of, a relistening to, the inflection of the interregnum itself that opens upon the potential for life in the break, within the break.

The interregnum's historical function has been to describe a space between monarchic reigns. Interregnum arose, particularly in Roman law, as a concept to "denote a time-lag separating the death of one royal sovereign from the enthronement of the successor."[6] This resulted in a "state of exception," when normal law was set aside, that then evolved into a transitional (and constitutive) gap in the law itself, a space for "public mourning for the death of the sovereign."[7] In a later European context, "interregnum" came to name "a breach of continuity in the normal executive reign of a sovereign power," the form by which it would designate in England the gap between Charles I's execution and Charles II's ascendance.[8] This interregnum is nothing but an exchange of and within sovereignty, the nod by which a crown passes between heads. This also, however, has the effect of making it the possible space of an utterly radical exception that, far from being constitutive of modern governance, would be the very suspended animation of sovereignty, both within and without it. An opening, a continuity, a mourning, and a new life.

For Giorgio Agamben, crisis points in politics rarely indicate a meaningful site where thoroughgoing change might take place, merely marking instead additional examples of the capacity for producing exceptions upon which sovereign power depends.[9] Where there is crisis or emergency, one finds in this view only "the opening of a fictitious lacuna in the order for the purpose of safeguarding the existence of the norm."[10] This is not unlike the depressing (but so far accurate) critique that each instance of resistance only helps tighten the coil of capitalist dominance. As Slavoj Žižek puts it, "Everyone 'resists' . . . so why not draw the logical conclusion that this discourse of 'resistance' is the norm today, and, as such, the main obstacle to the emergence of the discourse which would actually question the dominant relations?"[11] Activism and critical theory have not so far proved able to harness the fact that global capitalism itself "generates the excesses (slums, ecological threats, etc.) that open up the site of resistance,"[12] similarly failing to halt or even slow the acceleration of the "new barbarian capitalism"[13] spread through the death-making necropolitics of COVID governance. Is the interregnum, then, only another state of exception? Agamben said as much about the pandemic, in 2021's *Where Are We Now?*, though not in a way that does credit to his theory. Is the sense of hope and difference and kairotic action despite collapse doomed to always be precisely what sustains that collapse, propping up the sovereign order we know under the ever-present guise of a *now*, the crucial moment for action that will change everything and yet never does?

Again, the question of an interregnum is always a question of sovereignty. In modernity, the question of sovereignty is also always a biopolitical one, a question about the emergence of biopower, a "power over life"[14] through which the concern of politics becomes "the administration of bodies and the calculated management of life."[15] Thinking with biopolitics means asking what populations are legible in the political milieu and how they relate to the health of the social body, how knowledge is generated and institutions are produced in the maintenance of these populations. Over and above the sovereign power of lawmaking, economic policy, or militarization, sovereignty in the modern world is a biopolitical apparatus that attends to life in each of these fields. Biopower "creates the health and welfare of the population as a properly political problem"[16]—or rather, it creates populations as such and then renders sovereign decisions of how to manage their living and dying. In Achille Mbembe's paraphrase of Michel Foucault, "To be sovereign is to exert one's control over mortality and to define life as the deployment and manifestation of power."[17] Rather than emanating from solitary figures, biopolitical sovereignty issues heterogeneously in the institutions and ideologies that enforce and justify populational management. Here, "living increasingly becomes a scene of the administration, discipline, and recalibration of what constitutes health,"[18] the countless unlocatable decisions that enable and force populational groups to flourish and perish. Approaching the between-spaces of the interregnum through biopolitics, then, unveils how mechanisms of politics institutionalize and *produce* "life" and how it could be produced differently.

What might be sought here is sovereignty otherwise. With a biopolitical inflection, this becomes the possibility of how life itself, as the stakes and negotiated territory of any modern reign, might be otherwise organized and disorganized. Surely it is more than subjugation that we should hope to break, more than populational oppression, more than the rule of a particular political faction, more even than an ideology, more even than white supremacy, more even than capitalism. If the contemporary sovereign order as we know it is founded upon all of these (and so many more) stratagems for the management of life, we might seek not something entirely new, not something after biopolitics, but an *other* biopolitics. Any ethical politics must continue to involve the fostering of life, but analysis of our interregnal condition has so far missed the biopolitical texture latent here. The orderly upheaval of COVID (non)responses, of transantagonism, of police violence, is in each case a matter of populational differentiation. Thinking biopolitically, each of these must also be thought of as entailing managerial strategies calculated to enable the success of a particular vision of life by the removal and suppression of its supposedly contaminating forms. A different biopolitics, a biopolitics of the break, would instead ask for institutional, political, and intellectual strategies that cultivate life within the manifold textures emerging in these encounters, which would necessitate theoretical and practical projects of making possible global COVID survival (say, total vaccination), trans flourishing (say, institutionalized gender abolition), and safety before the law (say, dismantlement of the carceral and punitive state). Approaching these issues through biopolitics allows them to be thought together under the banner of discursive strategies for life. It also discards the notion that these are lists of tasks to complete; what we have instead are potential modes of redirecting power that remain to be thought.

The artifacts of culture have already begun this work. Literature teems with biopolitical, interregnal thought experiments. Take, for instance, Richard Wright's novel of flight from the white supremacist state, *The Man Who Lived Underground*. The work is an experiment of Blackness both beyond and inside biopower, of tunneling within its grounds. It lives in the *inter* of interregnum as an interring, a burial that is not death, not only death but life otherwise, burrowing through sovereign ordered space and seeking another way for living in the place of death. In the breakneck journey of the novel's

African American protagonist, Fred Daniels, from falsely accused murderer, to subject of police torture, to father of a newborn, to fugitive living in the sewers of his nameless city, to, finally, reemergent scion of truth and justice, Daniels re-sees his world as its commonplace links are defamiliarized. This means perceiving relations and space where before things had seemed joined (law and justice), as well as observing relations where before things might have appeared unconnected (law and torture). Throughout the novel, Daniels moves within this physical and ideological between space that is by no means empty as Wright theorizes how we might occupy the interstices of life and what is to be found there.

It is the long middle portion, in which Daniels does actually live underground and has little direct interaction with anybody, that dominates the novel. When Daniels escapes into the sewer, he perceives a break in the world; where there was one world, he now finds two: "He saw the steel cover moving slowly and then it clanged into place. He was still; the upper world was shut from sight and its sounds were muffled. The whispering rush of the water now droned louder, creating an illusion of another world with other values and other laws."[19] Daniels's retreat is a choice made under duress that expels him from the space of communal belonging, but it also allows him to secrete himself within the world's below, as the state above and around him continues its business. Precisely by disconnecting from the formal space of sociality, social relations and their ethics emerge with new clarity as Daniels observes life through the cracks and tunnels of his subterranean abode. His separation is also a closeness, as *The Man Who Lived Underground* experiments with Blackness beyond and within the biopolitical state, literally going within its grounds and living in its under and within.

As we continue to explore the space of interregnum, we must think this not as the task of creating a void, an empty space to start over, but as one of, like Daniels, probing deeper within the grounds of political space, where the synapses of law and life ravel and unravel. Along these lines, Marquis Bey has raised the inviting specter of "a nonplace where we might, finally, live," one that the fugitive practices of Blackness, transness, and feminism set for us the project of discovering.[20] For this we must seek "the space of the between": "Living in the space of becoming other than what we were is where living unbounded happens."[21] The interregnum continues to remind us that we *are* in such a between, making a path and carrying forward the diagnoses of inequity that are the toolbox of a biopolitical justice in which living otherwise is the project, not the deviation. In this way we emerge in the interregnum as a (non)space that might also go by the name of the *khōra*, that "receptacle," that "space which is eternal and indestructible, which provides a seat for everything that comes to be, and which is apprehended without the senses by a sort of spurious reasoning and is hardly an object of belief."[22]

Both the site that holds the creation of the world itself—in the mythology of Plato's *Timaeus*—and the nonsite we see only "in a kind of dream"[23] that has no definite place of its own, the *khōra* marks the world's betweenness, names the interregnum of the world itself, its uncertainty and its future. Far from a gap of emptiness, the interregnum as *khōra* is not the absence of sovereignty but its absolute presence, its gathering in the space of making difference.

To propose the interregnum as a gap, as a full break, would itself be to approach politics "in a kind of dream," to fantasize about setting aside the pain and life of the world and conjuring a new one. This would be to institute yet another binary, another "*bifurcation*."[24] This dream would be too fantastical, too facile—but so too should we beware the hopelessness of morbidity and infertility lurking in the Gramscian interregnum, in which "the old is dying and the new cannot be born,"[25] and its interpretations by such critics as Nancy Fraser, who in 2022 returned to Gramsci to contend that we are indeed in such an interregnum today.[26] If today's crises can be responded to through a programmatic socialist political vision—and either way, they *should*—it cannot be missed that with each revised plan of action the already-daunting list of tasks to be completed lengthens: reverse the effects of climate change, end global white supremacy, create systemic resources supporting gendered labor, unmake sexism and patriarchalism, put a stop to capitalism and its "entwinement of exploitation and expropriation,"[27] and so on. These are political concerns, and they must be approached with political projects in mind—with activism and legislation. And yet the question remains: If we respond programmatically, directly, within the terms of the crisis, will this really enable us to leave the space of the interregnum?

With this question in mind, we can revisit sovereignty in a manner that thwarts Agambenian negativity and the exception as rule, via the *khōra*. If the interregnum is a political condition or situation the primary quality of which is its capacity to highlight our position within, inter, between, the task is then not to create a new sovereign order (of socialism or the United Nations or whatever) to replace the old sovereignty but to make life possible in the between, to disorder the interregnum. Moten proposes that "perhaps political upheaval is in the nonlocatability of discontinuity,"[28] and such upheaval would be precisely the imprecise place for searching out life's otherwise. The interregnum is an opening, not for creating a new order but for fostering the ongoingness of political opening itself, for life lived otherwise, for new worlds. This is life in the *khōra*, the place that "displaces and disorganizes all our onto-topological prejudices," the place of "body without body"; as Fred Daniels witnesses in his time underground, "Everything secret is played out here."[29] Remaking the interregnum, rendering the landscape of contemporary sovereignty livable, open to life, rather than simply replacing it with another sovereign order, means reanimating it and rendering it endlessly plural.

The interregnum is the space where the body itself can become plural, where life that is excepted, excluded, and abandoned by statist biopolitical control, as well as life that has been constrained by the strictures of a well-meaning politics of identity, can come to be otherwise. As Bey writes, "If our aim is to not only 'contest' given ontological and ideological systems . . . but to *abolish* them, as black trans feminism calls us to do, we cannot simply reify all things as ever more and more marginalized identities."[30] This must be a biopolitical future, but it will be a very different one from any system derivable from the contemporary status quo. The interregnum is the dwelling place where bodies and life can be in flux, where an other politics remains always possible. Here the focus must lie, as Hil Malatino emphasizes, on a transness of becoming that can complement our understanding of identity.[31] No amount of doubling down on the populational categories by which sovereign biopolitical order institutes itself will overthrow that order. Interregnum as break and *khōra* is not only the place of displacement for sovereignty; it is (because of this) the place for disidentification, itself the (non)site of, as Jacques Derrida writes, "a third gender/genus,"[32] a place for regendering and transgendering and "fugitivity"[33]—and the question of gender is always also the question and the questioning of race,[34] identity, and life itself.

If I appear to have forgotten the seeming cynicism with which this essay began, I have not. We are not in any open space we could call by the name of a gap; we are not in *that* interregnum and should not wish to be. But we are in *an* interregnum. We all dwell in sovereignty's interstices—none of us simply matches the biopolitical categories by which we unavoidably define ourselves and are defined. Thinking in this break does not kill pain, does not overwrite the need for the dying to have care, does not displace the need for the homeless to have homes, does not obviate the necessity and urgency of enacting practical solutions for anti-trans violence, for anti-Black murder, for heading off the endless list of agonies made possible by the power we know. But it does show a way, not a single way, not a way that can ever be singular, but a means of carving paths into the terrain of the biopolitical logic that makes possible both populational oppression and its identitarian responses. Where biopower has heretofore been leveraged toward the ends of discretionary management, it might instead be exploded into an ethics of fostering life itself—from the brash pretenses of categorical regulation, then, into the mists of political life.

If we are to live within the regnum, clearing paths through an other way, it will be by making the impossible decisions of how to live life in the place of death. "I cannot think the notion of the way," Derrida writes, "without the necessity of deciding there where the decision seems impossible."[35] Rather than seeking to surpass the Gramscian "impasse by seeking a new order beyond it, what would it mean to assume it for what it is,"[36] to forge a way deeper within the impossible space of the interregnum? In this, "the interregnum could itself become the name of an alternative form of political synthesis."[37] We should explore this inter as the space of a new politics, not by taking upon ourselves the task of abolishing sovereignty but instead by othering it. As Malatino asks, speaking of interregnum as a space for nonteleological transness, "What possibilities open up when we cease to run toward promissory futures from pasts that we're (sometimes, literally) dying to leave behind?"[38] If sovereignty is the capacity to render decisions of exception to legal norms, we must seek something different and messier: the ubiquity of the exceptional space of the interregnum as the ever-inchoate space of every decision, of sovereignty itself. In this biopolitical otherwise every exception proves the exception, and sovereign are they who decide within the impossible, urgent collectivity of the spray of life how to subvert its categories. After all, this impossible, undecidable, interregnal period "may end up being the only time we have."[39]

Let us, then, hear Gramsci's familiar line differently. It is tempting to continue to read the lament that "the new cannot be born" as a concern of ideological natality—indeed, as an expression of properly biopolitical concern—an expression of how "general disbelief makes it impossible to reactivate the old ideologies, while cynicism and skepticism makes it all the harder to believe in any new propositions."[40] In the original Italian, the natal emphasis is clear: "il nuovo non può nascere"[41]—*nascere*, "to be born." If that "born," however, is read also as a bearing, a carrying, a natality that means being not only born but borne, borne up(on) (and *nascere* can also mean to "bear"[42]), then a newly ambivalent sense of "the new that cannot be born" rises into view. It is, in this sense, not a question of infertility nor of grief in the face of termination—or rather, it is not only these—but the more open-ended concern of how the new is to be carried, of who can hold it, of why it outweighs any possible burden. How is life itself to be newly born/e? This is to radically shift the terms of the Gramscian formulation: not at issue is the impossibility—the actual impossibility—that whatever would be new cannot come into life; instead, the new is living, it is in life, but it cannot yet be carried; it has not found who will host it.

We can, from here, reread Gramsci with a new inflection. The unparalleled betweenness of Paul Celan's poetry, which burrows within language, forging impossible connections between words, is especially appropriate here, not least because of the great care with which his poetry bears forth the tangled ethics of birth and the host, particularly in his poem "Great, Glowing

Vault," which ends: "The world is gone, I have to carry you"[43] ("Die Welt is fort, ich muß dich tragen"[44]). Here too there is the impossibility of life, the disappearance of the world itself, and the need to find a way to carry on. And here too the ultimate political concern—the ultimate biopolitical concern—might be said to be with natality as well, for "tragen" too implies birth and the bearing of children.[45] Yet again it is not only birth, not only the maternal question of creating new life, that is at stake here: it is how the world itself, how the space of political life, the break, the *khōra*, is to be held and borne. It is a line Derrida has made a great deal of, particularly in "Rams":

> when I owe it *to you*, owe it *to myself* to carry *you*, as soon as I speak to you and am responsible for you, or before you, there can no longer, essentially, be any world. No world can any longer support us, serve as mediation, as ground, as earth, as foundation or as alibi. Perhaps there is no longer anything but the abyssal altitude of a sky. I am alone in the world right where there is no longer any world.[46]

Is this not precisely the political condition of the interregnum? Our responsibility becomes not the founding of a new world or new political grounds but pursuing our responsibility to carry one another through this endlessly groundless space, to make life possible for others and ourselves, in the impossibility of this. Gramsci's lines become an injunction: we must bear the impossible responsibility for carrying new life, together. The question is not of breaking off, of breaking with life and politics and their conflation. It is of finding a way of bearing life within politics, within sovereignty, which will mean remaking the world—constantly, together. Can we bear life, life itself, anew? Can we bear life that is fully political but that escapes constantly from the bounds of the political as we know it—race, gender, sexuality, ability? Can we bear to bear this? And where will we carry it?

To close, then—to close in the middle, such is the essence of the interregnal provocation. When Moten urges us to think "in the break," this is not an injunction to try to produce some total rupture, where knowledge and life itself end in the hope that there is something like "justice" on the other side. Instead, what he asks is that we think within the space of transition, in the "moment between moments," a transition that is musical, that involves listening for the notes of the "universalization of discontinuity" that would usher in the endless flush of decisions before undecidability by which the work of making life possible might go on.[47] As we interrogate the interregnum, as we dwell in the inter that it offers, as we inter ourselves in it, we might do best to think of it as an intermezzo without end, as a place of displacement, for fidelity and infidelity, for hearing and looking, for playing in the space before the coming of difference. "Anyway," as Moten says, "this is just meant to trouble, by disseminating, the break or cut."[48] Not to force a break, not to break from the break, but to live in the break, to make life possible just there.

NOTES

1. Davis, "Thanatos Triumphant."
2. Moten, *In the Break*.
3. Moten, 85.
4. Babic, "Let's Talk."
5. Mandiberg et al., "Interregnum."
6. Bauman, "Times of Interregnum," 49.
7. Agamben, *State of Exception*, 65.
8. Theophandis, "Interregnum," 110.
9. For an alternative, see Agamben, *Open*.
10. Agamben, *State of Exception*, 31.
11. Žižek, *Welcome to the Desert*, 66.
12. Žižek, *Relevance*, 56.
13. Žižek, *Pandemic!*, 127.
14. Foucault, *History of Sexuality*, 139.
15. Foucault, 140.
16. Larrinaga and Doucet, "Sovereign Power," 520.
17. Mbembe, *Necropolitics*, 66.
18. Berlant, "Slow Death," 756.
19. Wright, *Man Who Lived Underground*, 53.
20. Bey, *Black Trans Feminism*, 94.
21. Bey, 103.
22. Plato, *Timaeus and Critias*, 43.
23. Plato, 43.
24. Balibar, "Out of the Interregnum."
25. Gramsci, *Selections*, 276.
26. Fraser, *Cannibal Capitalism*, 137.
27. Fraser, 47.
28. Moten, *In the Break*, 69.
29. Derrida, *On the Name*, 56.
30. Bey, *Black Trans Feminism*, 73.
31. Malatino, "Future Fatigue," 643.
32. Derrida, *On the Name*, 124.
33. Bey, *Black Trans Feminism*, 87.
34. Bey, *Problem of the Negro*, 10.
35. Derrida, *On the Name*, 83.
36. Theophanidis, "Interregnum," 119.
37. Theophanidis, 119.
38. Malatino, "Future Fatigue," 644.
39. Malatino, 657.
40. Theophanidis, "Interregnum," 112.
41. Gramsci, *Quaderni del Carcere*, 311.
42. *Cambridge Dictionary*, s.v. "Nascere."
43. Celan, "Grosse, Glühende Wölbung," 97.

44. Celan, 96.
45. Derrida, "Rams," 159.
46. Derrida, 158.
47. Moten, *In the Break*, 69.
48. Moten, 70.

BIBLIOGRAPHY

Agamben, Giorgio. *The Open: Man and Animal.* Translated by Kevin Attell. Stanford, CA: Stanford University Press, 2004.
———. *State of Exception.* Translated by Kevin Attell. Chicago: University of Chicago Press, 2005.
———. *Where Are We Now? The Epidemic as Politics.* Translated by Valeria Dani. New York: Rowman & Littlefield, 2021.
Babic, Milan. "Let's Talk about the Interregnum: Gramsci and the Crisis of the Liberal World Order." *International Affairs* 96, no. 3 (2020): 767–786.
Balibar, Etienne. "Out of the Interregnum." *openDemocracy*, May 16, 2013. https://www.opendemocracy.net/en/can-europe-make-it/out-of-interregnum/.
Bauman, Zygmunt. "Times of Interregnum." *Ethics and Global Politics* 5, no. 1 (2012): 49–56.
Berlant, Lauren. "Slow Death (Sovereignty, Obesity, Lateral Agency)." *Critical Inquiry* 33 (2007): 754–780.
Bey, Marquis. *Black Trans Feminism.* Durham, NC: Duke University Press, 2022.
———. *The Problem of the Negro as a Problem for Gender.* Minneapolis: University of Minnesota Press, 2020.
Cambridge Dictionary, s.v. "nascere." Accessed January 23, 2023. https://dictionary.cambridge.org/us/dictionary/italian-english/nascere.
Celan, Paul. "Grosse, Glühende Wölbung" ["Great, Glowing Vault"]. In *Breathturn into Timestead: The Collected Later Poetry*, bilingual ed., edited and translated by Pierre Joris, 96–97. New York: Farrar Straus Giroux, 2014.
Davis, Mike. "Thanatos Triumphant." *Sidecar*, March 7, 2022. https://newleftreview.org/sidecar/posts/thanatos-triumphant?pc=1428.
Derrida, Jacques. *On the Name.* Edited by Thomas Dutoit. Translated by David Wood, John P. Leavey Jr., and Ian McLeod. Stanford, CA: Stanford University Press, 1995.
———. "Rams: Uninterrupted Dialogue—between Two Infinities, the Poem." In *Sovereignties in Question: The Poetics of Paul Celan*, edited by Thomas Dutoit and Outi Pasanen, translated by Thomas Dutoit, 135–163. New York: Fordham University Press, 2005.
Foucault, Michel. *The History of Sexuality Volume 1: An Introduction.* Translated by Robert Hurley. New York: Vintage Books, 1990.
Fraser, Nancy. *Cannibal Capitalism: How Our System Is Devouring Democracy, Care, and the Planet—and What We Can Do about It.* Brooklyn: Verso, 2022.
Gramsci, Antonio. *Quaderni del Carcere.* 2nd ed. Vol. 1. Edited by Valentino Gerratana. Turin: Einaudi, 1975.
———. *Selections from the Prison Notebooks.* Edited and translated by Quintin Hoare and Geoffrey Nowell Smith. New York: International, 2020.
Larrinaga, Miguel de, and Marc G. Doucet. "Sovereign Power and the Biopolitics of Human Security." *Security Dialogue* 39, no. 5 (2008): 517–537.

Malatino, Hil. "Future Fatigue: Trans Intimacies and Trans Presents (or How to Survive the Interregnum)." *TSQ: Transgender Studies Quarterly* 6, no. 4 (2019): 635–658.

Mandiberg, Michael, Robin D. G. Kelley, Jayna Brown, and Tavia Nyong'o. "Interregnum." *Social Text* 39, no. 4 (2021): 83–101.

Mbembe, Achille. *Necropolitics*. Translated by Steven Corcoran. Durham, NC: Duke University Press, 2019.

Moten, Fred. *In the Break: The Aesthetics of the Black Radical Tradition*. Minneapolis: University of Minnesota Press, 2003.

Plato. *Timaeus and Critias*. Translated by Desmond Lee and T. K. Johansen. London: Penguin, 2008.

Theophanidis, Philippe. "Interregnum as a Legal and Political Concept: A Brief Contextual Survey." *Synthesis* 9 (2016): 109–124.

Wright, Richard. *The Man Who Lived Underground*. New York: Library of America, 2021.

Žižek, Slavoj. *Pandemic! COVID-19 Shakes the World*. New York: Polity, 2020.

———. *The Relevance of the Communist Manifesto*. Medford, MA: Polity, 2020.

———. *Welcome to the Desert of the Real*. New York: Verso, 2002.

2

Black and Indigenous Feminist Notes on the Interregnum

A Conversation with Alexis Pauline Gumbs and Leanne Betasamosake Simpson

Alexis Pauline Gumbs and
Leanne Betasamosake Simpson
with Beenash Jafri

Alexis Pauline Gumbs's and Leanne Betasamosake Simpson's works make critical interventions into our understandings of abolition and decolonization—crucially expanding our sense of futurity and possibility while simultaneously reckoning with ongoing forms of structural violence. Gumbs is a Black queer feminist poet, writer, and scholar whose recent publications include Survival Is a Promise: The Eternal Life of Audre Lorde *and* Undrowned: Black Feminist Lessons from Marine Mammals. *Simpson is a Michi Saagiig Nishnaabeg scholar, writer, and artist whose recent works include the novel* Noopiming: The Cure for White Ladies *and the music album* Theory of Ice. *We invited Gumbs and Simpson to be in conversation with one another to share their collective and collaborative wisdom on the interregnum. What does Black and Indigenous feminist thought teach us about the interregnum? In what ways does their wisdom critique and challenge the notion of the interregnum?*

BEENASH JAFRI: What are some visions you have for the future? What future-building work do you see or sense happening in our present?

LEANNE BETASAMOSAKE SIMPSON: Over the past few years, I've been thinking about what possibilities arise in this present moment from the responsibilities we have to each other and to all the life with whom we share this planet. It has been catastrophe after catastrophe in terms of the natural world and in terms of all of the ongoing crises and catastrophes that we're facing, whether we're talking about Palestine, trans folks trying to read stories to kids at libraries, abortion bans, anti-Blackness, pipelines, or deforestation. I found myself going back to this concept of the *biidaaban*, which I've written about quite a bit, and I can't stop thinking about it still: this idea that this present moment is a collapsing in of the past and of the future, the present as interregnum. In every minute of every day, there's this possibility that exists for us to build and make otherwise.

Going back to Anishinaabe thought, I've been thinking about biidaaban in my people's home, which is an ecotone, an area of overlap between two ecoregions or biological communities. It's also something that Michi Saagiig Nishnaabe recognized in our knowledge system. This area of overlap or ecotone is sometimes called "The Land in Between" and is between what's called the Canadian Shield and the Great Lakes–St. Lawrence Lowlands. There's an incredible diversity of species from both of these ecoregions in our area, on the north shore of Lake Ontario. I think of those areas of overlap *not* as borders, not as lines we defend violently, but as these zones of increased presence, zones of increased care, zones of increased diplomacy, of generative conflict, where every moment we're collaborating and making the kinds of realities we want to live in. Kina Gchi Nishnaabeg-ogamig is actually a rich meeting place of two distinct biological communities, living among each other to create this rich, diverse, productive ecology.

I started thinking of these interstitial spaces on a larger ecotone scale. Then I spent time at the shoreline—the shore of the lake, which makes sense because Michi Saagiig Nishnaabe are named because we spent a lot of time at the shores of the mouths of the rivers that drain into Lake Ontario. The shoreline showed me another pretty interesting area of overlap on a different scale: I have the water world. I have the terrestrial world. I have the sky world. Meeting and at the shore in constant flux. Of course what becomes obvious is the shoreline is never a line; it's a changing community in constant relation to the species and elements around it.

And then, just last week I went to my reserve, Alderville First Nation. People there have been restoring a tallgrass prairie for the last few decades. The idea that we have tallgrass prairies here as part of Ontario is something most people don't know about because the land is now all farmland and cities instead of forests, savannas, and prairies. In Aldervillle's tallgrass prairie and black oak savanna there are tiny areas of overlap: some places are tallgrass prairies, some are black oak savannas, some are black oak woodlots, and there's a beautiful gradient and flow to it.

I started to think of overlap and in-between spaces because the land taught me to see overlap not as a conflict but as a generative space. For me, the land and water systems that make up the planet are a teacher for those of us that want to come together in coalitions and make other worlds. The ecology (in a relational sense, not a Western scientific sense) of the planet is continually doing this all around us all the time. From this perspective, when states and corporations are intent on destroying life on the planet, they are also intent on destroying any existing templates for making otherwise.

The future I want already exists and is being perpetuated over and over and over again through this cycling of life, through *mino bimaadiziwin*. And our only job as humans is to not wreck that. It's just to fit into this preexisting network of life and to figure out a way of living where we are putting more energy and more life back into the system. So I now approach the future with more humility. I now approach world making with a little bit more humility. I don't need to sit around and think the kind of world that I want to make. That already exists with plants and animals and the water cycle and a whole bunch of things that I don't understand. My responsibility is to work within those planetary forces and make something where I and my human counterparts can live in balance with all those other beings.

ALEXIS PAULINE GUMBS: I'm really grateful for everything you said. Where I am now—Durham, North Carolina, which is fed by the Eno River and stewarded by Occaneechi band of the Saponi Nation and many other nations—was prairie, even though it's a place that's now known as forest and was colonized partially through the forestry industry....

There's a tiny prairie restoration project I got to witness. It blows my mind every time I think about this as an area of prairie, an area of bison, an area that if—well, this is how I know that time travel would also be space travel, right. The earth is not the same across time *or* space. There's something really humbling about that scale of space-time for me.

It's generatively destabilizing to know that this is not at all what it would have looked like without colonization here.

I'm also resonating with the shoreline piece. I identify as a shoreline person. That has to do with aspects of my ancestry: being somebody whose ancestors survived the middle passage, with a lot of ancestors in the Caribbean, and also being someone of Shinnecock ancestry, which literally means "the shoreline people." That meeting of worlds where land meets air, meets water, has always been a place where I encounter spirit. Intuitively I just trusted that; the shoreline is a place where I can hear spirit more deeply. I feel more connected at the shoreline to the actual existing multispecies system that I must be tapped into, and there's a quieting of the systems that capitalism is forcing me to try to fit into.

Now I have more words. I'm actually part of an art project with musician Toshi Reagon, geography theorist Danielle Purifoy, and planning theorist Danielle Spurlock called Eco-Tones, where we're thinking about those overlaps. There's always poetic resonance. I really do think that the universe is a poet.

Similarly, the way that I think about time is in alignment with what you're saying, Leanne. In my education I was taught, "Make a vision for the future!" and "Make it happen!" and "Make a difference!" As I have come into my forties, I've realized—well, one, that's exhausting. Two, it really does reveal a level of hubris that is totally unwarranted about what I can make happen. And it's out of alignment with what I know in my deepest self but also what I see modeled by my elders. I laugh about forty because I'm in the midst of completing—in my permissions process for—this new biography of Audre Lorde, that I've been writing over the past several years. And Audre Lorde identified as a high priestess of forty. She was like, "There's something that happens at forty!" She talked about feeling such a release of pressure, such a deep connection to a power bigger than her clever plans. And she would just lose it when people said they were turning forty. . . . And I turned forty while writing this biography of Audre Lorde. So I feel like she did in some ways, priestess my forty-dom.

In the transition between my thirties and my forties, I realized . . . , "Oh! I'm actually called to show up for the miracle, to continue to hold space for a possibility." And so, future building has transformed into daily practice. I'm looking at what are the daily practices that I can be in that allow me to be in the moment, to be in that meeting place that you describe for us and have been describing for us, Leanne, where the past and the future are folding in.

The scale of the daily practice has become important to me. White supremacy, colonialism, and capitalism—those are daily practices. The choices that I'm making around my relationship with the food system are happening every day, the things that we are compelled to do, even if it's the money that we pay to the power company, you know. All of those things are iterative and happen on a scale of again, again, again, again. And they seem small but . . . the impact is horrific, and we know this from all the catastrophes that Leanne mentioned. The absurd heat of the ocean in this moment, all of those things, are caused by these daily practices. It's a daily practice of forgetting that there are much older systems of ways that things have been done and that there's infinite possibility for how things could be.

I think about what Sylvia Wynter says is distinct and important about this time, as an intellectual historian and a person who's made it her project to think about: What are the systems of thought that made colonialism thinkable to the colonizers? She learned all the European languages so that she could [ask], "What could they possibly have been thinking? What made this thinkable as a definition of the human that is so profoundly inhumane?" She says that colonialism operates from this false universalism that tries to impose a European way of being over the entire planet, on every species, and on every body and to actually define species in a certain way—all of those things that are part of the colonial project. What she says now is that we actually have the opportunity to intentionally operate on a species scale. Because we are aware of things that are going on that we wouldn't be aware of in real time, that are happening in different climate zones, in different ecotones, in different spaces of overlap. So, we're not only in the process of how to be in relation to the species and the forms of life that we're in collaboration with physically where we are. We actually have the speed of communication at this point that offers a different operation of scale, which, she argues, makes it even more important that we don't continue with this false universalism.

BJ: What can we learn from other- or more-than-human worlds, both within these times of "in-between" (a.k.a. the interregnum) and in the future?

LBS: I like how much, Alexis, you talked about practices because within Anishinaabe thought, you are your practices—that's who you are, that's how you relate to the world, that's how you make the world. And those practices and their repetitive nature is something that I think propels you through the thirteen moons, that propels you through these larger lunar cycles and universal cycles. I like embodying practice because within Indigenous knowledge systems, it's that relational practice, it's that context, that is how you make meaning. That's how you make theory. This all starts to shift when we embody practice as a formation or a family or a community. When we start to come together, across differences, and figure out how to get the work done together. This is the fabric of Anishinaabe politics, making truths out of seven different perspectives through communal embodied practice.

One of the things that I try and do in my life is spend time engaging with embodied practice and the political theory it generates and figuring out ways of making those practices relevant and meaningful when the climate is under attack. This makes me very much reliant on this diversity of beings, because even if I'm in my tiny, tiny, tiny home space, I'm still sharing that home space with an infinite number of species, with an infinite number of beings.

One of the things I really loved about *Undrowned* was that I haven't spent very much time thinking with the ocean, because I don't spend very much time at the ocean. But when I was reading it, I was like, well, I spend a lot of time in these lakes and rivers which drain into Lake Ontario, which drain into the St. Lawrence River, which go right out to the Atlantic Ocean—so it's not very many degrees of separation either. I liked, actually, that I relied on you—as a Black feminist thinker and researcher and a poet that I trust—to bring me this knowledge that I didn't necessarily have access to or that was outside of my sphere of influence or my sphere of responsibility. I learned from you, though, that in my life, because I'm living in Kina Gchi Nishnaabeg-ogaming and because I've had elders and language in my life that I've always used that as a medium for understanding the world around me. And what I liked was that you learned all of this stuff from seals and whales—some of them who are also living in captivity—by being present and by being open, by witnessing, and by paying attention. That was generative to me in terms of not necessarily relying on a framing of an elder or a framing in my language, seeing in another layer or a deeper layer. We can learn things from the water, from the oceans and its inhabitants, by being open and paying attention.

Sometimes Indigenous movements get stuck, in that we get good at doing on the level of the individual, but it's more difficult to figure out collective practices, to work across difference and through conflict. I think my ancestors must have had amazing skills in managing conflict, differences of opinion, mediation, and generating consensus while living together in close range and in a fluctuating environment. When I'm out on the land with students building a community, it becomes very clear to us the skills that we're lacking as a community in terms of decision-making, bringing people together, and mediating conflict.

I'm interested in how we take embodied practices and grow them so that we're not alone—grow the commune around these practices—and how those practices shift and transform across communities and movements and how this changes and transforms knowledge that we're making together. It seems like there's something in that that generates the sorts of skills and the sorts of knowledge and the kind of theory and care that I think we need to connect to each other and connect and build, too, toward larger solidarities. Also, for me, it's just realizing continually how little I know and how much I rely on the practices and the knowledge of trans Anishinaabe living in downtown Toronto, or the wild strawberries that I'm sharing space with in my backyard, or to Alexis and your deep love of the ocean to make this whole larger system work.

APG: Exactly. We're learning from multiple species; we're learning in multiple languages; we're learning through so many forms of knowledge at the same time. There's infinite possibility at the level of bacteria, even on the scale of what is supposedly one life but that is not one life. In my so-called embodiment, there are so many bodies, all these species, and all these different bacteria... this huge collective that I barely understand, even though I move it around. There's so much to learn.

I was with one of my elders yesterday, and I'm thinking about how hot the ocean is. I'm thinking about these whales beaching. I'm always listening, and not to have the arrogance to say that marine mammals are always speaking to me, but I have so much to learn from marine mammals that I'm always listening.

This elder of mine, or elder sister, is a world-renowned menopause expert, and toothed whales are the other species that go through something called menopause by Western science. That's a construct in itself; all of that has this story. This is part of her calling, to shift the conversation around menopause and decenter a white norm in that conversation. Her name's Omisade Burney-Scott, and she said something similar to interregnum except she was talking about ceremony as a liminal space. The way that she thinks about menopause is as a ceremonial liminal space that is part of the process of becoming an elder in community in a particular way.

I was just this morning reading something that she wrote about what she means when she says "liminal" space. She's saying that in a liminal space there's this possibility of upheaval, of a transformed society, of different norms. There's all of this possibility in a liminal space that is really important.

Yesterday I was asking her very sincerely: Is this planet going through menopause right now? She was saying that, well, if it is, that's really exciting, because it is a place of possibility. Things could be different; regimes could be overturned; roles could be changed that aren't as they're supposed to be. And I'm excited too because so much needs to completely change. And what if it is led by the wisdom of elder women, those who have always stewarded the larger goal, the multigenerational imperative for love.

I've been wondering about these whales, the grandmother orcas who will just actually sink the ships of the billionaires. Or even these pilot whales, stranded off the coast of Australia the day before yesterday in the shape of a heart, and then actually broke their hearts? What happens when a whale or dolphin strands is, it crushes their organs, because their chest cavity is supposed to be floating in water. So when it's on land like that, it really is heartbreak that happens. In some sense, this puts me out of a job as a poet: it's not even metaphor anymore; it's very literal. What does it mean that the symbols that I have learned are showing up in this way across species?

I'm thinking about eldership, and I'm thinking about ceremonies for eldership. There is something really vulnerable in knowing that part of the ceremony for eldership is not knowing who you are, not knowing what's possible, and having to be in a place of not knowing in order to then arrive at a place where you can be empowered to speak on behalf of a multigenerational accountability. How do we think of eldership in an interspecies way as a young species on Earth? How do we think of planetary accountability in an eldership way, which would mean to respect the eldership of Indigenous communities?

There is a way that marine mammals are demonstrating eldership. What does it mean to publicly express your heartbreak and die in order for a message to be received? That's something that, to me, is *legibly* happening. And again, I don't want to say that because of its legibility to me it means it's the truth of marine mammals.... That's not at all necessary. What's necessary is my listening and our listening in an interspecies form of presence, and listening within our so-called species in a way that's informed by the interspecies scale of existence. I really agree with what Leanne was saying—what we can learn from more than human worlds is [that] in every second something is possible to learn. Like why does my leg itch right now? What bugs are in here? All of those things. There's always an opportunity....

LBS: I was thinking when you were talking about how [for] my whole life, elders have been talking. I don't want to say talking loudly because they never talk loudly, but they've been talking emphatically about what we are doing to the planet. And I remember elders that I've worked with, that are [now] in their eighties, remembering their grandparents and great-grandparents praying in the morning with the water, crying because the water was so dirty— and this would have been back in the 1800s. Indigenous peoples here—from the moment colonizers showed up and killed all the queer people, killed all the beavers, killed the white pines in the name of capitalism—they knew there was going to be a problem. They saw the problem instantly in this greed, this setting structures and hierarchies infused with violence in order to take as [many] natural resources as possible and feed it into a capitalist economy. They knew this was going to happen, and they used their words and their bodies, and they resisted. And I was thinking when you were talking about how quiet a lot of them are right now. Because they told us this would happen. It's heartbreaking to me. I remember Anishinaabe elders talking about this heat right now as a fever. So not menopause but a fever, because this system is injured because of the constant attack. And ... fevers cause damage; fevers cause further death. It's possible that we don't come out of this. The majority of the human world knew that things were going in the wrong direction, and it's been this small pocket of rich white men who hold all the power and who are able to be the architects of this present moment.

Every time you look at news—the headlines just in the last three days, from the whales, to the sea lions running out in the ocean, to the spiral and acceleration of destruction this July—it feels like it's been marked. But it's also been marked in a way that next July, this July, is going to look easy, right? Because we haven't met the present moment with the sort of large-scale mobilization that would be needed to intervene. It's depressing—and maybe you can find a way of practicing hope in this moment. But when you've got this group of pilot whales in the shape of a heart, breaking their hearts—how much more death do we need?

APG: ["Between regimes" is] a linear set up: "Here we are, and here's the between, and here's the next regime." But there's this layering, and there's this planetary scale of layering. As Leanne was just saying, there's actually a majority, and knowledge and reality and even a set of practices of resilience that is present right now. And there are these few rich white men who are hoarding resources and dealing death and exercising violent control.

How to interrupt that? It's almost like this evil force field. A frequency signal—maybe it's the kind of cartoons I watched when I was growing up!—but that frequency that's shutting off people from being able to be in relationship and actually interact and do what they know is right. But then the collective comes together, and they knock over that tower that's making that frequency. That's kind of how I think about it—that there's longevity of practice and of knowledge that the dominant systems are overriding just by being so painful and loud.

What I really wanted to say: in addition to the things I admire about Leanne's work and about the way you have prioritized collaborating with other Black feminists and all of the things that I really love about the way you move in the world, the thing that first got me and pulls me in is the depth of your listening. *Islands of Decolonial Love* was the first of your works that I learned about. It called me deeply. It's a work that for me was profound and different from anything I had ever read because all through—how is it that the listening itself can be present in every word, in between the words, in the repetitions, in the lines?

The depth of listening is so profound that it calls my own listening, and it opens this portal to hear something and feel something and actually be vibrationally impacted. Which is why it doesn't surprise me that you are also a musician and you collaborate with other musicians all the time. But then as I continued through the portal of *Islands of Decolonial Love* to engage the rest of the work, it is all listening. Your listening practice with your elders is the generative site that you're always actually connecting to with everything you create, which means you connect us to that listening. For me it's been a model for what is possible, for how important listening is, and I feel it even in this conversation of what makes it possible for us to listen across these different knowledges, to listen across species. It's the practice of intergenerational listening—listening to our elders, which was my first practice.

There is something vibrational—there is something about listening as a practice and a technology and a rigor that feels very central to me to what we're talking about here. So "between" is the depth of our listening such that we can actually tune in to the majority, the majority of species, the collectivity, the wisdom of our elders, the wisdom of each other's elders through each other, even though there's this terrible, loud, interrupting signal of violence that is present also. What would it mean to be able to listen so deeply that we get underneath it or beyond it or between the holes that exist in it? Maybe that's the between.

Either way, all I know is that it has something to do with listening. And, Leanne, you have been one of my teachers from a distance and through text about the power of listening and how it can show up. It seems like an impossible thing. It seems like a sci-fi thing: How could it be that your listening shifts a vibration in my body, right? Listening that you did years ago, but it's present in the ceremony of your work. And all these bacteria and every cell in this being over here [are] actually attuned and vibrating differently because of the depth of your listening. That seems like that shouldn't even be possible. But I'm a witness, because I experienced it, so I know it's possible. And I'm really grateful because it's an immersion that we need, and knowing it's possible feels like really good news especially in these depressing times.

LBS: When I was in my twenties, I was able to listen to this past generation of elders that have now passed on. They were so quiet; they rarely, rarely spoke, in part because they were constantly listening to what was going on around them—to the rustling of leaves, to birdsong, to the fire crackling. I remember them talking about how your voice is your instrument, and it's your vibration, and that if you're going to intervene in the universe with your voice, then you need to do that *weweni*—you need to do that very carefully—because you're putting out a vibration and a power that travels inside of people. It goes into bodies through ears, and it has a potential to transform.

I've often gone back to thinking about sound. If you're listening with your whole body to the sound [that] comes in through your ears, you're listening with your heart; you're listening with your spirit.

This is an important communication practice in networks. And when you were talking about how the space in between sets up this very linear sort of framing, I was thinking of myself and my body as this node in a network with this infinite number of relationships going off in all directions through time and space. Those points of connection, those vibrations, are often aural—they're often that sound.

That's an important theoretical intervention, methodology and method. It's not just hearing—it's not just the content of what's coming out of someone's voice. It's the quality of the voice; it's listening for specific things outside of yourself, a listening for resonance and dissonance, and I think it can be a really beautiful form of love and care. There is a practice of hope in deep listening.

BJ: What creative projects are you working on right now?

APG: This biography of Audre Lorde has totally transformed me. And it'll be coming out in August 2024. I've also been writing with paintings of Alma Thomas, who was a Black woman artist born in 1891, in Georgia, at the height of lynching. She is a color theorist. It's not always known, because her work is abstract, that she is a Black woman who is thinking about lynching, thinking about color in a way that is profoundly transformative.

And then the other thing I'm doing is just continual ancestral listening. It's part of my daily practice to go deeper into everything my elders, who are now ancestors, ever told me, to keep listening more. I feel like it's like keeping a door open to continue to learn from them and be guided by them. That is a thing that happens every day; that is the thing that must happen—and I think it's the most creative thing I can do, so far.

LBS: I have a few projects in various states. I have a book that is nonfiction called *Theory of Water*, where I think alongside water for a while. I'm also finishing the first draft of a kind of novel building up from some of the characters that started in *Islands of Decolonial Love* and were present in *Noopiming*, and that's currently called "The Breathing Lands," which is an Anishinaabe name and a Cree name for bogs—sphagnum moss bogs and peatlands. And then I'm about to switch gears and try to write another album.

3

A Reformation of a Communist Kind

Class Struggle after the "End of History"

Manu Karuka

In comparison to war, ending with the withdrawal of forces from the battlefield, Antonio Gramsci argued that political struggle is "enormously more complex." In political struggle, as in colonial warfare, "the victorious army occupies, or proposes to occupy, permanently all or a part of the conquered territory," while the defeated army is "disarmed and dispersed." As in situations of colonial occupation, however, the struggle continues on an altered terrain.[1] Gramsci's insights can provide us an opening to consider the end of the Cold War in the years 1989–1992.

Much grander than the end of the Cold War, Francis Fukuyama argued, 1989 marked the "end point of mankind's ideological evolution," through the "universalization of Western liberal democracy" as the "final form of human government." Claiming that "the class issue has actually been successfully resolved in the West," Fukuyama presented class struggle as an ideological relic of bygone times. Embedded in Fukuyama's argument about the end of history is an argument about the obsolescence of historical materialism. Fukuyama presented his argument as moving beyond "the materialist bias of modern thought," assessing the events of the year as a "victory of liberalism" occurring "primarily in the realm of ideas or consciousness." The "end of history," for Fukuyama, was the end of class struggle.[2]

The end of history, he argued, would mean the end of major conflicts between liberal democracies. War would be replaced by competition in the capitalist marketplace, regulated within the bounds of liberal democracy.[3] His argument carries a very definite geographic focus, proceeding from "societies in Europe and North America at the vanguard of civilization," which could lay claim to "the common ideological heritage of mankind." Fukuyama's end of history was not only the triumph of capitalism over socialism. It was also the "triumph of the West, of the Western *idea*," taking two forms: first, "the total exhaustion of viable systematic alternatives to Western liberalism"; second, "the ineluctable spread of Western consumerist culture." For Fukuyama, a "spectacular abundance" of "advanced liberal economies," and a corresponding "infinitely diverse consumer culture," fostered and preserved liberalism.[4] Arguing for the ultimate precedence of Hegel, Fukuyama invoked a philosophy reflecting an era when the European bourgeoisie had asserted its universality over the working classes of Europe and the peoples of the colonized world.[5]

Behind Fukuyama's triumphalism is the question of imperialism. For Fukuyama, 1989 bookended the twentieth century, which began and now returned to a state of "self-confidence in the ultimate triumph of Western liberal democracy." The inheritors of the so-called Great Powers, now calling themselves the G7, celebrated "an unabashed victory of economic and political liberalism." The end of history, for Fukuyama, was marked not only by the ideological defeat of communism but also by the electoral victories of "unabashedly pro-market and anti statist" conservative parties in Britain, Germany, the United States, and Japan. Meanwhile, the "bulk of the Third World," Fukuyama warned, "remains very much mired in history." All societies, he argued, need to "end their ideological pretensions of representing different and higher forms of human society," while, he predicted, international conflict would continue between the "historical" and the "post-historical" world. Finally, he warned, "the simple existence of communist China" constitutes a threat to liberalism, maintaining "an alternative pole of ideological attraction."[6]

Replying to his critics at the end of 1989, Fukuyama further developed the themes in his initial essay. The evolution of human thought about first principles governing political and social organization, he insisted, followed a clear historical and geographic trajectory "primarily from the First World to the Third, and not the reverse." Returning to threats to liberalism, Fukuyama focused on "difficult-to-assimilate immigrant populations" in France and West Germany, as well as the "politically dangerous" critique of liberalism from the Right, with its focus on moral and cultural "contradictions" within liberal societies.[7] Despite his triumphalism, Fukuyama acknowledged a danger from the extreme Right. Gramsci had noted the "reactionary and conservative tendencies" of the "old intellectual and moral leaders of society," during an earlier era. Facing the decomposition of the forms of culture and morality they had represented, "they loudly proclaim the death of all civilization, all culture, all morality," advocating state repression.[8] In a moment of seeming triumph, with the wealthy economies buffeted by serial recessions and the prospect of prolonged stagnation, a whiff of rot permeated the air.

In the preface to the 1990 edition of their book *Free to Choose*, Milton and Rose Friedman commented on a remarkable shift in political culture within the United States, "away from a belief in collectivism and toward a belief in individualism and private markets." A decade earlier, they continued, many had been convinced that capitalism "was a deeply flawed system that was not capable of achieving both widely shared prosperity and human freedom." In 1990, they argued, "conventional wisdom regards capitalism as the only system that can do so." Given this profound ideological shift, they suggested, what had seemed "utopian and unrealistic" in the book's first edition would appear to readers in 1990 "as almost a blueprint for practical change."[9] If recession and stagnation loomed, the answer was to unleash the animal spirits of the market.

In a November 1991 talk delivered at the Smith Center for Private Enterprise Studies at California State University, Hayward, Milton Friedman distinguished between economic, human, and political freedom. While capitalism was a "necessary" condition for human and political freedom, it was not in itself a "sufficient" condition for these freedoms. Friedman lauded Hong Kong as "one of the freest, if not the freest, of countries in the world," blessed with a free market that had arisen from the designs of British colonial officials, and "a great deal of human freedom" in the form of free speech and press freedoms. In one respect, Friedman conceded, Hong Kong had "no freedom whatsoever." In a curious formulation, he suggested that Hong Kong residents "did not choose freedom. It was imposed on them." This disjuncture between economic and political freedom also shaped his analysis of Chile, presenting the Pinochet dictatorship as a restoration of Chile's democratic process. As examples of economic freedom, Friedman offered colonial rule on the one hand and military dictatorship on the other. Against these spaces of economic freedom, Friedman alleged that India and other British colonies that had been "given" political freedom in the postwar era "have for the most part destroyed" economic and human freedom, concluding that economic freedom facilitates political freedom, but political freedom "has a tendency to destroy economic freedom."[10] For Friedman, democracy and the market exist in uneasy tension.

A few weeks later, Friedman delivered a talk at the Manhattan Institute, later published as the pamphlet *Why Government Is the Problem*. For Friedman, democracy could be best understood as a contract relation, and the individual citizen, an entrepreneur, making deals rather than participating in processes of collective governance. From this perspective, "the essence of freedom" lay in "free private markets." Such markets, furthermore, were the only truly democratic mechanisms available to organize decision-making, mechanisms to achieve "voluntary cooperation among people" marked by an absence of coercion and a shared belief that all participants "are going to be better off." In Friedman's presentation, the free market itself is indifferent to social identities, like race or religion, one of its "great virtues." The "free market," he concluded, was the most effective system "to enable people who hate one another to deal with one another and help one another." While Fukuyama argued for the centrality of ideas, Friedman argued, to the contrary, that ideas "take a long time and are not important in and of themselves," requiring external triggers to "provide a fertile ground for those ideas."[11] The weakness of organized political opposition sowed this ideological ground, and the expansion of police functions over everyday life preserved and extended this weakness, buying time for Friedman's ideas of "economic freedom" to take root.

Gramsci had critically assessed the Italian communist movement's actions in the period prior to the rise of fascism. Avoiding the "basic problem, the problem of power," the movement had instead diverted popular attention to secondary objectives, while "hypocritically concealing" ruling class responsibility for the crisis. As various social strata were radicalized in the throes of the crisis, the movement "gratuitously turned them into enemies" instead of making them allies.[12] Diversion, concealment, and disunity also shaped certain theoretical perspectives at the close of the Cold War. In their 1987 essay, "Post-Marxism without Apologies," Ernesto Laclau and Chantal Mouffe had anticipated Fukuyama's arguments about the obsolescence of Marxism, proclaiming that socialism needed to be reformulated through discursive struggles over rights and equality. Laclau and Mouffe presaged Fukuyama's argument that the principles of 1776 and 1789 cannot be transcended. "Post-Marxism" moves toward greater inclusion within the accepted boundaries of legitimacy within liberal democracy. Rather than a "direct attack upon the State apparatuses," Laclau and Mouffe advocated "the consolidation and democratic reform of the liberal State." Jettisoning class struggle, at the heart of their proposed transcendence of Marxism is a basic consensus with Fukuyama's position. For Laclau and Mouffe, struggle is defined by qualities of variety and autonomy that align neatly with Friedman's free private market, so apparently indifferent to social identities.[13] Gramsci had warned that copying the political methods of the ruling classes leads to "easy ambushes." A class that controls concentrated wealth, whose members control their time, is able to operate politically in fundamentally different ways than a class that does not control its own working day.[14] With the decline of working-class organizations, social organizations, which forge a shared common sense and values, producing the consent of the governed, are "left to the private initiative of the ruling class."[15] Post-Marxism counseled a bizarre kind of mysticism, predicting a transcendence of bourgeois power through the mechanisms of bourgeois power.

In his 1990 essay "Dislocation and Capitalism, Social Imaginary and Democratic Revolution," Laclau acknowledged his definitive agreement with Fukuyama, proposing that the end of a possible transcendence of liberal democracy could be understood just as well as the "beginning of history," when the promises of liberal democracy might finally achieve "full recognition."[16] In his 1992 book *The End of History*, Fukuyama would postulate that the dissolution of the USSR marked an achievement of a "higher rationality" on the part of its citizens, who "recognized that rational universal recognition could be had only in a liberal social order."[17] In her 1993 essay "Feminism, Citizenship, and Radical Democratic Politics," Mouffe clarified both the turn away from class struggle and the engagement within the framework of liberal democracy embedded in the call for post-Marxism, which she shared with Laclau. Class, in her approach, is a type of identity, an "equivalent articulation" with other identities, not a relationship within a given mode of production. Moving away from class struggle, she instead proposed a more amorphous model of struggle against "forms of subordination." Mouffe advocated a model of "radical and plural democracy," understanding citizenship as an identification with foundational principles of "modern pluralist democracy," namely, "liberty and equality for all." Left unaddressed is the specific class content of these principles. For Mouffe, a "radical democratic" approach is different from liberalism because it views the full realization of democracy as impossible. In a moment of bourgeois triumphalism, Mouffe counseled pessimistic concessions to bourgeois common sense.[18] Behind these counsels was an unspoken and unverified claim about the dynamism of capitalism itself in the 1990s. Prior to capitalism, Gramsci noted, the ruling classes "were essentially conservative," conceiving of themselves as "a closed caste." The rising bourgeoisie, as an open, dynamic class, presented itself as culturally and economically capable of absorbing all of society. The state form of the bourgeoisie reflected this dynamism and openness. Over time, however, as this process of dynamism ground to a halt, the state returned to relations of pure force. As competition is replaced by monopoly, and capitalism becomes moribund, the bourgeois class becomes "saturated." It stops growing, beginning to shrink. The bourgeois state in the era of imperialism reflects these patterns of decay.[19] What possibilities are obtained for a "radical, plural democracy" in the era of imperialism?

A 1990 conference at the University of Illinois, Urbana–Champaign, marked a turning point in the institutionalization of cultural studies within the U.S. academy. "At the very moment at which cultural studies begins to gain institutional recognition," Angela McRobbie noted in her concluding remarks, the critique of Marxism and the decentering of class relations shook its intellectual foundations. Seeking some bearings, McRobbie turned to Laclau's arguments that "antagonism is not inherent to capital, but based around external, contingent, and historical processes." Laclau, she continued, offered "a more democratic conception of social change" than the "essentially authoritarian notion of leadership" she found in the ideas of the "neo-Marxist" Gramsci. This might involve turning from the relations of production, for example, to focus on the inability of working people "to participate in the broader society" as consumers. The idea of radical, plural democracy, moreover, "need not imply greater state intervention in public life; it might involve less," while "the free market offers opportunities for new emergent identities." What was the role of the "organic intellectual," McRobbie asked, after the eclipse of class struggle? How would the loss of "that sense of urgency" shape the further development of cultural studies?[20] In his remarks at the Illinois conference, Stuart Hall questioned Marxist theory "for the model around which it is articulated: its Eurocentrism." Hall argued that intellectuals with commitments to emancipatory projects had a responsibility to transmit ideas and knowledge "to those who do not belong, professionally, in the intellectual class." Without the simultaneous operation of these "two fronts" of theory and communication, Hall insisted, "you can get enormous theoretical advance without any engagement at the level of the political project."[21] Gramsci defined the intellectual as a "permanent persuader." After the "end of history," what was the intellectual persuading?[22]

In 1991, the central government of India, under the Congress Party, opened India's domestic economy to international finance capital, a policy of "liberalization." The impacts of this policy would fuel a wide-ranging and devastating crisis across the Indian countryside. At the end of 1992, Hindutva forces demolished the Babri Masjid, a historic mosque in Ayodhya, in a brazenly criminal act of collective violence. The winter of 1992 also saw the publication of Dipesh Chakrabarty's essay, "Postcoloniality and the Artifice of History." Conceding to Fukuyama that "the end of history is in sight for us in India," Chakrabarty focused on "'history' as a discourse produced at the institutional site of the university." His critique framed "'Indian' history itself" in "a position of subalternity," arguing that "one can only articulate subaltern subject positions in the name of this history," while acknowledging that this position left him open to charges of "nativism, nationalism, or worse . . . nostalgia." In this historical context, Chakrabarty's focus on the "Bengali Hindu middle class, the bhadralok or 'respectable people,'" considerably sharpens the sense of nativism, nationalism, and nostalgia to be glimpsed in his curious kind of "middle-class" subalternity, so far removed from Gramsci's own methods and concerns.[23]

Gramsci had assessed a failure to anticipate the fascist triumph in Italy, because struggle took place over doctrinal principles rather than over concrete social relations.[24] Chakrabarty would admit the real danger of "an Indian 'Hindu' fascism," in a 1995 essay, while contending that this danger was "sometimes exaggerated." Insisting that "modern problems of Hinduism and caste" were inseparable from the social order instituted by British colonialists and then preserved by Indian nationalists, Chakrabarty described the former USSR and India as imperial structures.[25] What was the evidence for this claim? For Gramsci, class consciousness, developed through engaging the state (whether defending, attacking, or seeking to overthrow it), is a necessary component for an accurate understanding of the state.[26]

In a pair of astonishingly prescient talks, the first given on December 27, 1992, in Calcutta and the second in early December 1993 in Hyderabad, Aijaz Ahmad took up these questions. Cautioning against transporting ideas developed for a specific moment of struggle, Ahmad nonetheless asserted that a certain kind of ghostly resonance with the Indian situation could be found in a careful reading of Gramsci. While Chakrabarty described the subaltern studies project as an attempt to think past an assumption of failure in Indian history, Ahmad insisted that Gramsci could speak to the Indian context in the 1990s precisely because Gramsci was, himself, concerned with a particular kind of failure in Italian history, a "paradox of great civilizational depth combined with endemic national fragmentation." Analysis suffers not only from Eurocentric assumptions but also from assumptions that capitalists are the source of democracy, and the oppressed and exploited classes, its objects. It is insufficient to "provincialize Europe," in other words. It is also necessary to provincialize the capitalist class. Rather than the "prototype of all bourgeois revolutions," Ahmad pointed out, the French Revolution was in fact "a very notable exception." The increasing conservatism of the bourgeoisie across Europe following the French Revolution spurred a wave of national revolutions through alliances between the bourgeoisie and the aristocracy, presenting a united front against the threat of worker-peasant insurgencies.[27]

Reading Gramsci from India in 1992, Ahmad identified resonances between the historical legacies of the Catholic Church and "High Brahminism" (which predated European colonialism by centuries), both of which sought to homogenize belief systems and social practices, assuming positions of cultural supremacy, as well ideological guardianship of "systems of tributary exploitation of the peasantry." Gramsci's focus on the Risorgimento could be connected to nineteenth-century reformist movements in India, oscillating between "the twin attractions of indigenist, often obscurantist, revivalisms on the one hand, and the empty 'cosmopolitanism' of the Anglicizers on the other." Missing, in these reformist movements, was any discussion of revolutionizing the relations of production. Ahmad insisted that ideological struggle against Hindutva would need to engage traditions of struggle inherited from precolonial antibrahmanical movements, alongside the legacies of the nationalist movement. Together, he argued, these histories imprinted the spiritual and political consciousness of tens of millions of rural households across India, shaping democratic traditions that had developed out of centuries of class struggle in southern Asia. Ideological struggle in itself was insufficient to defeat Hindutva. To be credible, "ideologies of secularism and democracy" would need to take concrete form through struggles to radically restructure property relations and systems of governance, giving the popular classes "a real, tangible stake in the anti-Fascist struggle." The critical rejection of "nation" as a political category conceded the ground of social struggle. It marked a particularly sharp failure (in a Gramscian sense) during a period of rise for the extreme right.[28] "Nation," Ahmad emphasized, is not a thing. Like "class," "nation" is a process. It is a terrain of struggle.

To critically examine nationalism, in a Gramscian sense, requires us to study historical trajectories of class struggle, understanding liberal democracies and liberal nation-states as particular outcomes of longer histories of classes in motion. Likewise, the Gramscian concept of "consent." Ahmad reminds us that Gramsci's immediate concern was not consent to parliamentary democracy but consent to fascism. Gramsci struggled with how to best understand mass consent in Italy for the fascist project of Mussolini and how to combat it. Similarly, in "Americanism and Fordism," Ahmad points out, Gramsci wrote about consent not to "liberal democracy" but to the capitalist mode of production (in Friedman's terms, consent to economic, not political, freedom). For Gramsci, capitalist hegemony in the United States during the high era of liberal imperialism, the first phase of Jim Crow, was produced at the point of production by industrial management, not in the realm of "culture."[29]

Fascism, Ahmad insisted, is a kind of nationalism, competing with the historical traditions invoked by other forms of nationalism, such as anticolonial nationalisms. Fascist movements unify diverse social strata by distilling the lingering "rot of an anachronistic history," endowing these new unities with "power, purpose, and intellectual location." In India, at the heart of this lingering rot was a "masculinist mobilization, in the name of a unitary Hinduism." The image of the family was crucial to Hindutva, drawing in its strictly all-male fronts through the centripetal forces of patriarchy. In India, even after the destruction of Babri Masjid, a certain complacency about the fascist threat led many to "feel free to carry on with our sectarian habits," focusing critical efforts within the hermeneutics of theory or against the organized Left.[30]

Gramsci understood Italian fascism as a particular resolution of the structural crisis of Italian capitalism. Its success derived from its ability to mobilize different regional, class, and social sections of Italian society in its favor.

The rise of extreme right movements in India, Europe, and elsewhere in the late 1980s occurred alongside the development of academic critiques of "the nation" as a political category and the deterioration of class analysis. As in the era of classical fascism, this took place in a period of capitalist stagnation, but this resurgent fascism now followed a retreat from social democracy in the wealthy industrialized countries, the dismantling of radical nationalism in recently decolonized countries, and the demise of mass communist parties in western Europe. After the 1991 "liberalization" of India's economy to finance capital from around the world, leading academics conceded the ideological ground to international finance and its local representatives rather than contributing to an intellectual project that addressed the impacts of this policy on the working class and the peasantry (the overwhelming majority of Indian society) or the situation of "expectation and hope" among the small capitalists of India's cities and countryside, who formed a core constituency of organized Hindutva.[31]

Hindtuva's rescripted nationalism, with its mythos of an eternal, strong nation, marked a repudiation of the anticolonial project, a willing subordination to imperialism. Although Hindutva developed in conditions specific to India, its rise in the early 1990s, Ahmad argued, exemplified a general tendency across the world at that moment. Movements of the extreme Right stabilized the twin defeat of communism and anti-imperialist nationalism, cementing "the triumph of imperialism in a moment of capitalist stagnation." In this historical moment, he continued, neoliberal economic policies combined with "irrationalist populism" to provide "a general solution for the period of stagnation." Reading Gramsci can help situate these developments in a longer historical trajectory. For Gramsci, as Ahmad points out, it was only in May 1871 that the French bourgeoisie, after its decisive victory over the commune, was able to stabilize its rule, thanks to a new imperialist economy fueled by colonial wars in Africa and Asia. Contra Fukuyama, with his presentation of a timeless French Revolution as the end point of humanity's ideological evolution, Gramsci understood that the defeat of the Commune entailed the final exhaustion of the dynamics first unleashed in 1798. These are the terms—defeat of the working class and the rise of a new imperialist economy—not some timeless "liberal democracy," that lurked behind Fukuyama's thesis.[32] The celebrant of mass murder dressed in professorial tweed.

Reading Gramsci in order to reflect on the demands of the moment, Ahmad insisted on clarity about Gramsci's own project as a communist militant, "a leader of the largest proletarian uprising that occurred in Europe" following World War I and the Bolshevik Revolution. Rather than a departure from Marxism, Gramsci's entire body of work "had the single purpose of reconstituting a Leninism" appropriate to the specific conditions of Italy, a "largely peasant, indifferently industrialized society—in the face of Fascism." Projects like subaltern studies presented Gramsci "essentially as a *thinker*, a maker of *concepts*," whose ideas could be detached from the political project in which they emerged. Gramsci analyzed the cosmopolitan conditions of traditional intellectual life in Italy, separated by language (Latin) from the language of everyday life (the vernacular), shaping an intellectual outlook divorced from the everyday lives and aspirations of the popular classes. In the early 1990s, Ahmad wrote, a "leftwingish culturalism" posed politics "as an autonomous realm with no necessary relation with class politics," forwarding all-encompassing concepts as alternatives to historical materialist understandings of social relations, wielding these concepts as weapons "to attack the organized Left."[33]

Fascism, Ahmad argued, has two faces. On the one hand, it involves massive cultural and ideological upheaval, deploying a "machinery of terror" across society. On the other hand, fascism involves a comprehensive economic restructuring, achieving transformations the bourgeoisie had been unable to achieve through the existing channels of the liberal state. In this process, large segments of the capitalist class are brought over to the side of fascism. Widespread passivity among the working classes and the peasantry, and simultaneous political and social initiative in the hands of the professional classes and small business owners, facilitates the rise of this "pathological nationalism." To combat fascism, Ahmad maintained, it is necessary to remember that conservatism "is born not only from privilege and the will to protect that privilege, but also from the experience of pain and the fear of future pain." Amid "near-universal misery" in working-class and poor communities across India's cities, the RSS (Rashtriya Swayamsevak Sangh) offered "compensatory hallucinations of power," to address real and perceived suffering.[34] In such a situation, Ahmad insisted, fascism can only be fought through "the organization of a collective human agency which addresses the linkages between moral reform and the transformations of material life." Fascism, in other words, can only be fought with class struggle.[35]

The "death of old ideologies," Gramsci wrote, takes the form of a generalized skepticism, leading to a kind of politics "which is cynical in its immediate manifestations." Conditions of crisis distill the most rarified realms of thought to questions of hunger and survival, raising "the possibility and necessity of creating a new culture."[36] Thirty years after the apparent "end of history," the task of intellectuals committed to processes of liberation remains to educate, to persuade, and to organize. In many ways, it also requires a reconstruction. As Ahmad concluded in 1993, "An antifascist struggle requires ... that complex thing for which Gramsci often used the cryptic term 'Reformation'—a Reformation, that is to say, not of a religious kind, but of a communist kind. For our own time, this word 'Reformation' can only mean the refounding, in the post-Soviet era, of a new communist movement actually capable of becoming a 'collective intellectual' for the anti-Fascist forces in general, and thereby to help initiate a new century of revolutions."[37] In the interregnum between the "end of history" and the present moment, we have come closer to the suicide of our species, whether through nuclear war, ecological destruction, or the intensification of mass starvation. In the meantime, forces of the extreme Right have been successfully employing the mechanisms of liberal democracy, including the judiciary and electoral processes, to consolidate power within and across countries. In this context, Gramsci's "new culture" and Ahmad's "reformation of a communist kind," both projects of renewing and extending class struggle, have become not just possibilities but necessities for the future of humanity.

NOTES

1. Gramsci, *Selections*, 229.
2. Fukuyama, "End of History?," 3–18, 4–6, 9.
3. See Kautsky, "Ultra-Imperialism."
4. Fukuyama, "End of History?," 3, 8.
5. Gramsci, *Selections*, 258–259.
6. Fukuyama, "End of History?," 10, 11, 13, 15–16, 18.
7. Fukuyama, "Reply to My Critics," 21–28, 22, 24, 26, 28.
8. Gramsci, *Selections*, 242n42.
9. Friedman and Friedman, "Foreword," x–xi.
10. Friedman, "Economic Freedom," 2–6.
11. Friedman, *Why Government*, 15–16, 18.
12. Gramsci, *Selections*, 225n20.
13. Laclau and Mouffe, "Post-Marxism without Apologies," 104–105.
14. Gramsci, *Selections*, 232.
15. Gramsci, 259.
16. Laclau, "Dislocation and Capitalism," 64.
17. Fukuyama, *End of History*, 202, 205.
18. Mouffe, "Feminism, Citizenship," 372, 376–380, 382.
19. Gramsci, *Selections*, 260.
20. McRobbie, "Post-Marxism and Cultural Studies," 719–720, 722–725.
21. Hall, "Cultural Studies," 280–281.
22. Gramsci noted the devolution of universities amid crisis conditions of political, cultural, and spiritual decay to purely rhetorical intellectual work divorced from local concerns and specificities. Gramsci, *Selections*, 228.
23. Chakrabarty, "Postcoloniality," 1–5, 9, 11, 13, 16–20, 22–23.
24. Gramsci, *Selections*, 225.
25. Chakrabarty, "Modernity and Ethnicity," 3373–3375, 3378–3379.
26. Gramsci, *Selections*, 275.
27. Ahmad, "Fascism and National Culture," 221, 224, 226, 250, 251, 252; Hobsbawm, *Age of Capital*, 15–16, 32–34.
28. Ahmad, "Fascism and National Culture," 223, 241, 263. See "Notes on Italian History" and "Americanism and Fordism" in Gramsci, *Selections*.

29. Ahmad, 235–236.
30. Ahmad, 230–232, 243, 271.
31. Ahmad, 230, 293, 257.
32. Ahmad, 237, 293–294.
33. Ahmad, 227, 229, 237, 238, 248.
34. The Rashtriya Swayamsevak Sangh (RSS), the world's largest self-declared fascist paramilitary organization, is a key organization of the Hindu nationalist movement. Its political front, the Bharatiya Janata Party (BJP), is the current ruling part in India. See Noorani, *RSS*.
35. Ahmad, "Fascism and National Culture," 243, 257, 261, 300.
36. Gramsci, *Selections*, 276.
37. Ahmad, "Fascism and National Culture," 264.

BIBLIOGRAPHY

Ahmad, Aijaz. *Lineages of the Present: Political Essays*. New Delhi: Tulika, 1996.
Chakrabarty, Dipesh. "Modernity and Ethnicity in India: A History for the Present." *Economic and Political Weekly* 30, no. 52 (1995): 3373–3380.
———. "Postcoloniality and the Artifice of History: Who Speaks for 'Indian' Pasts?" *Representations* 37 (Winter 1992): 1–26.
Friedman, Milton. "Economic Freedom, Human Freedom, Political Freedom." *Smith Center for Private Enterprise Studies*, November 1, 1991, 2–6.
———. *Why Government Is the Problem*. Palo Alto, CA: Hoover Institution, 1993.
Friedman, Milton, and Rose Friedman. "Foreword to the Harvest Edition." In *Free to Choose: A Personal Statement*, ix–xii. San Diego: Harcourt Brace, 1990.
Fukuyama, Francis. "The End of History?" *National Interest* 16 (Summer 1989): 3–18.
———. *The End of History and the Last Man*. New York: Penguin, 1992.
———. "A Reply to My Critics." *National Interest* 18 (Winter 1989/1990): 21–28.
Gramsci, Antonio. *Selections from the Prison Notebooks*. Edited by Quintin Hoare and Geoffrey Nowell Smith. New York: International, 1971.
Hall, Stuart. "Cultural Studies and Its Theoretical Legacies." In *Cultural Studies*, edited by Lawrence Grossberg, Cary Nelson, and Paula Treicher, 277–294. New York: Routledge, 1992.
Hobsbawm, Eric. *The Age of Capital: 1848–1875*. London: Sphere Books, 1975.
Kautsky, Karl. "Ultra-Imperialism." *Die Neue Zeit*, September 1914: 908–922.
Laclau, Ernesto. "Dislocation and Capitalism, Social Imaginary and Democratic Revolution (1990)." In *Post-Marxism, Populism, and Critique*, 30–65. London: Routledge, 2015.
Laclau, Ernesto, and Chantal Mouffe. "Post-Marxism without Apologies." *New Left Review*, November/December 1987, 79–106.
McRobbie, Angela. "Post-Marxism and Cultural Studies: A Post-Script." In *Cultural Studies*, edited by Lawrence Grossberg, Cary Nelson, and Paula Treicher, 719–730. New York: Routledge, 1992.
Mouffe, Chantal. "Feminism, Citizenship, and Radical Democratic Politics." In *The Return of the Political*, 74–89. New York: Verso, 1993.
Noorani, A. G. *The RSS*. New Delhi: LeftWord Books, 2019.

Temporality and the Interregnum

4

"Freedom is Near!!!"

Insurgent Punctuations in Chester Himes's Plan B

Yumi Pak

Chester Himes opens *My Life of Absurdity* (1976), the second volume of his autobiography, with the following credo:

If one lives in a country where racism is held valid and practiced in all ways of life, eventually, no matter whether one is a racist or a victim, one comes to feel the absurdity of life. Racism generating from whites is first of all absurd. Racism creates absurdity among blacks as a defense mechanism. Absurdity to combat absurdity.[1]

With a writing career spanning from the 1940s until his passing in 1984 and as a contemporary of James Baldwin and Richard Wright, Himes is both venerated and denigrated for his contributions to Black literatures, with critics paying particular attention to the queer and queering thematic in his novels and his eventual turning toward hardboiled fiction. Perhaps this turn occurs in part because of what he calls absurdity or what he considers patently absurdist: the impulse to find meaning and logic in life and the simultaneous inability to do so. He states that, with the publication of *The End of a Primitive* (1955), he realized that although he had believed he was writing a novel "about the deadly venom of racial prejudice which kills both racists and their victims," he had in fact written a novel of absurdity.[2] The titles of his two-volume autobiography, published in 1971 and 1976, respectively, mark a shift in Himes's thinking. In moving from *The Quality of Hurt* to *My Life of Absurdity*, he locates the febrile blooming of absurdity from pain. From the depth of that deep pain—"I was beginning to bleed," he writes in *The Quality of Hurt*, "but I had not bled enough"—to the peak of the absurd, Himes requires his readers to understand racialized violence as all-pervasive but also seemingly random, as simultaneously within the terrain of structural power relations and in excess of them, in the unmanageable terrain of that which cannot be made to make sense.[3]

In this essay, I argue that the notion of an interregnum as an interruption of normative linear time is an absurd one because, as numerous scholars working on and around the intersections of structural power have long argued, an acceptance of such a concept of time privileges an epistemological standpoint of liberalism over all others and simultaneously forecloses the possibilities of different modes of resistance.[4] Roughly forty years prior to the publication of *My Life of Absurdity*, Antonio Gramsci offers a definition of the interregnum, writing that a rift has appeared between "the great masses" and "their traditional ideologies" and that "in this interregnum a great variety of morbid symptoms appear."[5] In this reading of the passage of time, the ruling class now leads through "coercive force alone," and thus an eruptive pause emerges, wherein "the old is dying and the new cannot be born."[6] Gramsci wonders if, in this parsing of linear time, new ideologies will eventually emerge, potentially to unseat those that came before. The span in between the death of old ideologies and the birth of new ones is fecund with the potential of unmooring and collapse; a liberal reading of the term, however, presupposes the assumption that time runs in linear fashion from past through present to future. Our contemporary discourse of liberalism runs slipshod over such a definition of the interregnum, adding yet another layer of expectations: that as time passes, things must only get better.

In response, I turn to Himes's final novel, *Plan B*, as a site where he challenges his readers to see two different forms of interregnums, one shaped by plot and the other by what I call his "insurgent punctuations." *Plan B* marks the conclusion to his Harlem Detective series; beginning with *For Love of Imabelle* (also published in the United States as *A Rage in Harlem*) and ending with *Blind Man with a Pistol*, the first eight novels' publication dates span roughly a decade, from 1957 to 1969, and are the reasons behind Himes's international fame as the foremost chronicler and satirist of Harlem noir. While at first he is reluctant to embrace this fame, instead wanting to be known for his more "literary" fiction, ranging from *If He Hollers Let Him Go* (1945) to *The End of the Primitive* (1955), Himes eventually does begin to see his Harlem Detective series as critical to his career, going so far as to question why there aren't more Black writers working in the genre of hardboiled fiction.

An unquestioned acceptance of the interregnum as initially defined above is always limited, whereas more dynamic and fluid conceptualizations of the term challenge the simple move from the old to the new, the past to the future, the barbaric to the civilized. If we imagine the interregnum as a kind of in-between, I ask us to consider what is mobilized in that pause. Take, for example, the trans studies scholar Hil Malatino's argument that while

> typically understood as a moment between state regimes, or the moments between state failure and the installation of a new system of power, the meaning of the interregnum shifts if we refuse to place emphasis on what was and what might be, and instead focus on the pause, the interim, as a moment of foment, generation, complexity, and fervor, rife with unexpected partnerships, chance events, and connections fortuitous and less so—a space of looseness and possibility, not yet overcoded and fixed in meaning, signification, or representative economy.[7]

Malatino's work generously makes space for readers to understand how campaigns like It Gets Better are meaningful but at the cost of foregrounding LGBTQ identities as nonintersectional: in other words, the campaign imagines that all those who are queer are queer in the same way. Implicitly aspiring to the future when "it" will be better, campaigns like these imagine life between the recognition that one is queer and/or trans and the moment post-transition as a binary: the former is wretched, the latter is "better," and the time in between is nothing more than a waiting game. As Malatino argues, however, there is something of "foment, generation, complexity, and fervor" in that space and time.

I hold Malatino's work close to that of Kara Keeling's, especially to her arguments in *Queer Times, Black Futures*, wherein the very structure of her text takes up the question of how Black, queer, and Black queer studies' frameworks and their accompanying conditions of possibility interrupt Gramsci's definition. Refusing to adhere to the notion that the "lack of a perceptible future as a problem to be solved or a crisis to be addressed, or a cause for pessimism or optimism," Keeling instead argues for us to read "the cut of Black existence" and how "it might cleave an opening in the present order of meaning and being" and reveal the multiple orders of meaning and being that also concurrently exist.[8] The organization of Keeling's book makes a practice out of her theorizing, as she intercuts her chapters with explorations of Herman Melville's novella, *Bartleby the Scrivener* (1853). The first such interruption she titles an "Interregnum," the second an "Interlude," and the final an "Intercession." In "Interregnum," she writes that in her theorizing of the Black and queer possibilities of the interregnum, new relations do not emerge linearly. Rather, the interregnum is a space that can be read as "too soon, too early, or too late to achieve new relations" but one in which "such relations may still be immanent."[9] Keeling illuminates how the titular character queers and confounds not only the other characters but also the logic of Wall Street. She states that Bartleby "provokes a confrontation with opacity, incommensurability, (un)accountability, radical contingency, and the impossible from within the logics of Western philosophy."[10]

Interestingly, the novels wherein I see most clearly Himes's grappling with Gramsci's, Malatino's, and Keeling's arguments on the interregnum belong to a genre that seems to uphold normative and linear time—that is to say, in hardboiled fiction, criminals are sought and more often than not caught by world-weary detectives who work through the evidence. His Harlem Detective series epitomizes the genre, where we are invited to witness the aftermath of the crime (and sometimes the crime itself), the gathering of evidence, and the final confrontation with the guilty party. Written at the behest of Marcel Duhamel, the editor of Edition Gallimard's publishing imprint Serie Noire, nearly all nine volumes in the collection star Coffin Ed Johnson and Grave Digger Jones, two Black detectives who live and work in Harlem. Coffin Ed and Grave Digger contest Megan Abbott's definition of the (white) detective as one who occupies the "murky space . . . between conventional society and a criminal underclass" as instead, the murky space is between upholding an unjust system and providing justice to those for whom it has long been denied.[11] The two men belong to Harlem, where Himes locates "the Mecca of the black people," in which "the black people have the past and the present, and they hope to have the future."[12] As befitting hardboiled fiction, the neighborhood of Harlem figures as prominently as the femmes fatales, the pimps, the police, and criminals, all archetypes who make up the seething mass of "the yearly accumulations of thousands of unlisted odors embedded in the crumbling walls."[13] For Coffin Ed and Grave Digger, Harlem is "not merely something [they] inhabit, but something that inhabits [them]. They understand interiority itself as a built structure, as 'imagination merely made.'"[14]

In late 1968, Himes wrote to his friend John A. Williams, "I have now commenced on the wildest and most defiant of my Harlem series, which will wind it up and kill one of my two detectives."[15] Extracting from this manuscript, he also wrote five short stories—"The Birth of Chitterlings, Inc.," "Pork Chop Paradise," "Tang," "Celebration," and "Prediction," of which the latter three were published in 1972. Yet *Plan B* was never published in English during Himes's lifetime; indeed, it was both unpublished and unfinished when he passed in 1984. Almost no mention of the book is made in either volume of his autobiography: only briefly does he share that he is writing it and that it was "gradually heading for disaster."[16] Instead of completing *Plan B*, Himes turned his attention to *Blind Man with a Pistol*, which many see as somewhat of a companion piece to his final novel. Drawing from Phil Lomax's anecdote that gives the novel its name, Himes's penultimate Harlem Detective novel diverges wildly from his earlier ones, pulling together disparate crimes and characters in a literal riot while Coffin Ed and Grave Digger spend their time shooting rats. "Can't you men stop that riot?" demands Lieutenant Anderson, to which Grave Digger responds, "It's out of hand, boss." Bewildered at the turn of events, Anderson mutters, "That don't make any sense," and Grave Digger gets the last line of the novel: "Sure don't."[17] Yet even with its unwieldy plot, the proliferation of seemingly unconnected and random characters and the refusal to solve the crimes committed, Himes makes the authorial decision to complete this absurd novel while abandoning *Plan B*.

Why might this be?

Structurally, *Plan B* progresses in a much more linear temporal and narrative fashion than *Blind Man with a Pistol*. The novel opens with a Black man, T-bone Smith, receiving a package that contains an ancient M14 rifle. Accompanying the gun is a note: "WARNING!! DO NOT INFORM POLICE!!! LEARN YOUR WEAPON AND WAIT FOR INSTRUCTIONS!!! REPEAT!!! LEARN YOUR WEAPON AND WAIT FOR INSTRUCTIONS!!! WARNING!!! DO NOT INFORM POLICE!!! FREEDOM IS NEAR!!!"[18] Recognizing the gun as an army weapon, T-bone declares he wants nothing to do with the gun, because "I done served my time."[19] Here, I read Himes's collapsing of space and time; while "time" for T-bone can mean either his enlistment with the U.S. Army or incarceration, the proximity of freedom—"NEAR"—is what causes him to invoke the past: "I done served."

With the arrival of this rifle, we also have the entrance of Coffin Ed and Grave Digger into the narrative, and as Himes's intrepid detectives work to learn who has supplied T-bone Smith with this weapon, Himes veers into the secondary backstory of how Chitterlings, Inc., came to be. A long-abandoned plot of land by the Tombigbee River in Mobile, Alabama, which once belonged to the Harrisons, a slave-owning family with questionable sexual mores, lies in rot until Tomsson Black (originally christened George Washington Lincoln), a convicted Black man whom Himes alternately identifies as a rapist / former Black Panther Party member / Marxist sympathizer, buys it under the guise of his business, Black for Blacks, Inc. He explains to prominent Black leaders in the United States that "this project would be non-profit making, and that its sole purpose would be that of employing indigent blacks and taking them off the relief rolls and other forms of white charity," harkening back to a rhetoric akin to that of personal responsibility espoused by conservative leaders.[20]

As Chitterlings, Inc., begins masquerading as a pig farm and Black rises to power, more and more "mystery guns" crop up in the United States, resulting in the death of white people throughout the country. At first, the response from white liberals is one of guilt, of a "masochistic desire" for punishment.[21] Soon enough, this gluttonous wallowing shifts to righteous indignation and the insistence on white innocence: they want the killings to make sense rather than continuing—as they label it—as the slaughter of "innocent, unengaged, unknown white strangers."[22] The response from both juridical and extrajuridical formations are, as to be expected, multiple and extravagant, ranging from lynchings to riot tanks decimating entire blocks in Harlem, from failed calls to reinstate slavery to the practice of Jim Crow–like restrictions. At the conclusion of the novel, Coffin Ed and Grave Digger discover that it is Tomsson Black who is sending these guns out, only addressed to Black men, and that it is Black who "had acquired ten million guns and a billion rounds of ammunition, and once they had all been distributed and blacks had become familiar with their use and in the tactics of guerilla warfare . . . issue[d] an ultimatum to the white race: grant us equality or kill us as a race."[23] During their confrontation, Coffin Ed pulls his gun on Black, vowing to protect his family and friends from the ensuing white violence that Black's rebellion has created. In a surprising move, Grave Digger pulls his own gun on his old friend and partner, saying, "You can't kill, Black, man . . . I'd rather be dead than a subhuman in this world."[24] When Coffin Ed refuses to stand down, Grave Digger shoots him in the head; in the next sentence, Black executes Grave Digger in the same manner.

A reductive reading of Himes's abandonment of this novel is that he could not face killing off the two characters for which he is best known; it is telling that the original and unfinished manuscript ends at the moment before the detectives figure out who is responsible for the mystery guns, mere pages before their nearly simultaneous deaths.[25] As Michel Fabre and Robert E. Skinner write in the introduction to *Plan B*, Coffin Ed's and Grave Digger's deaths are tantamount to "literary suicide and one can well understand why Himes became stalled and could not carry the book through to publication during the early 1970s."[26] While this can be one interpretation of why this text remained unfinished (in favor of *Blind Man with a Pistol*), I wish to focus on the failure of Black's insurrection. Yet rather than focusing solely on Black's justification and rationale for Plan B—in which "B" stands for "Black"—I want to offer a few readings of Grave Digger's blunt statement to Coffin Ed, complete with typo: "You can't kill, Black, man."[27]

The typo of these dual commas, whether placed there by Himes, Fabre, or Skinner or the editors, offers us two distinct readings of this statement depending on the correction. Hypothetically, first consider the correction in this way: "You can't kill Black, man," where it becomes a statement that confirms Grave Digger's commitment to Black's seemingly revolutionary principles. A second and potentially more evocative correction: "You can't kill, Black man," which would then shape his statement as one that moves beyond Tomsson Black's misreading of the situation at hand. Black admits that he did not anticipate the following questions—"Why should black men act any different from white men in a similar situation? . . . What was the difference between a Black man and a white man whose antecedents had lived under the same society and with the same values and beliefs for three and a half centuries?"[28] If we take Grave Digger's statement as "You can't kill, Black man," this becomes a potential answer for Black's questions: the difference between a Black man and a white man, it seems, is that no matter what, Black armed resistance will not result in enough deaths for revolution. While white men, women, and children can be and are killed in *Plan B*, Grave Digger's sorrowful explanation of the situation to Coffin Ed points to the inevitable and always present failure that accompanies insurrection.

The dual commas also do double duty: a comma represents a brief pause, and the two of them in the statement also work to set apart the word *Black* from the rest of the sentence. In other words, I read both the comma and the commas as punctuations of interregnum, rife with the possibilities of reading into them Gramsci's morbid symptoms of disrupted and eruptive time. As Jennifer Devere Brody writes, punctuation is "neither speech nor writing; art nor craft; sound nor silence. . . . Punctuation performs as a type of (im)material event or, perhaps, as a supplement."[29] The commas supplement and direct our reading, interrupting—or performing Keeling's Black cut—into the linear and temporal sentence structure of Grave Digger's statement. They force a speech act without actually being speech.

This is perhaps why Himes is unable to complete the novel: to do so, to search for a logical conclusion to the narrative of a race war, is akin to admitting that revolution writ large is nigh impossible. Read in this way, Grave Digger's shooting of Coffin Ed is less an uncharacteristic move against his partner and friend and more a recognition of the symptomatic anti-Blackness that reduces them to nothing more than vermin exterminators in an absurd world. Grave Digger's recognizes that this system is incapable of meting out justice, as are the detectives themselves; this understanding accompanies Himes's recognition that the genre of hardboiled fiction is also unable to offer an eternal reprieve to his characters, resulting in their termination. The only answer, from Grave Digger's and Himes's points of view, is death. To quote Toni Morrison's *Playing in the Dark: Whiteness and the Literary Imagination*, they both take to heart that "the master narrative could make any number of adjustments to keep itself intact."[30] While I do not wish to overdetermine the significance of the novel being unfinished at the time of his death, the fact that it was, in some ways, solidifies its existence as the disruptive fissure in Himes's publications. The series, in other words, remains caught on a comma.

Plan B is discordant from Himes's "Negro Martyrs Are Needed," published in *The Crisis* in 1944, where he writes, "Martyrs are needed to create incidents. Incidents are needed to create revolutions. Revolutions are needed to create progress." The aim of such a revolution "is the enforcement of the Constitution of the United States . . . a revolution by a racial minority for the enforcement of the democratic laws already in existence." Moreover, "revolutions are not necessarily brought about by force of arms. They may be successfully accomplished by the manifest will of the people. In the event of a Negro American Revolution it is to be hoped there will be no shooting." By the time he is writing *Plan B*, however, Himes espouses that "in order for a revolution to be effective, one of the things that it has to be, is violent. . . . In any form of uprising, the major objective is to kill as many people as you can, by whatever means you can kill them, because the very fact of killing them and killing them in sufficient numbers is supposed to help you gain your object."[31] How to account for this radical shift? Is it the wars and revolts unfurling on the international stage, in Vietnam, in Algeria? The establishment of the Black Panther Party for Self-Defense in Oakland, California? The Black Power Movement in London, England? Or perhaps it is Himes's own permanent relocation to France (and later Spain), because, as he writes in 1969, he "felt [he] would have a better chance to survive in some other country. . . . All [he] wanted to do was live—*to keep alive*."[32] And thus while Himes's definition of revolution as armed struggle is borne out in *Plan B*, as the unmarked guns and unmarked shells point to the indisputable fact that the weapons are meant for political assassinations, "You can't kill, Black, man."

I wish to propose one other means of reading the dual commas in that sentence. Significantly, while Tomsson Black sends the first gun to T-bone, it is actually T-bone's common-law wife, Tang, who understands precisely what is occurring. T-bone recoils from the nearness of a promised freedom, insisting on his time served; his illiteracy means that he cannot read the note. Instead, it is Tang who reads the note and proclaims, "We gonna be free! . . . That'll chip a white policeman two ways, sides and flat. That'll blow the white out of whitey's asshole," directing the reader's attention directly to the whiteness of policing in the United States.[33] T-bone is flabbergasted at this response; Tang merely responds, "You wanna uprise, don't you? . . . You think I wanna sell my pussy to whitey all my life?"[34] As the situation escalates, she declares, "I shoulda known, you are whitey's slave; you'll never be free."[35] Those are her last words; immediately after, T-bone stabs her, and "she crumpled and fell and died, as she had known she would after she first saw the enraged look on his face."[36]

To reiterate before continuing my reading of Tang, Tomsson Black arms only Black men—the shooters Himes lists include a student, a Baptist minister, a Black nationalist, a father, a handyman, a doctor, a HEW (Department of Health, Education and Welfare) administrator, and, in the two large-scale shootouts within the novel, an unnamed, half-naked Black man and a janitor. It is the last character who, of all the ones listed, comes closest to explicitly stating outright what is at stake in Black's plan: "He had waited four hundred years for this moment and he was not in a hurry. . . . He knew his black people would suffer severely for this moment of his triumph," but "he would have to believe that although blacks would suffer now, there would be those who would benefit later."[37] The deaths of the unarmed man and janitor result in patently absurd situations: the former's literal explosion from a 105 mm shell, shot from a tank, results in an "immediate horror . . . so great the mind could not accept it. The mind recoiled from it. Some of the white cops found themselves laughing uncontrollably."[38] The absolute violence of the moment causes the retreat of sensibility. Meanwhile, the janitor's death results in the stock market crashing: "The dollar fell on the world market. The very structure of capitalism began to crumble. Confidence in the capitalistic system had an almost fatal shock. All over the world, millions of capitalists sought means to invest their wealth in the communist east."[39]

In the space of this absurdity, the character who reads the uprising as holding revolutionary potential is Tang. She is the one who sees most clearly the issue at hand: T-bone's demands are for equality or death. While it is easy to overlook as a minor plot point, I turn to the question she poses to him: "You think I wanna sell my pussy to whitey all my life?"[40] For Tang, what she calls an uprising is not defined through the upholding of the Constitution or the recognition of equal status; rather, it results in the destruction of a social and economic world order that is maintained through the selling of her body, that has been maintained through the enduring fungibility of Black female bodies. Literally named after the slang terms for female genitalia, her language explicitly connects her prostitution with chattel slavery when she accuses T-bone of putting "[her] on the block to sell [her] black pussy to poor white trash," to "go down into Central Park and trick with some white man so they could eat."[41] The invocation of the block upholds her incredulous belief that T-bone cannot see what she sees: that an armed uprising holds the possibilities of eradication of the world and, simultaneously, the creation of new one and that *these two events are already occurring* in the pause that we might read as an example of Keeling's "queer temporality," a Black and queer reading of the interregnum that "governs errant, eccentric, promiscuous, and unexpected organizations of social life."[42] To phrase it slightly differently, I turn to Terrion L. Williamson's argument that we must "consider black social life from the vantage point at which it is lived."[43] Black situates equality or death as the only two outcomes of revolution. For Tang, however, her embodied knowledge and lived experience solidify in the most principled rationale for the uprising—the concomitant obliteration of capitalism and racism, one that cannot exist without the other, played out on her body.

Himes believed, at one point, that "the black man can destroy America completely, destroy it as a nation of any consequence. It can just fritter away in the world. It can be destroyed completely."[44] Yet what comes to light, at least in *Plan B*, is that this frittering and destruction have no chance of succeeding because Tomsson Black's understanding of the interregnum is akin to a liberal reading of such—in the in-between and moving toward the "better" that Malatino critiques. Better for whom? It is clearly not better for Tang, as there is no space allowed for her intersectional critique of the violence articulated in *Plan B*. In Tang, I see how we must read "the domain of the symbolic" (for what does Tang stand in?) "in relation to the material foundations" (and how has Tang arrived to be here?).[45] Insurrection, when affixed to Black masculinity in *Plan B*, can only be read as *being*, staying, in the condition of possibility that extends only insofar as it imagines the coming of a new world rather than a consideration of what might already be. "You can't kill, Black, man."

I do not wish to produce a romantic reading of *Plan B*: Tang always dies, at the hands of her husband/pimp, in the least spectacular fashion because her weapon, the first of Black's guns, weighed with the significance of what she ascertains, is also loaded with misreading. Yet I want to end here by suggesting that the marginalized figure of Tang embodies a promise of an uprising that refuses the narrative rather than rewriting it, that sees the Black cut, that sees "foment, generation, complexity, and fervor" as already here. Her last words to T-bone are "You'll never be free."[46] For Tang, "You can't kill, Black, man" is written true; I read her as that misplaced comma that disrupts Himes's masculinist revolution, the "crumpled" mark that disorganizes and reorganizes Grave Digger's statement and forces us to focus on the pause. She and that second comma—and she *as* that comma—function as "a key role in our quotidian movements and missteps by stopping, staying and delaying the incessant flows of information to which we are subject."[47] Keeling situates Bartleby's passivity as the directing force of Melville's novella; I read Tang as the comma, the interregnum, that disrupts Himes's focus on the impossibility of revolution in an absurd world. What is the freedom she desires, the freedom that is near? In a novel so steeped in the absurd, only she dares to speak the obvious: that a politics of revolution must call out how merely *rewriting* the master narrative is absurdity writ large.

NOTES

1. Himes, *My Life of Absurdity*, 1.
2. Himes, 1.
3. Himes, *Quality of Hurt*, 73.
4. This kind of reading also expands a formative reading of time and history in historical materialism and cultural studies, that of Walter Benjamin's Angel of History, who faces backward while the debris of progress—violence—mount at his feet.
5. Gramsci, "Wave of Materialism," 276.
6. Gramsci, 276.

7. Malatino, "Future Fatigue," 644.
8. Keeling, *Queer Times, Black Futures*, 174.
9. Keeling, 41.
10. Keeling, 109.
11. Abbot, *Street Was Mine*, 3.
12. Himes, *Blind Man*, 20.
13. Himes, *Plan B*, 51.
14. Fuss, *Sense of an Interior*, 5.
15. Himes, *Plan B*, ix.
16. Himes, *My Life of Absurdity*, 363.
17. Himes, *Blind Man*, 191.
18. Himes, *Plan B*, 8.
19. Himes, 8.
20. Himes, 150.
21. Himes, 105.
22. Himes, 129. Himes seems to be saying, to borrow from Fanon, that they are incapable of comprehending his edict that if one argues that all Black people are the same, the only reply must be that all white people are the same.
23. Himes, 200.
24. Himes, 202.
25. The rest of the manuscript is reconstructed from a detailed outline, first in French by Michel Fabre in 1983 and then in English by Robert Skinner in 1993.
26. Himes, *Plan B*, xxix.
27. Himes, 202.
28. Himes, 200.
29. Brody, *Punctuation*, 3.
30. Morrison, "Romancing the Shadow," 51.
31. Himes, *Plan B*, xxi.
32. Himes and Williams, *Dear Chester, Dear John*, 50.
33. Himes, *Plan B*, 8, 9.
34. Himes, 9.
35. Himes, 11.
36. Himes, 12.
37. Himes, 174, 175.
38. Himes, 66.
39. Himes, 182.
40. Himes, 9.
41. Himes, 10, 4.
42. Keeling, *Queer Times, Black Futures*, 19.
43. Williamson, *Scandalize My Name*, 15–16.
44. Williams, *Dear Chester, Dear John*, 46.
45. Hall, "Formation of Cultural Studies," 23.
46. Himes, *Plan B*, 11.
47. Brody, *Punctuation*, 6.

BIBLIOGRAPHY

Abbot, Megan. *The Street Was Mine: White Masculinity in Hardboiled Fiction and Film Noir*. London: Palgrave Macmillan, 2002.

Brody, Jennifer DeVere. *Punctuation: Art, Politics, and Play.* Durham, NC: Duke University Press, 2008.

Fuss, Diana. *The Sense of an Interior: Four Writers and the Rooms that Shaped Them.* London: Routledge, 2015.

Gramsci, Antonio. "'Wave of Materialism' and 'Crisis of Authority.'" In *Selections from the Prison Notebooks of Antonio Gramsci*, edited and translated by Quintin Hoare and Geoffrey Nowell Smith. New York: International, 1971.

Hall, Stuart. "The Formation of Cultural Studies." In *Cultural Studies 1983: A Theoretical History*, edited by Jennifer Daryl Slack and Lawrence Grossberg. Durham, NC: Duke University Press, 2016.

Himes, Chester. *Blind Man with a Pistol.* New York: Vintage Books, 1989.

———. *My Life of Absurdity: The Later Years.* New York: Thunder's Mouth, 1976.

———. *Plan B.* Jackson: University of Mississippi Press, 1993.

———. *The Quality of Hurt: The Early Years.* New York: Paragon House, 1971.

Himes, Chester, and John A. Williams. *Dear Chester, Dear John: Letters between Chester Himes and John A. Williams.* Edited by John A. Williams and Lori Williams. Detroit: Wayne State University Press, 2008.

Keeling, Kara. *Queer Times, Black Futures.* New York: NYU Press, 2019.

Malatino, Hil. "Future Fatigue: Trans Intimacies and Trans Presents (or How to Survive the Interregnum)." *TSQ: Transgender Studies Quarterly* 6, no. 4 (November 2019).

Morrison, Toni. "Romancing the Shadow." In *Playing in the Dark: Whiteness and the Literary Imagination.* New York: Vintage, 1993.

Williamson, Terrion L. *Scandalize My Name: Black Feminist Practice and the Making of Black Social Life.* New York: Fordham University Press, 2017.

5

Police-Time

Tia Trafford

Future Remain the Same

Stephen Lawrence was eighteen when he was stabbed to death by a group of white racists in southeast London. His best friend Duwayne Brooks later described his murder as "like a lynching from the days of slavery." Speaking amid Britain's home office hostilities and institutionalized anti-Blackness, Doreen Lawrence also located her son Stephen's killing within what Derek Gregory terms the "colonial present":

> [The police] treated the affair as a gang war and from that moment on acted in a manner that can only be described as white masters during slavery.... Everything in this country has Black people who have played a part in it.... We helped to make the National Health Service what it is today, we have good transport, you name it and we have been a part of it.... My feelings about the future remain the same as they were when my son was murdered. Black youngsters will never be safe on the streets.... The police on the ground are the same as they were when my son was killed. I am hearing killing on the streets and in the back of police vans and it is clear that nothing has changed.[1]

Considering the content of this statement and Doreen Lawrence's later invocation that "nothing has changed," I want to read the phrase "future remain the same" as not only an expression of feeling. I read "future remain the same" as also expressing the colonial present by situating anti-Black violence across the reverberating spatio-temporalities of colonial modernity.

The colonial present thereby does not only index how trajectories of slavery, colonialism, and imperialism continue into the present. But also, the colonial present indexes how colonial modernity shifted to accommodate formal equality while leaving its frameworks unexamined and the plantation system reorganized rather than ended.[2] That "future remain the same" does not collapse histories into analogy; nor does it suggest that history is static. Rather it centers how, as Frank Wilderson writes, "[Black people] are policed all the time and everywhere."[3] Both abstract and intimate, the universality of Black policing is embedded and entrenched across the world to the extent that, as Rinaldo Walcott puts it, "deaths at the hands of police and other state actors and substate actors are so frequent and so numerous as to be a normal part of Black life."[4] Attending to the death of Stephen Lawrence in this context is articulated as a multifaceted moment *within*: transatlantic slavery, plantation, apartheid, segregation, colonization, dependency of the Global North on the labor of peripheral nations, the police van.

This chapter reconsiders modernity's claims to progress by centering its coherence with the universality of anti-Black policing. Many have focused on modernity's racialized temporalities, arguing that the chronopolitical exclusion of Black people promotes a future as white destiny.[5] Here, I show how the irrevocability of Blackness indexes a fissure within modernity's teleology. For the architects of modernity, history's sequentiality relies on both the inescapably regressive status of Black Africans and their eventual annihilation. So the problem of modernity is not a white destiny that excludes all others; it is that white destiny is both necessary and impossible.

The aporia of white destiny sets in motion its indefinite postponement by fraught technologies of temporality that police and enclose Blackness to produce a limited and stalling progress. The concept of the interregnum signals time's stagnation as crisis or condition. Here, I am primarily interested in the attempt to suture white progress—*as reform*—to Black stasis *as both crisis and condition*. The stuttering oscillations of temporality foreclose interregnal possibilities insofar as the concept suggests something hopeful, a breaking free from, which I argue could only possibly hold within it a return. The universality of anti-Black policing forms both the unthinkable condition of modernity's futurity and its irredeemable failure to petition the future.

Police Reform

The pitiful Metropolitan Police response to the 1993 murder of Stephen Lawrence was investigated by the Home Office, which found the force to be institutionally racist. The 1999 Macpherson Report produced by this investigation was perhaps the most significant call for police reform in recent British history. The finding seemingly represented a significant shift from the Scarman Report, of nearly two decades earlier, that had investigated the 1981 Brixton uprising. Then, Lord Scarman had blamed "tensions" between Black communities and the police on perceptions of institutional racism and the nature of Black family structures, while conceding that there were a few bad apples within the police force. Scarman spoke of "understandable" failures of Black communities to deal with oppression and poverty, suggesting that unemployment and family structure lay at the root of the uprising.[6]

In contrast, Macpherson argued for action to be taken across police and social agencies. The report called for seventy reforms to policing and criminal law in addition to suggestions for reforming local government, the National Health Service, and the school system. At the time, the report was widely decried by stakeholders in white supremacy, but over time those reforms are said to be embedded in a reformed police force. In 2020, for instance, Metropolitan police chief Cressida Dick stated that they had embraced Macpherson's challenge:

> I was the person charged with implementing the recommendations and I'm very proud of what we did. I think we've come a very, very, very long way.[7]

The repetition here—"very, very, very"—indicates both movement and punctuation. Social progress is indexed to a dialectical relationship between police as institution and the progressive social movements from which oppositions to specific instances of policing arise. The temporalities of progress and reform are compressed in this incantation that would confine anti-Black policing to the past.

As critics have long argued, reforms embedded in policing operate as part of a machinery of deferral through which progress can be produced and measured within the frameworks of liberalism.[8] But this suggests a more deeply embedded problem. Resistance to police is dealt with insofar as reforms are the process through which oppositions to police can be internalized and policing remade. Reforms are counted as progressive insofar as they are also the stasis of return and "making good with" an anti-Black state. Calls for reform embed a promise of progress into a political time that will never arrive.

As such, "police reform" can be considered as a conjunction that not only defines and delimits police opposition with consequences that ensure the deferral of progress by oscillating around stasis and progress but also encapsulates a fundamental temporal operation of colonial modernity that thrives on the anti-Black violence that forms its condition of possibility.

Anti-Blackness *as* Time

It is often supposed that history was brought into being through colonial modernity insofar as linear temporality was produced through its categories.[9] That a sequential form of temporal order—of progression, development, and expansion—was set *against* the state of nature (embodied by Black African people) and *toward* a future determined by (European) man.[10] Blackness is both necessary to and also positioned outside of time—as anachronistic and subject to nature's caprice.[11] Concepts of backwardness and pastness provided a framework that justified colonialism as part of the process of evolution toward modernity.[12] The sequentiality produced ensures that Black African people would perpetually be in a position of "catching up" to white time or consigned to a regressive past. The myth, accepted by both critics and advocates of imperialism as a civilizing mission, is therefore that the force of imperial conquest imposed backwardness on the colonized.

We find this articulated by the philosophical architects of modernity. For example, Black people, according to Immanuel Kant, "have by nature no feeling that rises above the ridiculous," and so without "capacity to act in accordance with concepts and principles," they are incapable of the reason that could underwrite freedom and history.[13] G. W. F. Hegel also judged that history proper begins only with the Caucasian race.[14] The incapacity of Black Africans to determine a universal order from nature causes their enslavement to arbitrariness.[15] Humanity is here defined through the cultural achievement of history. Hegel writes that "what we properly understand by Africa, is the Unhistorical, Undeveloped Spirit, still involved in the condition of mere nature."

So here, Hegel shares Kant's insistence that rational law is the basis of freedom requiring the subordination of naturalness to order as progress. Black Africans are bound to their senses and so incapable of the negation of the given that would be required to distance themselves from nature and become part of history. They are trapped within immediacy. Hegel formulates a conception of "the African" that is of time but not in time.[16]

The binding of the political remaking of the world within the present is possible on condition of future novelty. It is important to foreground that, for philosophical modernity, the future cannot merely be given but must be constructed since futurity is not by itself necessarily novel. Change occurring through contingency and chance must therefore be subordinated to *progress* that is built through the actions of human reason. Any supposed "civilizing mission" of imperial expansion must then re-form the earth through culture in accord with reason and law, recursively embedding the global development of history. In Kant's later work, the actions of reason are thereby understood as a constructive project that turns the material of the earth into the world:

"Without man all of creation would be a wasteland, gratuitous and without final purpose."[17] This project is teleological. Development from a "lawless state of savagery" is intertwined with a developmental theory of natural order that promises the remaking of the earth in the image of a Europe to come.

We see this in Kant's cosmopolitanism, which has usually been understood as a kind of gradual perfectibility in which the goal of history lies with the global ordering of humanity under universal principles of law and morality. For example, Robert Louden suggests that Kant is committed to all humans eventually sharing a common destiny.[18] But this global ordering of humanity is to be enforceable under violence against any society not yet deemed to have escaped the "lawless state of nature."[19]

This prepared the path for Hegel's dialectical movement through history toward freedom understood as a correlation between the rational human mind and the institutions that humans create.[20] Hegel is concerned to see how history and culture set in motion the process of reason's self-realization in the world. World history is constituted through the integration and absorption of alterity through a process of negation and the overcoming of prior civilizations that consolidates advanced forms of culture. European culture emerges as a series of dispositions of reciprocal limitation and adjustment along a racialized hierarchy of perfectibility that relies on the progressive manufacture of the earth as the world. This is a generative relationship of *poiesis* between reason and its external scaffolds that is also reliant on a story of progression and the temporality of a world to come.

As Andrea Long Chu suggests, for Hegel, world history is the dialectical process through which freedom is actualized in the form of the rational state.[21] This dialectic is inherently expansive, moving to envelop a world and, as Hegel writes, "push beyond its own limits . . . in other lands, which are either deficient in the goods it has overproduced or else generally backward in industry."[22] This is justified since "only certain races produce peoples,"[23] as Hegel wrote, so "one must educate the Negroes in their freedom by taming their naturalness."[24] Deracination, enslavement, and plantation work formed the basis of "education" for Hegel.

Finding its culmination in Hegel, the hierarchy of perfectibility attributes universal moral properties to white Europeans, which relies on exclusions and the subordination of Europe's "others." As such, the so-called education and imperial support offered require the deferral of progress through a logic of endless postponement.[25]

The Impossibility of White Destiny

Frantz Fanon's analysis of the dialectic pushes beyond this now standard critique, which centers a humanity foreclosed by the European as the "universal measure, that is, as the bodily, mental, and societal actualization of universality."[26] The binding of the Black African into temporality cannot be processed as a chronopolitical exclusion that focuses on the endless deferrals of a "freedom to come that never comes, continually postponed."[27] "The settler makes history," Fanon writes: "He is the absolute beginning, 'This land is created by us.'"[28]

Wrenching history into being such that modernity's novelty could be unshackled from nature's contingency requires rupture with, rather than exclusion of, Blackness. The impossibility of ordering the symptomatic disorder ensconced in the Black African ensures the universalization of anti-Black violence, but it also indexes colonial modernity's aporia: anti-Black violence is the necessary motor for white destiny.

Race is irrevocable for Kant: "Race, when once it has taken root and extinguished the other seeds, resists all further transformation because the character of race at one point became dominant in the generative power."[29] Any commitment to the progression of the human species cannot possibly involve Black people, who "infect or compromise the very idea of humanity as Kant conceived it."[30] As sketched above, for Hegel world history is produced through the subordination and dialectical overcoming and subsequent absorption of alterity. The condemnation of Black Africans to absolute alterity and regression thus requires imperial intervention that could ensure the global advancement of civilization. But Hegel agrees with Kant's judgment that "Negroes . . . cannot move to any culture,"[31] since their "condition is incapable of any development or culture, and their condition as we see it today is as it has always been."[32] Denied the possibility of development, Black Africans are "frozen in the mode of immediacy."[33]

There is a fissure within modernity's teleology. Fanon draws attention to the fact that "at the basis of Hegelian dialectic [is] an absolute reciprocity that must be highlighted."[34] The dialectical machinery of history operates through mutual recognition with alterity moving to reinvent both past and present as a process of overcoming by sublation. The attempted sublation of prior stages requires both shared purpose and ground with the subject of a recognition because a "one-sided activity would be useless."[35] But situated in the plantation and colony, Fanon argues that where for "Hegel there is reciprocity; here the master laughs at the consciousness of the slave."[36] Rather than forming an alterity that can be sublated and unified, Fanon argues:

> The colonial world is a Manichean world. . . . The colonialist turns the colonized into a quintessence of evil. . . . The "native" is declared impervious to ethics, representing not only the absence of values but also the negation of values. He is, dare we say it, the enemy of values. In other words, absolute evil.

So considered from within Hegel's vision of history, dialectical circuity is shut down, making the "two-way movement unachievable."[37] The abrogation of history from the Black African must operate by rupture such that Blackness cannot possibly be recognized. But "in effecting this deprivation, [the white man] disables himself from entry into the recognitive process."[38] The Manichean world of mutual exclusion—of absolute oppositions that cannot be unified, neither interdependent nor interpenetrating—indexes a nondialectical antinomy that short-circuits historical progress.[39]

If modernity were to be eventually capable of achieving its asymptotic goals, it would seem to require not the dialectical progression of the entire species but the annihilation of those who were deprived of entry.[40] However, the movement of history itself requires the irrevocably atemporal status of Blackness:

> eternally aligned with the status of immediacy, of corporeality, serving as the Other, as that which must be sublated or superseded in order for self-identity—of Europe, of the male—to be realized.[41]

The logics of colonial modernity seem to require the destruction of their own conditions. Put bluntly, temporal progress would require the annihilation of those it requires as its basis for defining time.[42]

Explicating Fanon's argument, M. R. Habib clarifies this point:

> By placing Africa in a permanent state of nature, in a perpetual state of being-in-itself, [Hegel] simultaneously divests subsequent historical stages of the ability to develop through any truly dialectical interaction with the stages that they supersede.[43]

The problem of modernity is not a white destiny that excludes all others; it is that white destiny is both necessary and impossible.

Infinite Postponement

As such, attention is drawn away from dismissal, or philosophical analysis of history's fissures and modernity's problems. Rather, embedded within the colonial situation, their aporetic form both conditions and confounds resolution. This is to say that the tendency and drive of colonial modernity toward extinction would create "a void which empties foreign domination of its content and its object: the dominated people," as Amílcar Cabral put it. The urge to destroy the colonized would "amount to the immediate destruction of colonization," as Fanon asserted, citing Jean-Paul Sartre. Modernity's dependence on those it requires as its basis for defining time indexes a terminal aporia in which history is driven through the management and staving off of anti-Black genocide. What it sets in motion as a project of infinite postponement is therefore not characterizable as the white paternalist or temporizing universalism in which freedoms are endlessly deferred. Rather, this is an infinite postponement of the progressive political structure of the world as white destiny.

Taking this dependence and postponement as a spiraling point of entry into the colonial present is inimical to temporalities of succession and repositions the phrase "future remain the same."[44] The fragile dependencies of the colonial present employ practices of reform and social inclusion not as a progression but as an operation of the attempted suture of white order.[45] Indefinite postponement operates through the movement of social inclusions and exclusions in a supposedly dialectical motion as a process of *reformist* management reliant on anti-Black violence.

For example, the 2021 Sewell Report chartered by the Conservative Party, seemingly to appease itself (and all stakeholders in white supremacy) after antipolice protests earlier in the year, similarly announced that we have reached the end of institutionalized British racism. Emerging in response to the murder of George Floyd by the Minneapolis Police Department officer Derek Chauvin, Britain's protests were barely acknowledged before they were sanctioned for their violence by Prime Minister Boris Johnson.[46] Set in another moment of potential destabilization of the police-public compact, the report stated that incremental progress is beyond doubt, drawing attention to the relationship between progress and fatalism:

> You do not pass on the baton of progress by cleaving to a fatalistic account that insists nothing has changed.[47]

Attending to anti-Black violence operates as a fatalism in this logic, attempting to cleave stasis against progress.

Reforms are often felt as stasis and deferral. Cue the multiple reports, articles, and statements analyzing progress ten years, twenty years, forty years on. These engagements implicitly reify a notion of progressive policing, making room for reform's dialectical movement to grind into motion once more. So, in seeming opposition to the Sewell Report, a Home Affairs Committee report published in July 2021 considered the Macpherson Report twenty-two years later, bemoaning how a representative police force would not be reached at the current rate of progress for another twenty years.[48]

The oscillation continues. The 2021 Home Affairs Committee report called for renewed attention on Macpherson's suggested reforms and targets, centering the need for diversity within the policing and criminal justice system, and attention to stop-and-search disparities. As if in conversation with Doreen Lawrence and the Sewell Report, Labour MP Yvette Cooper discussed the report as follows:

> We have found that in too many areas progress has stalled.... Without clear action to tackle race inequality we fear that, in 10 years' time, future committees will be hearing the very same arguments that have been rehearsed already for over 20 years.[49]

The dividing line between reform and a politics of equal-opportunity law and order is tipped out as a continuum along the binary of stall and progress. They are together productive of a state whose benevolence and viciousness are modalities of the colonial present.

Time as Fatal

I have suggested that the conjunction "police reform" expresses the temporality of progress as stasis—operating as a primary engine through which policing can be infinitely expanded and embedded into the everyday. Reformism is the logic of supposed dialectical progress, but that process indexes the continued attempt to suture white order under police.[50] The inertia and petrification of the colonial situation, which is characterized in the Sewell Report as "cleaving to a fatalistic account," is here both violence's cause and effect.

The production of time as fatal (as perpetuated death) operates through a fatalism (as permanent state of nature) that is both necessary and illegitimate for colonial modernity.[51] Insofar as the concept of the interregnum rests on prior progress and potential breakthrough, its possibilities and demands would therefore be routed through police reform. The structure of novelty is dependent on an impossibility that sutures temporality to dialectical stutter between fatalism and stasis. Valorizing the "radically" new is thus born of a desire to both reify and deny the conditions through which the world itself requires continual founding and refounding.

As such, there is no progressive possibility for Blackness in the absence of violence, just as there is no possibility for modernity to petition a future in the absence of Blackness. But, far from indexing stasis and fatalism, the temporality of "future remain the same" indexes a sprawling temporality that is unthinkable as temporality (or at least within temporalities marked by progress), while also providing the conditions and context for the construction of temporality as such.

NOTES

1. Lawrence, "Statement."
2. See Gray, "Now It Is Always," 41; Hartman, *Scenes of Subjection*, 119; Sharpe, *In the Wake*, 73.

3. Wilderson, "We're Trying," 46.
4. Walcott, *Long Emancipation*, 12.
5. For examples, see the references in notes 9–12.
6. See Smith, "Unravelling the Thatcherite Narrative."
7. Braddick, "Met Is Not."
8. Shange, *Progressive Dystopia*, 4.
9. Mills, "Chronopolitics of Racial Time"; Hesse, "Racialized Modernity."
10. Mignolo, *Darker Side*, 151.
11. Hanchard, "Afro-Modernity."
12. Johnson, "Possible Pasts," 485.
13. Kant, *Anthropology, History, Education*.
14. Bernasconi, "With What Must."
15. Jackson, *Becoming Human*, 112.
16. Jackson, 112.
17. Kant, *Opus Postumum*.
18. Louden. *Kant's Impure Ethics*.
19. Kant, *Perpetual Peace*, 98.
20. Habib, *Hegel and Empire*, 6.
21. Chu, "Black Infinity," 416.
22. Hegel, *Philosophy of Right*, S246. See Hirshman, "On Hegel."
23. Hegel, *Philosophy of Mind*, 47.
24. Cited in Stone, "Hegel and Colonialism."
25. Brendese, "Black Noise."
26. Da Silva, *Toward a Global Idea*; Bhabha, "'Race,' Time."
27. Chu, "Black Infinity," 417.
28. Fanon, *Wretched of the Earth*.
29. Kant, cited in Bernasconi, "Will the Real Kant," 13–22.
30. Bernasconi.
31. Hegel, *Lectures*, S67.
32. Hegel, *Reason in History*, S190.
33. Habib, *Hegel*, 81.
34. Fanon, *Black Skin, White Masks*, 191.
35. Hegel, *Hegel*, S182.
36. Fanon, *Black Skin, White Masks*, 39.
37. Fanon, 92.
38. Habib, *Hegel*, 68.
39. In particular, see Marriott, "Judging Fanon."
40. See Bernasconi, "Will the Real Kant"; Harfouch, *Another Mind-Body Problem*.
41. Habib, *Hegel*, 80.
42. Agathangelou and Killian, *Time, Temporality, and Violence*.
43. Habib, *Hegel*, 68.
44. Hartman and Wilderson, "Position of the Unthought."
45. Hartman, *Scenes*.
46. BBC News, "George Floyd."
47. Commission on Race and Ethnic Disparities, *Report*.
48. Home Affairs Committee, *Macpherson Report*.
49. White, "Racism in Policing Remains."
50. Rodriguez, "Reformism Isn't Liberation."
51. Agathangelou and Killian, *Time, Temporality, and Violence*.

BIBLIOGRAPHY

Agathangelou, Anna M., and Kyle D. Killian, eds. *Time, Temporality, and Violence in International Relations: (De)fatalizing the Present, Forging Radical Alternatives*. New York: Routledge, 2016.

BBC News. "George Floyd: Boris Johnson Urges Peaceful Struggle against Racism." BBC News, June 9, 2020. https://www.bbc.co.uk/news/uk-politics-52973338.

Bernasconi, Robert. "Will the Real Kant Please Stand Up." *Radical Philosophy* 117 (2003): 13–22.

———. "With What Must the Philosophy of World History Begin? On the Racial Basis of Hegel's Eurocentrism." *Nineteenth Century Contexts* 22 (2000): 183–184.

Bhabha, Homi. "'Race,' Time, and the Revision of Modernity." *Oxford Literary Review* 13, no. 1 (1991): 193–219.

Braddick, Imogen. "Met Is Not Institutionally Racist, Says Commissioner Cressida Dick." *Evening Standard*, August 13, 2020. https://www.standard.co.uk/news/crime/cressida-dick-met-not-institutionally-racist-a4524421.html.

Brendese, P. J. "Black Noise in White Time: Segregated Temporality and Mass Incarceration." In *Radical Future Pasts: Untimely Political Theory*, edited by George Shulman, Mark Reinhardt, and Romand Coles, 81–111. Lexington: The University Press of Kentucky, 2014.

Chu, Andrea L. "Black Infinity: Slavery and Freedom in Hegel's Africa." *JSP: Journal of Speculative Philosophy* 32, no. 3 (2018): 414–425.

Commission on Race and Ethnic Disparities. *The Report*. 2020. Accessed on March 14, 2022. https://www.gov.uk/government/publications/the-report-of-the-commission-on-race-and-ethnic-disparities/conclusion-and-appendices.

Coulthard, Glen S. *Red Skin, White Masks: Rejecting the Colonial Politics of Recognition*. Minnesota: University of Minnesota Press, 2014.

Da Silva, Denise F. *Toward a Global Idea of Race*. Minneapolis: University of Minnesota Press, 2007.

Fanon, Frantz. *Black Skin, White Masks*. Translated by Charles L. Markmann. London: Pluto, 1986.

———. *The Wretched of the Earth*. New York: Grove, 2004.

Gray, Biko Mandela. "Now It Is Always Now." *Political Theology* (June 2022): 1–15. https://doi.org/10.1080/1462317X.2022.2093693.

Hanchard, Michael. "Afro-Modernity: Temporality, Politics, and the African Diaspora." *Public Culture* 11, no. 1 (1999): 245–268.

Harfouch, John. *Another Mind-Body Problem: A History of Racial Non-Being*. Berlin: Global Academic, 2018.

Hartman, Saidiya. *Scenes of Subjection: Terror, Slavery, and Self-Making in Nineteenth-Century America*. New York: Oxford University Press, 2010.

Hartman, Saidiya V., and Frank B. Wilderson. "The Position of the Unthought." *Qui Parle* 13, no. 2 (2003): 183–201.

Hegel, G. W. F. *Hegel: The Phenomenology of Spirit*. Oxford: Oxford University Press, 2018.

———. *Philosophy of Mind*. Translated by W. Wallace and A.V. Miller. Revised by M. Inwood. Oxford: Oxford University Press, 2007.

———. *The Philosophy of Right*. London: Hackett, 2015.

———. *Reason in History*. London: Macmillan, 1953.

Hesse, Barnor. "Racialized Modernity: An Analytics of White Mythologies." *Ethnic and Racial Studies* 30, no. 4 (2007): 643–663.

Hirshman, Albert O. "On Hegel, Imperialism, and Structural Stagnation." *Journal of Development Economics* 3 (1976): 1–8.
Home Affairs Committee. *The Macpherson Report: Twenty-Two Years on Home Affairs Committee.* 2021. Accessed on March 14, 2022. https://publications.parliament.uk/pa/cm5802/cmselect/cmhaff/139/13902.htm.
Jackson, Zakiyyah Iman. *Becoming Human.* New York: New York University Press, 2020.
Johnson, Walter. "Possible Pasts: Some Speculations on Time, Temporality, and the History of Atlantic Slavery." *American Studies* 45, no. 4 (2000): 485–499.
Kant, Immanuel. *Anthropology, History, Education.* Edited by Günter Zöller and Robert Louden. Cambridge: Cambridge University Press, 2007.
———. *Opus Postumum.* Cambridge: Cambridge University Press, 1993.
———. *Perpetual Peace and Other Essays.* London: Hackett, 1983.
Lawrence, D. "Statement to the Home Office." *The Guardian*, February 24, 1999. https://www.theguardian.com/uk/1999/feb/24/lawrence.ukcrime.
Louden, Robert B. *Kant's Impure Ethics: From Rational Beings to Human Beings.* Oxford: Oxford University Press, 2000.
Marriott, David. "Judging Fanon." *Rhizomes* 29 (2016). http://www.rhizomes.net/issue29/marriott.html.
Mignolo, Walter. *The Darker Side of Western Modernity.* Durham, NC: Duke University Press, 2011.
Mills, Charles W. "The Chronopolitics of Racial Time." *Time and Society* 29, no. 2 (May 2020): 297–317.
Rodriguez, Dylan. "Reformism Isn't Liberation, It's Counterinsurgency." *LEVEL: Abolition for the People Series*, October 20, 2020. https://level.medium.com/reformism-isnt-liberation-it-s-counterinsurgency-7ea0a1ce11eb.
Shange, Savannah. *Progressive Dystopia: Abolition, Antiblackness, and Schooling in San Francisco.* Durham, NC: Duke University Press, 2019.
Sharpe, Christina. *In the Wake: On Blackness and Being.* Durham, NC: Duke University Press, 2016.
Smith, Evan. "Unravelling the Thatcherite Narrative: The 1981 Riots and Thatcher's 'Crisis Years.'" *New Historical Express*, January 9, 2013. https://hatfulofhistory.wordpress.com/2013/01/09/unravelling-the-thatcherite-narrative-the-1981-riots-and-thatchers-crisis-years/.
Stone, Alison. "Hegel and Colonialism." *Hegel Bulletin* 41, no. 2 (2020): 247–270.
Walcott, Rinaldo. *The Long Emancipation: Moving toward Black Freedom.* Durham, NC: Duke University Press, 2021.
White, Nadine. "'Racism in Policing Remains an Issue, 20 Years after Macpherson Report,' Say MPs." *Independent*, July 30, 2021. https://www.independent.co.uk/news/uk/home-news/racism-policing-home-affairs-committee-b1893324.html.
Wilderson, Frank, III. "'We're Trying to Destroy the World': Anti-Blackness and Police Violence after Ferguson." In *Shifting Corporealities in Contemporary Performance*, edited by Marina Gržinić and Aneta Stojnić, 45–59. London: Palgrave Macmillan, 2018.

6

Blackness and Disability Justice in Pandemic Times

A Conversation with Therí A. Pickens and Sami Schalk

Therí A. Pickens and Sami Schalk with SAJ

Therí A. Pickens (New Body Politics, 2014; Black Madness :: Mad Blackness, 2019) and Sami Schalk (University of Wisconsin–Madison) are joined by SAJ in a conversation to explore futuring work that holds Black disabled people with love. This conversation takes up a central question: How do we think about building futures and the work it takes to get there? We shared perspectives on the interregnum from writing, teaching, care work, and community building, ultimately exploring and exploding the interconnected threads of time, space, bodily materiality, and action.

SAJ: Academic theorizing and social and cultural meaning-making are built around both organized abandonment of and unabandoned violence against Black body/minds. This knowledge shapes thinking on the interregnum, epochs and breaks, temporalities, and the need for utter transformation. In counter: the significant body of ongoing work to expand our collective horizon of possibilities, in the face of simultaneous oppressive work to "patch" or "prevent" any kind of socio-structural break. I hope that there is a chance today to consider and discuss how Black, disabled, mad, fat, crip, queer, and trans activists, artists, and thinkers approach this horizon of possibilities. To begin, how are you currently thinking about temporality and time and, perhaps, this idea of "break"?

SAMI: When thinking about our current moment, I'm still always thinking in terms of pandemic time-temporality and pandemic time; I think a lot about pace and speed; there are so many ways that it feels like we've been in this forever and it also feels like no time at all. In particular, I was thinking about the end of the world and whether or not that's where we're headed in many different ways and, because I'm in conversation with Therí, thinking about Octavia E. Butler and *Parable of the Sower, Parable of the Talents,* and the way that Butler represents the speed of apocalypse as not always fast. It's slow until it's not. I've been having more and more of those moments lately, particularly around climate change, where it was snowing in April here but then it was also ninety degrees in May. Or I've been kayaking here (in Madison, Wisconsin) more, and the algae that's normally here at the end of the summer is here in May, and it's already too gross to swim in the lakes here. So I'm seeing these ways that I'm clocking the change that feels kind of slow because it's seasonal and yet also fast that all of a sudden we're here. The pace feels slow and then fast but also unpredictable, in particular regarding climate change. In that same way of the gated community coming down in *Parable of the Sower,* I think that climate crisis is that moment when "now there's a fire and you have to leave." Some of my friends are in Los Angeles, and they had to leave their homes. Or there's a hurricane, and you have to leave. But it feels like we're always slowly creeping towards it, and you just don't know when it's suddenly going to be fast with immediate danger.

THERÍ: One of the things that I really like about being in conversation with Sami is that it feels like we are two sine/cosine graphs that sometimes meet up and sometimes deviate in really productive ways. I think that right now being in an English department, trying to work for a more antiracist curriculum, we're having to rethink periodicity, and part of the difficulty of that paradigm is that it's the geography that English departments are built on. They're built on the geography of the United Kingdom and the United States, and they're also built on a periodicity that starts in the U.K. and continues into the U.S. That particular intellectual mapping is contingent on dividing time in a certain way. And to do away with that also means that you have to, for the sake of practicality, divide the curriculum in another way, but you also then have to trouble what the time periods look like—whose time are you keeping? If I'm thinking about something like crip time or "CPT, colored people's time," then there's an entirely different temporality at stake. I'm not sure that a Black history would usefully divide U.S. history into the time periods that we usually think of. If you are thinking about queer Black history—so we're both in pride month and Black music month at the time of this conversation—what does it mean to trace a time period from, say, Prince's time, which is obviously different from Michael Jackson's time, which is obviously different from the now-departed Tina Turner's time? When I think about temporality, I think about pace and speed, and I'm also thinking about the nature of whose time we're on.

I think trying to consider how to live within this space also means consistently resetting your idea of *when* you are. There's another addition to this, an interjection of Michelle Wright, who says that Blackness is not a "what" but a "when."[1] So *when* are you Black? *When* are you disabled? *When* are you both? Because that time is also contingent on space. My Blackness is not the same in Maine as it is in New Jersey, is not the same in academic conferences as it is with my family. The when is also contingent on a where, as well as contingent on what time is supposed to do in that moment. Is it supposed to keep you on track as a speaker? Or is it supposed to just lapse because the family event technically starts when some person gets there with their dish? Or so-and-so is on the grill. I'm thinking very much of summer events. I think just trying understand when and where we are is much more flummoxed if you're keeping track of time based on a Black disability framework or a Black queer one, anything nonwhite and non-Western, all of the litany of those of us thus far not included.

SAMI: And I think of the specificity of experiences that the time you were just talking about—there's that material thing of "When do we eat?" Well, we eat when this person does their thing, and that's what it is. Or we eat when the brisket is ready; it's gonna cook until it's cooked.

THERÍ: Low and slow.

SAMI: That's right, low and slow every time. I also think about flexibility—and maybe Therí you want to talk about your work on Black madness. I think about trauma and the way that shifts our experiences of time. What's on my mind is that recently I got a bunch of childhood things from my mom, and I was rereading my high school journals, because I journaled daily through high school and into college. And it can take me right back there. There were ways that I had to say to myself, "You are no longer an insecure, scared teenager. It is OK." Or times that I had to put that down because it was taking me out of time or taking me to a different time that I actually don't want to be in anymore. There's a lot to that around triggers and activated states in general, where folks are elsewhere and that elsewhere isn't necessarily place but also time.

THERÍ: It's funny to hear you say that because I journaled all through high school as well, but in 2007, after a pretty huge argument with a family member, I threw all my journals out. I regret that decision every day of my life.

But I think having the object and being able to time travel, as it were, is a different experience of trauma and madness and difficulty mental health-wise as well. I started journaling when I was twelve, which is when I received my diagnosis of myasthenia gravis. Those memories are really fragmented. And there's a utility sometimes I think to the forgetting that time allows. It can be quite useful to understand the concept of the mad Black as a concept that is very unresolved and nonlinear and always in process. And there's also, I think, a desire (for some people falling into that category) for closure and for the ability to tie the bow, close the loop, put a period at the end of a sentence. But there's also a kind of frightening in-process part of what it means to never close the chapter or to close it very loosely only because you have to move into a different time period, say, adulthood—which is the worst -hood I've ever been in. I want to move. So there's also a kind of loose definition of time that can force you to shut and force you to create a regna, to live inside an interregnum. Your adolescence is a long interregnum or can be particularly in the U.S., where college is understood as an extended adolescence as opposed to a gateway to adulthood. Thinking about mad Blackness as in process can be frightening as well as freeing. Because there's also the possibility of letting go when you feel like letting go. Or letting go arbitrarily, which has its own merits.

SAJ: I notice this in your most recent books, a sort of moving relationship to time that you're describing, in the sense that there is an opening up of possibility or maybe a refusal of closure that also shapes how I see your work in *Black Madness :: Mad Blackness*, Therí, and there is also a very generative push in *Black Disability Politics*, Sami, for—I wouldn't say closure but specifically a direction towards transformation. I've been thinking and holding these two as—what do the anarchists say? A diversity of tactics. But also the Black freedom politics of "by any means necessary." The opening and the pointedness of your approaches as parallel ways of thinking about Black disabled time and transformation. It also reminds me of Moya Bailey's work.[2] Do time travel, time transformation, or varied kinds of movement and time (not just slowness) sit alongside an ethical approach to pace?

THERÍ: Ethics is a useful mode for thinking about the question of how we ought to be to each other, or how people have decided to be toward each other given the confines of ableism, white supremacy, et cetera. It strikes me that given all those confines, one of the ethical things is to take people as they come to you, which means that they're coming to you with a different time than perhaps the one you're living in. So, pace in an Intro to African American Literature course, the students always say it's too fast. And I'm thinking,

"I don't really want to linger in the slave narratives the way that you all seem very comfortable here for some odd reason. I don't wanna stay here." I hate teaching the first part, pre-1910, because it always forces me to be in a time that is deeply traumatic, but it is also a time that the students believe themselves to be very familiar with. They think they know about enslavement in a way that they don't think they know about the Depression or in a way that they already know that they don't know about the mid-twentieth century. And there's a desire to stay in the period that is intellectually familiar and also allows them to say, "This is just like today." They collapse time. For me, the ethics of that is to not linger as much as they'd like in terms of texts but not go too quickly in terms of concept either.

The pace of teaching is actually keeping multiple temporalities in mind. The temporality of the syllabus moving from, say, Lucy Terry to James Weldon Johnson or Nella Larsen, that wide expansive time between the eighteenth century and the early twentieth. Then also moving intellectually at a pace that is quite slow, only getting to four or five major concepts because it is a 100-level class. And then there are also some students keeping a heightened time because they're more advanced students, and they are doing the optional reading, and so they're bringing themselves into the present as well as into the past. Some of them are doing theoretical readings, some of them are combining information in one class and another, so I've got their time to keep track of, and I've got my own time to keep track of: where I'm at emotionally vis-à-vis the material, where I'm at intellectually vis-à-vis the material, and then also where I'm at that's outside of class because this is not my area, and so my intellectual commitments at any given semester or year are definitively not slave narratives. So keeping track of all of those and also trying to be ethical means that they are certain parameters that I put up: a contract-graded syllabus where there's a bare minimum and anyone who wants to go above that will do what they wish, and also requiring that they meet with me. Being ethical in my position of power requires more time. And being ethical between historically marginalized groups, depending on the nature of power, is not the same as being ethical where the distribution of power and privilege is so heavily imbalanced. There's that as an example of ethics and what they look like, and I think about that a lot with regard to teaching because it's a hard thing to do in the spaces that some of us are forced to do them in.

SAJ: Thinking about taking people at the time they are in, which is not necessarily your own, reminds me of Black queer disability organizing, for example, Peoples Power Assemblies NYC, which deliberately had marches and actions led by disabled people, to set the pace for everyone by being in front.

I'm wondering what other kinds of lenses or lessons, strategies or tactics, that the activists or artists or theorists that you've engaged with offer for us? Perhaps thinking through time and pace but also beyond that.

SAMI: I'm glad Therí took it to teaching. I was thinking about movement stuff because I think that there are several phrases that come out of movement work around this idea of pace and speed that really bring up the questions for me around individual experiences of temporality and pace. And then what Therí was highlighting, of what happens when we're moving as a collective whether that is short-term, like a semester, or that is longer-term, movement building. How do we consider these power dynamics within whatever the collective is? In disability justice we have to think about "leave no one behind," so there's the practice of disabled folks being up front; they determine the pace in a march, for example. That's a very concrete example, but there are other ways we can think about what it means to leave no one behind in our organizing and moving at that pace. In transformative justice work, we talk about moving at the speed of trust in terms of relationship building, and that for me is one that really makes clear the individuality of pace because some of us don't trust very easily. It takes a long time for us to genuinely trust a person, and that's shaped by individual identities and experiences, including trauma. So when we talk about the ethics of pace, that is still something that has to be determined within individual and collective groups. I think sometimes my earnest students who really want the world to be different, they want one clear cut rule of How To Do the Thing. The thing is that all those rules have to adapt depending on who's here, who's in the room right now, and who are we trying to reach. Because not everyone is involved in every single thing. Moving at the speed of trust is this key concept that really highlights that pace is individualized, to be figured out between whomever. And things can't be forced to move any faster than the slowest person.

THERÍ: The other thing we come up against is that there's the ideal for how we wanna work with people and how we're planning on interacting, and—to return to Octavia Butler—there's also the nature of outside pressures. For each one of her novels, she's got a kind of internal pressure that the character is up against and an external one. She loves time-based pressures, something that's pending. So *Fledgling*, for instance, has that "must find the people that want to kill me before they kill me" aspect of it that speeds things along. And then there's the three-day council of judgment that also speeds things along. I think reading Butler gives you a sense of what the strategies are when the ideal situation is not possible. I think one of the things that makes her work so difficult to represent on-screen is that most of her characters are very practical and not necessarily very warm. They aren't necessarily the ones in the movement that have the baked goods and present you with a strategy in a way that you may feel affirmed and heard. It's like, "This is what we have to do to get the shit together because we're facing apocalypse or death or aliens." So there's that as sort of looking to fiction for strategies because fiction is made in a controlled environment, and so you get a chance to brainstorm. Sami, I don't remember what year this was, but the Shaping Change conference with Moya and—

SAMI: 2016?

THERÍ: OK, so we were there with someone who asked, "How do you create movements with people when you love them but don't like them, or when you care about them but find it difficult to be among them?" That's been a question that's governed the way that I try to understand what these strategies look like. Like in the academy: being a professor is a job, but in the workplace, "family" is one of the most dangerous metaphors. What's the strategy when you deeply care about the same things, and they're related to justice, and they're related to and impactful for how people are living their lives, but what's the strategy when you cannot be your chair's sister? I defy her to call me her sister, but I would be lying if I didn't say I didn't care deeply about the same things that she does. I think Butler as an artist-theorist offers those sets of strategies, ways to think about those things.

Another artist-theorist-activist that I'm engaged with is Fred Moten, whose work is so elastic, and I think between the poetry and the theory are these spaces. One that he's theorized as "the cut" or "invagination," with all that that implies and entails, he's asking fundamentally the question: What happens in the between space? Where's the resistance there? How is resistance created and processed and then activated? And he openly talks about this, of having a son with autism, which means that he is operating consistently on crip time and operating in the space, as it were, between what people understand to be agreed-upon, unspoken social norms and the availability of people's bodies/minds to meet those norms and whether or not they should. I think as an artist, what he offers is a kind of place to sit. And I think of whenever there's a television series with magic, there's always a place where the characters get pulled to that is everywhere and nowhere. It's this nowhere space—not the sunken place—but somewhere where all the magic exists at once, but they can't do anything with their powers. I think what Moten offers is a place to kind of rest there in the elasticity. But also there's always an urgency to that space, the characters usually have to get out and do something, and Moten's work doesn't lose a sense of that urgency even with the oneiric quality of his writing.

SAMI: Many of us in disability justice are thinking about the pandemic as a mass disabling event on multiple levels, including folks who have long COVID, but also the yet-to-be understood effects of COVID. We're seeing more young folks with dementia, people in their twenties and thirties, and we're seeing more children with diabetes who had COVID. We don't yet understand the direct and indirect impact of the virus on bodies or the impact on society as a whole. For example, how many folks were, either intentionally or by force, delaying medical care for months to years because hospitals weren't able to do surgeries or because it was such a risk to go to a doctor if it wasn't life-threatening? People were putting things off. It will be years to really understand what it meant for many folks to essentially not have health care for this period. And, of course, there's trauma and grief. I think about some of my friends that lived in New York and at one point had a refrigerated truck with dead bodies posted outside of their apartment building because they couldn't bury people fast enough. All my friends who were frontline workers, doctors and nurses, what they were experiencing. There's all these ways that folks are being disabled physically, mentally, and now we're just being told "go back, it's fine, it's normal, it's good. Let's keep going. Let's keep up the pace." And actually kind of make up for the pace when we slowed down.

    A strategy that I've been thinking about lately, particularly as a person who has had more disabled people in my life in the last few years, including a partner with long COVID, is disability doula-ing or crip doula-ing. This concept comes from Stacey Park Milbern, who coined the term, and Leah Lakshmi Piepzna-Samarasinha.[3] Crip doula-ing is helping bring someone into disability community and disability identity, whether that's someone who has been disabled for a long time and is just now developing a more political lens for that or, in the wake of this mass disabling event, people who are figuring out being newly disabled. There are sometimes conflicts, with folks with long COVID saying, "We need more money for research and cure," and longtime disabled people being like, "Oh, babies, oh, sweet, sweet things, with your belief that the medical industrial complex will save you. Please, come with us." This can happen sometimes in not very kind ways; disabled people are still hurt and traumatized ourselves, so when we see folks who we believe could be part of our community distancing themselves and saying, "We don't need access and accommodations, and we don't need long COVID to be recognized as a disability. We need treatment, cure, medical research; we need money for that"—it can be really challenging for longtime disabled organizers. We really are in a moment where the U.S. health care system has not yet fully collapsed, but it's on the brink. This is a moment when crip doula-ing, bringing people into community and sharing disabled wisdom about care networks and tools that we use outside of the state, which very clearly is not going to save us, feels very important. A lot of that is very individualized work but a strategic approach can focus on getting people into community faster, because there's just so many who need that information.

I'm seeing a variety of ways that people are doing crip doula-ing either directly in relationships or by putting out informational things in more mass audience ways, which I think of as still crip doula-ing. Tons of other disabled people can give you advice whether or not they have the same disability as you, like helping people realize, "Oh yeah, canes are a thing," or sharing strategies for handling fatigue. Watching the emerging long COVID community interact with disability justice communities leaves me asking, "How do we gently bring folks in?" And my work centers Black disabled folks, so how do we do it without a bunch of white disabled people just screaming at Black people and other people of color that they're disabled and need to get that and get it now? It took me a really long time to come into my disability identity, and that was partially shaped by my relationship to white disabled people who would say things like, "Just call me when you finally admit it." And I didn't like that attitude, the way that some people would condescendingly tell me who I am versus just offering me space to figure that out in community; it made me want to pull back even further. Right now feels like a really important time before whatever the next major world-falling-apart crisis is, to really try to bring folks into that care and political community around disability.

SAJ: Just taking a second to name that we hear this: desire both for community-building and also space and time and gentleness as part of that. Community as *not* just a group of white angry people yelling, "Get on the same page as me." Community as attentive to where and when you are at. I love crip doula-ing as a way to practice this. Thank you for bringing Stacey Park Milbern's work into this space. I wonder to what extent the Harriet Tubman Collective has been doing some of that?

SAMI: Yeah, absolutely. I think by coming together and virtually organizing, the Harriet Tubman Collective was the beginning of a creation of a Black disability-specific community. And frankly, my interviews with many of those folks for the book was what got me to finally be able to talk about myself as disabled in a more public way. They were reflecting so much of my experience back to me and also making really useful—while still kind and open—arguments about the importance of identifying as disabled as Black people, publicly, especially when we're leaders. Candice Coleman who works for Access Living in Chicago said something in my book to the effect of, "This is a tool. We want to bring people into community, not because identifying as disabled is the goal but being in community where you can learn that these things you're experiencing are not you, it's not your fault, you are not alone, there are strategies." The community connection is the goal, and identity is a path into community.

Generally, when people say, "I'm disabled," in disability justice communities, we're like, "Great, come on in." We don't police. We don't ask for your paperwork. When you use certain words, it's a way of finding each other. That was one of the things that really helped me shift, to think, "Yeah, what I want is to find community." And even though I've been part of disability studies communities for a long time, it really took me coming into Black disability activism specifically that helped shift my own understanding. Crip doulaing is part of a network of personal support that happens in disability communities. A loved one of mine got a new diagnosis, and I hit up my network to be like, "Who do we know that I can connect this person to that may be closer to their specific diagnosis?" That network of support and connection that happens behind the scenes, that care work that happens, it doesn't have to be face-to-face; it can happen over text or Facetime, even if you live in the same city. Sometimes we both can't get out of bed, so we've gotta connect outside of just face-to-face. And these activist networks are crip doula-ing networks in various ways.

SAJ: Exploring the impact of connection on people's real lives—this troubles and exceeds the limits and flaws of the ocularity of representation, much like the artist-theorists you explore, Therí. Connection exceeding representation. Yet the health care system collapse is happening perhaps simultaneously with the limit of social media as an infrastructure for connecting so that we are perhaps isolated, siloed, more than ever, and must struggle to connect. Once again, the labor for something that should be a social structure is falling on the people who need it the most, but then also in my experience, there can be something enormously beautiful that is created out of that.

THERÍ: It's really beautiful to hear the energy and the possibilities that are present in these other spaces. I think it's also important to acknowledge not everyone has access to that. So I think in hearing that I was like, "Oh wow, I'm so glad that exists," and then also sort of wracking my brain to figure out where I'm getting that, and it's not always possible. While there's also great hope there, there's also the flipside of that.

SAMI: Yeah, I think about how Leah Lakshmi Piepzna-Samarasinha talks about how it's important to not just represent care networks as being this magical, rainbow, glitter solution because sometimes everyone is in a flare-up, or everyone can't access it, or the network is just down, strained, strapped.[4] I think Leah even says something like, "Sometimes care networks are just a bunch of people screaming and crying at each other." Community is actually not an end goal but a continual process of people changing and people becoming more disabled and having different needs. So community is this ongoing, shifting network, and I think that it's important to recognize that it is not perfect and not always rainbows and sunshine and not possible for everyone as our world is now. Like, who is likable? Who has public-facing capacity? Those folks might have the most support, but what about the cranky people that don't want to make a bunch of friends? How are they also going to be in community? How do we be in community with one another and not necessarily all be besties but still genuinely show up for one another? [It] is an ongoing process question, because it takes a lot of work. People have different capacities, and folks with higher capacities can forget that and assume that people just don't care about making and maintaining connections and doing "the work," whatever "the work" is in that particular moment.

NOTES

1. Wright, *Physics of Blackness*.
2. Bailey, "Ethics of Pace."
3. Piepzna-Samarasinha, *Care Work*.
4. Piepzna-Samarasinha, *Future Is Disabled*.

BIBLIOGRAPHY

Bailey, Moya. "The Ethics of Pace." *South Atlantic Quarterly* 120, no. 2 (2021): 285–299.
Pickens, Therí. *Black Madness :: Mad Blackness*. Durham, NC: Duke University Press, 2019.
Piepzna-Samarasinha, Leak Lakshmi. *Care Work: Dreaming Disability Justice*. Vancouver: Arsenal Pulp, 2019.
———. *The Future Is Disabled: Prophecies, Loves Notes, and Mourning Songs*. Vancouver: Arsenal Pulp, 2022.
Schalk, Sami. *Black Disability Politics*. Durham, NC: Duke University Press, 2022.
Wright, Michelle M. *Physics of Blackness: Beyond the Middle Passage Epistemology*. Minneapolis: University of Minnesota Press, 2015.

Spaces of the Interregnum

7

Decolonizing Gender

Reading Interregnum in the Colonial Disruption of Matriliny

Anna Karthika

Interregnum in the Colonial Arc of Gender

Colonial encounters have been replete with moments where human lives were brought together to create a history that categorized those lives for asymmetrical purposes. The colonial historiography captures the episteme of a time that was dictated by the idea of resemblance in understanding encounters rather than embracing the notion of difference, particularly of hierarchy when those encounters transformed from the curiosity of a traveler to one that committed to gaining mastery over the Other. This was constitutive of the coexistence of excluded and subjugated bodies of people outside of the European liberal subjects—that is, white, androcentric, male, heterosexual, and capitalist subjects—within the folds of European universalism transpired into colonized territories. The loss and exile of history of these excluded bodies have been manifestly homogenized by the "figure" of Europe impelling on the necessity to read the "history from below" in an exigent manner.[1]

To Dipesh Chakrabarty, historicism "is what made modernity and capitalism not look simply global but rather as something that became global, *over time*, by originating in one place (Europe) and then spreading outside it."[2] The logic of historicism is then entangled in a process of continuity, the instance Chakrabarty writes as the one that placed everybody else outside an "imaginary waiting room of history"; the waiting being that of "the realization of the 'not yet' of historicism."[3] It is in this idea of the "imaginary waiting room of history" that this chapter articulates the concept of interregnum as a continuing phenomenon. For Chakrabarty, Europe is not just a cartographic representation of a geographical location rather a particular way of thinking linked to codes, principles, and standards that originate in the European Enlightenment, which assume non-Western societies as places that cannot be attributed to the telos of progress and history but of "stagnation" and "backwardness." Importantly, this way of thinking furthers the idea that non-Western societies remain perfectly translatable to Western terms of European universalism where they are constantly measured against the questions, what would be their notions of equality, if they were ever exposed to liberal thinking and what kind of modernity would they have if they had any?

Such non-Western societies, therefore, remain in the "imaginary waiting room of history," expected to aspire to a future, that of Europe. In the backdrop of an unchallenged translation of the non-West in the ambit of an uncritical transfer of ideas, practices, and historiography in a single direction from the West to the non-West, interregnum is the "always ever in the 'waiting room of history'" living in the absence of history, the absence of theory, and the absence of originality.[4] This interregnum is not temporary, the "in-between" or provisional. It remains a perpetual specter that has failed to unpack both the West and non-West to realize that in-betweenness is the conversation between them. The interregnum perpetuates an understanding that concepts emerging from European and American social and political philosophy carry with them the potential for universalization, but the same is not assumed for theories and philosophies emerging in non-Western societies. Therefore, in disrupting the prolixity of Eurocentric history, the enduring specter of interregnum ought to be deconstructed within the discourse of decolonization demanding a critical inquiry from the Global South on the experiences of colonized bodies under Western, imperialist knowledge production. This demand of the discourse of decolonization is legitimate because the codes of Eurocentric Enlightenment thinking were deciphered on the colonized bodies toward dehistoricizing them and shaping them through the ciphers of Western, colonial gender norms of heteronormative sexed bodies.

This chapter aims to underscore that the methodological craft of the discourse of decolonization is significant in rethinking the concept of the interregnum. To think from one's own locale is the position that is being insisted here in reading the interregnum—that is, to privilege one's own location—recognizing the spatial and temporal arrangements, which permeate all traveling theories that transcend the Eurocentric universalism with specific but heterogenous, multiple non-Western places and histories. An interpretation of interregnum is, therefore, firmly invoked in the decentering of the West through a decolonized exposition of gender. If the West is understood to have been built on the erasure of its own premodern history and defined as the antithesis to the Other, then decolonization of gender is compelled to challenge the Eurocentric universalism of Western Enlightenment defining West/non-West.[5] In this chapter, the decolonization of gender is read through the obliterated histories of a matrilineal past creating a discursive Other in relation to the modern conception of body[6] *defined* by power historically and discursively (legally, biologically, socially, etc.). The attempt, here, is to explore matriliny as one of the multiple sites unraveling the unfiltered violent character of colonial knowledge project in its articulation of colonial categories and classifications within the changing juridical-administrative policies and sociopolitical practices defining a new gender typescript in the colonized Indian subcontinent. The site of matrilineal historiography becomes an internal site of non-Western knowledge tradition in studying interregnum in the colonial arc of gender.

The historical project of shaping the modern body in Kerala—the coastal, peripheral southwest state in India, which started with a series of subtle colonial moves to abolish matriliny as a social structure in this region since the end of the nineteenth century and beginning of the twentieth century, invokes a reading of interregnum from the specificity of the heteronormative order of gender formation in matriliny. The idea of the modern body is historically constructed through the imperialist narratives of the Other following the historical encounter between (colonial) modernity and the body of the "native" Other in Kerala. It evolved in Kerala since the nineteenth century in a constant colonial attempt to tame and obliterate its constitutive outside—that is, other diverse nonheteronormative imaginations of the body specific to Kerala's history of matrilineal family kinship. The body, especially its sexual aesthetic, became the focus of the historical project of shaping the modern subject.[7] This facilitated recasting matriliny in order to construct patrilocal family as the base unit for the society in Kerala to enter into modernity.

Colonial Compass Disrupting Matriliny

On the southwest coast of India, there resided the "most lecherous and unchaste nation in all the Orients," wrote Linschoten, a Dutch traveler from the seventeenth century, as noted by G. Arunima.[8] They were the Nairs[9] of Malabar, which currently constitutes the northern part of Kerala.[10] It is not just the "excesses" of Nair women who took "series of lovers, oftenin one night," that shocked the European minds, according to G. Arunima, for promiscuity among men and women defined the Nair community, but it was "the absence of 'chastity and shame' in Nair women" that was difficult to conceive.[11] This exoticized polyandrous tradition of not having fixed husbands but having the entitlement and liberty to do what they please with themselves enchanted the Europeans who traveled to the coast of Calicut in the sixteenth century in the northern part of Kerala.[12]

In the nineteenth century, nearly 50 percent of the "Malayali[13] population, of different castes and communities, were matrilineal."[14] The interregnum coincided with the formation of modern gender identities during this time in Kerala, which was "implicated in the project of shaping governable subjects who were, at the one and same time, 'free' and already inserted into modern institutions."[15] By the end of nineteenth century, the texture and practices of the Nair and the royal households of Kerala were completely erased. It was British colonial dominance that ultimately shaped Malayalee modernity, particularly when intense efforts were made to "reform the customary practices and hierarchies of particular castes and give shape to 'modern communities.'"[16] The body, especially its sexual endowments, was and continues to be critical to the historical project of shaping the modern subject.[17]

In the matrilineal Nair household, known as the *taravad*, particularly of the Malabar region of Kerala, the centrality of women in the structure of households has been far more stable in comparison to the southern region of Travancore, Kerala. The women belonging to Nair subcastes were claimed to have certain sexual freedom, but seemingly only entered hypergamous liaisons, desirably with Brahmin men of the upper caste in the form of the *sambandham*—a relationship shaped without any expectation of its longevity or permanence, often considered "skewed."[18] The female line of inheritance of the collective property was bereft of paternal instincts and affection, as there wasn't any father-son relation in these households. For example, under *taravad*, land was owned collectively and inherited through female lines. Marital homes and the institution of marriage did not have decisive roles in Nair social arrangement.[19] This arrangement was considered beneath the civility of British colonial agents, who deemed the sexual freedom of Nair women to be of a promiscuous nature, and the want of paternalistic sentimentality was beyond the comprehension of the androcentric imperial temperament of colonizers.[20]

An early intervention from the British colonial government came when a new law was initiated instilling in the man the responsibility of providing for the wife and children—a law insensible to the Nair *taravad*, where the natal family provides for the woman and her children.[21] This resulted from the Malabar Marriage Act of 1896, which designated relationships in the nature of the *sambandham* to be instituted into monogamous marriages.[22] Until then women did enjoy access and control over economic resources, and their sexual freedom, in the form of polyandry, was acceptable to Nair families.[23] The last quarter of the nineteenth century saw educated Nair men who were colonial intermediaries and collaborators demanding reforms in the marriage system and individual rights to property. Their response embraced a colonial critique that essentialized "native" bodies, within the folds of the Western androcentric, bourgeois, heteronormative, capitalist, and white patriarchal structure of male dominance.[24] The "native" Indian elite, educated, heterosexual, upper-caste Hindu men compelled the "native" colonial subjects to heteronormative gendered notion of sexed bodies. Therefore, the cultural discourse of nationalist historiography was disinclined to oppose the imperial project's assertion that bodies outside of heterosexual, patriarchal, upper-caste, bourgeois, monogamous marital relations ought to be disciplined in order to prepare them to be fitting colonial subjects.

The enactment of the Malabar Marriage Act in 1896 was considered the first and most important step in the direction of abolishing all nonmonogamous, nonnormative conjugal relationships in the region and was an event that occurred amid an imperialist liberal discourse of progress, freedom, and individual identity. Prior to the bill, a Nair woman would enter into an "alliance" (or *sambandham*) with a man of her choosing.[25] The reference to this history here is not to romanticize Kerala's lost matrilineal past, but as Gayatri Gopinath suggests, "despite its destruction at the hands of the colonial and postcolonial legal apparatus, traces of Kerala's alternative organization of gender and the various sexual practices . . . continue to be apparent."[26] Emphasizing the historical contingency of the colonial project of shaping the modern body, Gopinath quotes Deepa V.N. who argues that "Kerala's matrilineal past points to the historical relativity of the construction of the 'modern' family in Kerala as patrilineal, nuclear and monogamous and the variety of practices which have existed outside of this."[27] This invokes a certain assumption of a modern idea of colonial bodies subjecting them to colonial modernity of ideals emerging in Europe reordering "native" subjects into an interregnum, that is, the "imaginary waiting room of history" with the decline of matriliny and the foundation to a new heteronormative gender characterization of colonized bodies. From this ensued intrusive and invasive practices directed on nonnormative, nonprocreative, nonheterosexual, and alternate bodies and sexualities in an attempt to control sexuality, desire, and possibility.

Sambandham, the prcolonial customary institution that framed sexual relations between men and women in the matrilineal system, was not recognized in the official discourse of the colonial state as a legally valid relationship, that is, as constituting marriage. It was denied legal status on the grounds that it did "no more than create a casual relation, which the woman may terminate at her pleasure."[28] For the colonial authorities and Christian missionaries standing on the pedestal of virtue and moral righteousness, the idea that "the 'husband' failed to acquire property in the 'wife'" or to acquire the right to exercise, discipline, and regulate her body "did not conform to the dominant conception of sexuality, held together by male dominance and female subjection."[29] This modern shift away from matrilineal kinship was accompanied by a shift in the idea of the female body to the Victorian ideal, dehistoricizing the colonial bodies into the interregnum of the "imaginary waiting room of history."

The angular reading of colonial modernity, thus, reflects on Nivedita Menon's argument that modernity has not been "unambiguously emancipatory," and it has "eradicated spaces of relative autonomy and produced new forms of subjection."[30] The marriage law of 1896 tied marriage to provisions that would facilitate and recognize a new form of family/household focused importantly on conjugality.[31] To establish the primacy of conjugality to any form of family, women had to be "marked" differently or recast as monogamous, "chaste," and dependent on husband and father—both of whom were, in the matrilineal discourse, legal nonentities. The representation of female bodies as sexualized bodies of women of male/husband's desire is certainly acquired from the "capitalist patriarchal" vocabulary of colonial governmentality. The women of matrilineal families came to embody the anticolonial rebel body representing the undisciplined female body, which in the interregnum was unsettled by the collapse of histories of colonial bodies as the Eurocentric production of universal heterosexual norms was established. Colonial capitalist order has been, unequivocally, anchored in heteronormative sexual-relation patriarchal marriage laws to ensure the economic dependence of women in matrilineal families on their husbands, as an ultimate means of control over female sexuality.

Dialectic of Gender in Reading Interregnum

The erasure of the history of the colonial body can be read as a microcosm of the interregnum as defined in this chapter. The thoroughly gendered distinction between "man" and "woman" has translated itself into sexual exchange between the domestic body of the woman and public body of the man.[32] An example here is the colonially informed reforms by the nationalist elite men in India reflected in a particular history of dress reform in Kerala.[33] Toward the end of the nineteenth century, the colonial denunciation of Indians as "degenerate and barbaric" had become an irrefutable fact for the emerging modern, educated Malayalee population, especially the elite, upper-caste, bourgeoisie male populace.[34] They responded fiercely through extensive publications in print media, a tangible representation of interregnum conceived in the patriarchal capitalist ideology of the colonial print culture distinguished by colonial modernity.

In addition to merely interpreting Victorian moral values, this space of Malayalam writing and publication in late nineteenth and early twentieth-century Kerala offered to reform the moral constituency of both the body and the individual of the colonial subject to attain "modern" and "progressive" ethics and ideals of Eurocentric universalism. The target, once again, was the female body. This modern redefinition can be discerned in the sexual imageries of the fetishized female body that began to emerge in modern Malayalam literature. The transformation of matriliny in Kerala was an upshot of the colonial hegemonizing drive for gender configuration to strictly enforce heterosexual binary codes of maleness or femaleness, in the gender insertion of normative male and female behaviors to create ideal imperial subjects.[35] This was furthered through journals brought out by the missionaries and later through other newspapers and journals claiming to articulate the "public interest."[36]

Women's magazines in Malayalam promoted the idea of replicating the English lady through the promotion of domestication and motherhood. The magazine, *Keraleeya Sugunabodhini*, in 1892, declared, "We will publish nothing related to politics," and they intended to include such topics as "writings, that energize the moral conscience, cookery, biographies of 'ideal women' and 'other such enlightening topics.'"[37] As late as, 1926, yet another women's magazine, *Mahila Mandiram* firmly argued, "A woman's role was as mistress of the (husband's) household, and as caretaker and that she should leave everything else to the superior competence of men."[38] The emergence of the institution of the "public space" as a site of men's "competence" perpetuated the colonial idea and ideal of the female body into the interregnum. The political ideological change of the Victorian imperialist project meant that the social respectability of women from the emerging middle classes was being "defined in counterpoint to the 'crude and licentious' behaviour of lower-class women."[39]

This meant a class differentiation on the basis of "sexual mores for women" in accordance with the emergence of the "new bourgeoisie," which inscribed its identity "on the bodies and souls of women" to churn the proper lady through sexual morality on Indian society.[40] In colonial India, this translated into upper-class/caste representation of the sanitized, "respectable" women framed in terms of sexual virtue and chastity contained within the monogamous conjugal unit.[41] Colonialism initiated heterosexual gender patterns on the "native" bodies, delegitimizing premodern customary family structures through criminal law, medical jurisprudence, and literary production.[42] It also erased the presence and lived experiences of female bodies outside of marriage, nonnormative and nonheterosexual bodies, labeling them as "deviant bodies." The technologies of power articulated by colonial governmentality produced the grid of "heterosexual matrix" altering and disciplining the "deviant" colonized body in an attempt to create their suitable colonial subject.[43]

Rethinking the concept of the interregnum in terms of a continued history of the making of the modern body, triggered by the colonial state's abolition of matriliny and perpetuated by the postcolonial Indian state, is critical to decolonize "gender." Decolonizing gender would mean to resist, counter, and dismantle different disciplinary regimes through a social articulation of multiple bodies against an accumulation of racist, casteist, and ethnicity- and class-based gendered hierarchies. For Chandra Talpade Mohanty, "Decolonization involves profound transformations. . . . It is a historical and collective process . . . the creation of new kinds of self-governance but also 'the creation of new men' (and women)."[44] Knowledge thus produced in postcolonial historiography concerning forms of social and cultural organizations transcends the boundaries of the nation-state. It calls for new outlooks for understanding a methodology of historiography that could no longer be explained by a homogenous and hegemonic Eurocentric epistemology cast in the reading of interregnum in this chapter. Mohanty further asserts, "Decolonization coupled with emancipatory collective practice leads to a rethinking of patriarchal, heterosexual, colonial, racial, and capitalist legacies."[45] This assertion, certainly, reflects in postcolonial history writing, where the quest of sociohistorical reach exceeds the physical boundaries of Europe, dissociating from its production of knowledge, "provincializing Europe" and the interregnum caused by it.[46]

In the cultural hegemony of Western imperialist knowledge production, Oyèrónké Oyewùmí notes that "Eurocentrism is the racialization of knowledge" in which "male gender privilege as an essential part of European ethos is enshrined in the culture of modernity."[47] Decolonization of gender, then, stresses an explanation of the asymmetrical perceptions of the Other, especially of gendered female bodies in the Global South. The bodies that transgressed the interregnum of gendered colonial discourse of power accounted for those histories, which were detached from the histories of the hetero/homo binary-gender notion of imperialist sexed bodies. It is against this backdrop that the assertion of the term "body" against "gender" takes its central position. In postcolonial societies, gender is an undeniable and concrete tool of Western, imperialist knowledge framing the manifold bodies of the "natives." The compulsory and systemic deployment of heteronormative gendered notions steered toward the erasure of those bodies proved "deviant" to the moral codes of the colonial heterosexist, racist, and bourgeois patriarchy and confined in the "waiting room of history." Reading sexuality in Kerala is, thus, a particular kind of critique of the conceptions and norms that control the body in the colonial contexts wherein the West tends to conceive bodies from a Eurocentric liberal and universalist perspective, but an analysis of the "deviant" bodies opens up the discussion to decolonizing questions of gender, sexuality, and desires of the body.

NOTES

1. Chakrabarty, *Provincializing Europe*, 5.
2. Chakrabarty, 7.
3. Chakrabarty, 8, 16.
4. Nigam, "Decolonizing the Mind."
5. Raghuramaraju, "Rethinking the West."
6. Throughout this chapter "modern body," "colonial body," and "modern colonial body" are alternatively used to refer to the same heteronormative idea of the body, which emerged historically since the nineteenth century. In addition, "the idea of the body" and "the body" are used alternatively to the extent that the body, as a psychosomatic and sociopolitical reality, is inseparable from "its idea," how it is conceived, redefined, and shaped historically and discursively. Thus the "idea of the body" means "the body" in its historical unfolding.
7. Devika, "Aesthetic Woman," 460.
8. Arunima, "Matriliny and Its Discontent," 157.
9. In the archetype of Indian caste structure, Nairs are supposedly Sudras, the lowest in the caste hierarchy, but unlike the rest of India, there is considerable fluidity to Nair caste identity. According to Robin Jeffrey, they are

> the lords of the country, guardians of the public wealth; they wielded the distinctive privileges of the Kshatriya. . . . These distinctive privileges . . . added their close bond of union with the Nambuthiri Brahmin . . . point to their unmistakeable pre-eminence.
>
> Nairs weren't egalitarian and consisted of many sub-castes or lineages: those of "royalty," of local chiefs, of village headman, or of "commoners" who acted as retainers of the first three or of Nambuthiri Brahmins.

Jeffrey, *Decline of Nair Dominance*, 13.

10. Arunima, "Matriliny and Its Discontent," 157.
11. Arunima, 157.
12. Pillai, *Ivory Throne*, 12.
13. Malayali or Malayalee/Malayalees are an ethno-linguistic group of people residing in the state of Kerala in India.
14. Menon, *Sexualities*, xx.
15. Devika, "Aesthetic Woman," 461.
16. In Devika, "Being 'In-Translation' in a Post-Colony," 182–183.
17. Devika, "Aesthetic Woman," 461.
18. Jeffrey, "Matriliny, Marxism, and the Birth of the Communist Party in Kerala, 1930–1940," 80–81.
19. Jeffrey, "The Decline of Nair Dominance," 15.
20. Liddle and Joshi, "Gender and Colonialism," 522.
21. Liddle and Joshi, 523.

22. Liddle and Joshi, 523.
23. Pillai, *Ivory Throne*, 181.
24. Chatterjee, *Nation and Its Fragments*.
25. Gopinath, "Unruly Visions," 38.
26. Gopinath, 38.
27. Deepa V. N. in Gopinath, 190.
28. Kodoth, "Courting Legitimacy," 383.
29. Kodoth, 383.
30. Menon, *Sexualities*, xvi.
31. Kodoth, "Courting Legitimacy," 356.
32. Devika, "Aesthetic Woman."
33. Devika, "Aesthetic Woman," 463.
34. Chatterjee, "Colonialism, Nationalism," 622.
35. Devika, "Aesthetic Woman," 462.
36. Devika and Sukumar, "Making Space," 4471.
37. Pillai, *Ivory Throne*, 186.
38. Pillai, 186.
39. Tharu and Niranjana, "Problems," 8.
40. Tharu and Niranjana, 8.
41. Devika, "Aesthetic Woman," 471.
42. Devika, 471.
43. It was in the location of what Judith Butler calls "heterosexual matrix" that colonial modernity's discourse of power erased the history of unstable identities in precolonial India. The "heterosexual matrix" refers to "a sort of grid produced by institutions, practices and discourses . . . through which, it appears to be 'a fact of nature' that all human bodies possess one of two fixed sexual identities, with each experiencing sexual desire only for the 'opposite sex.'" Menon, *Seeing like a Feminist*, 69–70.
44. Mohanty, *Feminism without Borders*, 7–8.
45. Mohanty, 8.
46. Chakrabarty, *Provincializing Europe*.
47. Oyewùmí, "Conceptualizing Gender," 1.

BIBLIOGRAPHY

Arunima, G. "Matriliny and Its Discontent." *India International Centre Quarterly* 22, no. 2/3 (Summer-Monsoon 1995): 157–167.

———. *There Comes Papa: Colonialism and the Transformation of Matriliny in Kerala, Malabar c. 1850–1940*. New Delhi: Orient Longman, 2003.

Chakrabarty, Dipesh. *Provincializing Europe: Postcolonial Thought and Historical Difference*. Princeton, NJ: Princeton University Press, 2000.

Chatterjee, Partha. "Colonialism, Nationalism, and Colonialized Women: The Contest in India." *American Ethnologist* 16, no. 4 (1989): 622–633.

———. *The Nation and Its Fragments: Colonial and Postcolonial Histories*. Princeton, NJ: Princeton University Press, 1993.

Chatterjee, Partha, and Anjan Ghosh. *History and the Present*. London: Anthem, 2006.

Chatterjee, Partha, and Nivedita Menon. *Empire and Nation: Selected Writings*. New York: Columbia University Press, 2010.

Devika, J. "The Aesthetic Woman: Re-forming Female Bodies and Minds in Early Twentieth-Century Keralam." *Modern Asian Studies* 39, no. 2 (May 2005): 461–487.

———. "Being 'In-Translation' in a Post-Colony: Translating Feminism in Kerala State, India." *Translation Studies* 1 (2008): 182–196.
———. *Her-Self: Early Writings on Gender by Malayalee Women, 1898–1938*. Kolkata: Stree, 2005.
———. *Imagining Women's Social Space in Early Modern Keralam*. Thiruvananthapuram, India: Centre for Development Studies, 2002.
———. "Rethinking 'Region': Reflections on History-Writing in Kerala." *Contemporary Perspectives* 2, no. 2 (July–December 2008): 246–264.
Gopinath, Gayatri. *Unruly Visions: The Aesthetic Practices of Queer Diaspora*. Durham and London: Duke University Press, 2018.
Jeffrey, Robin. *Decline of Nair Dominance: Society and Politics in Travancore (1847–1908)*. New Delhi: Manohar, 1994.
———. "Matriliny, Marxism and the Birth of the Communist Party in Kerala, 1930–1940." *The Journal of Asian Studies* 38, no. 1 (November 1978): 77–98. https://www.jstor.org /stable/pdf/2054238.pdf?refreqid=fastly-default%3Afb0a56139b160d71cfad7f90309 ed217&ab_segments=&initiator=&acceptTC=1.
Kapur, Ratna. "Dark Times for Liberal Intellectual Thought." *Profession* (2006): 22–32. https://www.jstor.org/stable/pdf/25595825.pdf?refreqid=fastly-default%3A80a2936e 5198fcd63b7ead2aa9bf9508&ab_segments=&initiator=&acceptTC=1.
Kodoth, Praveena. "Courting Legitimacy or Delegitimizing Custom? Sexuality, *Sambandham*, and Marriage Reform in Late Nineteenth-Century Malabar." *Modern Asian Studies* 35, no. 2 (May 2001): 349–384.
Liddle, Joanne, and Rama Joshi. "Gender and Colonialism: Women's Organization under the Raj." *Women's Studies International Forum* 8, no. 5 (1985): 521–529.
Menon, Nivedita. *Recovering Subversion: Feminist Politics beyond the Law*. Urbana: University of Illinois Press, 2004.
———. *Sexualities*. London: Zed, 2007.
Menon, Nivedita, and Aditya Nigam. "Disciplining Theories, Indisciplined Worlds: Doing Research in the Global South." In *Getting the Question Right*, edited by Mahmood Mamdani, 51–74. Kampala: Makerere Institute of Social Research, 2013.
———. *Power and Contestation: India since 1989*. New Delhi: Orient Longman, 2007.
Mohanty, Chandra Talpade. *Feminism without Borders: Decolonizing Theory, Practicing Solidarity*. Durham, NC: Duke University Press, 2003.
Nigam, Aditya. "Decolonizing the Mind." *Kafila*, August 15, 2013. https://kafila.online /2013/08/15/decolonization-of-the-mind/.
Osella, Caroline, and Filippo Osella. *Men and Masculinities in India*. Cambridge: Cambridge University Press, 2012. http://dx.doi.org/10.7135/UPO9781843313991.
Oyewùmí, Oyèrónké. "Conceptualizing Gender: The Eurocentric Foundations of Feminist Concepts and the Challenge of African Epistemologies." *JENA: A Journal of Culture and African Women Studies* 2, no. 1 (2002). https://pdfs.semanticscholar.org/af57 /1563763fd8f5ad20a21ee6b64c69906282c1.pdf?_ga=2.172399715.1592430338.159967 5773-434013723.1599675773.
Pillai, Manu S. *The Ivory Throne: Chronicles of the House of Travancore*. Noida: HarperCollins *Publishers* India, 2015.
Raghuramaraju, A. "Rethinking the West." *Third Text* 19, no. 6 (November 2005): 595–598. https://www.tandfonline.com/doi/pdf/10.1080/09528820500381343.
Ruvalcaba, Héctor Domínguez. *Translating the Queer: Body Politics and Transnational Conversations*. London: Zed Books, 2016.
Said, Edward W. *Orientalism*. London: Penguin, 2003.

Sarkar, Tanika. "Rhetoric against Age Consent: Colonial Reason and Death of a Child-Wife." *Economic and Political Weekly* 28, no. 26 (1993): 1869–1878. https://www.jstor.org/stable/pdf/4400113.pdf?refreqid=fastly-default%3A2854182cca6620f7621914470c0f047b&ab_segments=&initiator=&acceptTC=1.

Spivak, Gayatri Chakravorty. "Can the Subaltern Speak?" In *Colonial Discourse and Post-Colonial Theory: A Reader*, edited by Patrick Williams and Laura Chrisman, 66–111. Hemel Hempstead Hertfordshire, UK: Harvester Wheatsheaf, 1994.

Tharu, Susie J., and K. Lalita. *Women Writing in India: 600 B.C. to the Present*. New York: Feminist Press at the City University of New York, 1991.

8

Banana Republicans and the Capitol Riot

Jorge E. Cuéllar

> This is how election results are disputed in a banana republic—not our democratic republic.
>
> —George W. Bush, January 6, 2021

> ¿Cuál es la república bananera ahora?
>
> —*Publimetro*, Colombia, November 6, 2020

> Who's the banana republic now?
>
> —*Daily Nation*, Kenya, January 8, 2021

Imperial Hypocrisy

There are only a handful of terms that can be utilized to prismatically and transhistorically understand the many generations of U.S. empire in the Americas. One of them, emerging as a direct product of corporate-first foreign policy and a deeply unequal interstate process in the long era of the Monroe Doctrine, is the concept of the *banana republic*. This term, immediately recognizable as gross political mismanagement, backwardness, and underdevelopment, serves to index over one hundred years of U.S. empire building, labor discipline, and racial subjugation across the hemisphere. It remains a widely used shorthand to describe corrupt governments, democratic backsliding, and one-dimensional agrarian economies worldwide. As we observed in the wake of the U.S. autocoup on January 6, 2021, the notion of banana republic quickly became a discursive shortcut for politicians as they scrambled to make sense of what was a clear-cut, nativist, conspiracy-driven, fascist insurrection.

In this chapter, reflecting on the legitimation crisis laid bare by the Capitol Riot, I am concerned with the racial work of the term *banana republic* and how it makes intelligible real-time U.S. political decay. I suggest that banana republic is an interregnal concept that can serve to measure the depth of the U.S. political disarray prompted by the Trump administration and its mobilizing of the Big Lie. As a U.S.-made term, *banana republic* is a crucial keyword of U.S. empire and remains indispensable for identifying the functional continuities of U.S. racial capitalism from the era of the banana to our twenty-first-century interregnum.

Firstly, as a periodizing concept, the banana republic evokes the greatest hits of U.S. imperialism: from its recurrent campaigns of destabilization, annexation attempts, to the era of corporate colonialism where foodways, politics, and national futures became monopolized by foreign entities. It conjures the era of Gunboat Diplomacy and the nearly three decades of Banana Wars that the United States waged to protect its political and financial interests in the Americas. Like a reflection in a funny mirror, the Monroe Doctrine also produced different but parallel mutations, such as the Roosevelt Corollary, the Good Neighbor Policy, a smattering of memoranda refining Monroe's supremacist vision, to even providing the central framework to the Cold War, as clearly practiced in the counterinsurgency campaigns across Central America.[1] Even now, it remains an underexamined template for policy approaches, such as the Obama-Kerry Doctrine and Donald Trump's America First. As part of the U.S. unconscious, the banana republic cuts across partisan foreign policy and continues to symbolize the United States' endless quest for securing global hegemony and preserving capital advantages abroad. This view, integral to U.S. national common sense, also evidences a deep hypocrisy at the core of the United States' political formation. At once signaling ineptitude, the banana republic emblemizes the United States' global stratagem: using military and economic power as coercive tools, coupled with lofty, if empty, pluralist language to ensure consent for its leadership.

The Capitol Riot was a disruptive event. While its long significance will surely be reckoned with, it immediately yielded a plethora of curious responses from inside the United States and across the globe. This chapter contends with the content of these in-the-moment reactions. It proceeds in three parts to make sense of how the banana republic was utilized discursively, to naturalize and eventually dismiss the political diagnosis that the events of January 6 delivered to U.S. democratic capitalism. First, I turn to the early twentieth-century origins of the term *banana republic* to situate it within the history of U.S. empire making, drawing out how it melds with present-day U.S. common sense. From this early modern period, wherein U.S. liberal democracy solidifies its most central political values, *banana republic*, too, finds its way into the U.S. political vocabulary to understand U.S. capitalist triumph as civilizational progress. Here, I remark on why the term was revivified to domesticate the chaos of the January 6 insurrection. After this brief history, I turn to a handful of responses that emerged in the aftermath of the riot and locate the operative assumptions at work here about Third World life, political behavior, and corrupted culture. I then contrast these with the rebellious responses of non-U.S. populations who pointed to the racialized, white supremacist specificity of the *banana republic* as a demeaning, insulting political term.

Counterpunching U.S. empire, global others sarcastically commented on the Trumpian self-coup and ridiculed the Capitol Riot along with its revanchist, conspiracy-driven dupes. Characterizing the events of January 6 and its attendant discourses as revealing the American interregnum, I propose banana republic as a concept that helps demystify this uncertain, calamitous, anxiety-ridden period. The banana republic allows us to anchor this interregnal period in a specific moral chronology and imperial mythmaking central to the formation of U.S. political culture. It is, as Cedric J. Robinson might say, a part of the "counterfeiture" and the "new racial catechism" set into motion in the early twentieth century as hordes of peripheral jungle savages became the raw material, the racialized and gendered fuel, for enriching U.S. empire. Simultaneously, a dishonest politics in the form of national fictions emerged to make it all cohere.[2] The banana republic then, suggested here as a device to understand the present interregnum—as an irresolvable crisis of legitimacy—reveals how the United States as a polity frames itself in relation to the rest of the world. Deploying a discourse of civilizational difference—racially, politically, and economically—U.S. nationalism reactivates its imperial imaginary, utilizing racist theories of underdevelopment in times of legitimation crisis.[3] In this sense, the panicked, politesse turn to the banana republic as a reaction to the shock of the Capitol Riot is almost a classic instance of what Antonio Gramsci called "morbid symptoms" or "morbid phenomena," here appearing as a clutching to political simplifications in denial of the obvious exhaustion of U.S. democratic forms.[4]

A Bruised Banana

As an explainer, the banana republic solidified the view that political dysfunction is endemic to foreign nations and "other" people, an exteriority to U.S. political culture. The term had its genesis in 1904, in writer O. Henry's fictional "Anchuria," which stood in for early twentieth-century Honduras, and has since been elaborated through academic and public writings to explain the very problem it labels: the underdevelopment of nations, political retrocession, dictatorship, "backward" agrarian cultures, and as a periodizing concept to signal the era of corporate-first foreign policy that held a lasting monopoly in the agricultural commodity chain.[5] One of the major legacies of the banana republic in the realm of popular culture is found in the enduring stereotype of the "tropical" nation like the "politically wobbly"

Honduras, Jamaica, Guatemala, the Dominican Republic, or "corrupt" Panama, whom are all interchangeable, as if plagued by the same banana disease. These nations, particularly from Latin America but also from Africa and tropical Asia—the banana plantation archipelago—have come to stand in for the devolution of "other" political cultures. To U.S. politics, the banana republic signals the rule of "tinpot dictators," of unstable and incorrigible regimes stubbornly dependent on single-crop economies and whose sole outputs are agriculture and low-skilled labor: bananas, coffee, soy, sugar, and cacao.[6]

In our interregnum, that rudderless period wanting in political alternatives, the banana republic has reemerged, mobilizing imperialist imaginaries to explain away the present weaknesses of the U.S. political system.[7] Similarly, listing O. Henry as an example of the globalization of romantic adventurism in the world historical novel, literary scholar Edward King writes, "The timeless spaces of romance began to fill up with particularities of modern politics and commerce," which, it follows, led to imperial neologisms like "banana republic."[8] Imbued with complex global meanings, the term was again summoned to designate the Capitol Riot as unbecoming of the United States. Unsurprisingly, in a moment of generalized shock, this was a desperate attempt to make sense of the hijacking of electoral politics by homegrown antidemocratic forces, who were being encouraged by party officials, members of Congress, donors, and activists.

Following January 6, 2021, much banana talk emerged in U.S. public discourse. Most visibly, former president George W. Bush turned to its moralizing power to describe the incoherence and irrationality of the riotous, uncivilized scene that unfolded on the National Mall. Ahistorically, politicians, journalists, and pundits too repeated the banana republic trope—in all its economic, racial, and political insinuations—to make sense of Capitol events, relying on its loaded meaning to express their disapproval at the assault on U.S. democracy that took place on holy ground. Together, these produced banana republic chatter across social media, leading to a smattering of articles, memes, and debates aimed to clarify the problematic origins of the term.[9] Despite the discourse, few of these explained why so many would invoke the contentious term to address, or partly alleviate, the wounding of national self-esteem. These "crudely neophobe and conservative" thoughts like "banana republic" suggest, as per Gramsci, the presence of an ideological and commonsensical truth at the source of the expression: a superiority complex informed by imperial belonging and ethnonationalist self-imaginings. The turn to crude phrasings like Congressman Mike Gallagher's "this is banana republic crap" is not just a glimpse into how a particular political stratum views itself—as racially privileged and celestially ordained arbiters of democracy—but rather it illustrates how a temporary inversion of political order exposed an intolerable, festering contradiction.

By relying on age-old tropes like banana republic, the Capitol Riot revealed the "general form of thought"—the common sense—of the interregnum. This "American interregnum" finds its origins in U.S. empire building, in ongoing capitalist extraction and interventionist foreign policy. In 2020, these couplings yielded migratory flows, endless war, and generalized precarity, maintaining the underdevelopment of the same racialized nations made dependent in the banana republic era. Effectively, the reactions to the Capitol Riot revealed the length that U.S. politicians will go to tame political chaos, despite it plainly being hypocritical and ahistorical. Evident in the global responses to January 6, the same tropicalized barbarians adversely invoked to produce U.S. political meaning tacitly recognized the very pattern by which their natural subservience is assumed. In this crisis moment of bruised hubris, U.S. ethnonationalism could offer nothing more than the lazy, racist, stereotypical cartoons elicited by the banana republic: of an undifferentiated, uncultured mass of Central and South Americans, Caribbeans, Africans, and Asians of jungle origin—Indigenous, Black, or some other mongrel hybrid—whose unruly, unstable, barbaric political cultures and half-formed infantile institutions the United States has always measured itself against. However, even in rearticulating this civilizational difference on January 6, identifying oneself with the planet's leading nation proved hopeless and ineffective, an appeal far too cryptic to an enraged, mobilized whiteness.

Thus, in turning to the banana republic, influential political voices sought to reign in the runaway insurrectionists, calling for calm and order. They reminded protesters and the observing public of the proud civility that defines the "true" United States, one that was not represented in the riot. In a doubly useful move, officials expressed condemnation and distanced themselves from the aggressive, low-class, indecent mob that shared more with banana barbarians than with upstanding Americans. Even president-elect Joe Biden shored up the United States' falling esteem among the global public, salvaging some dignity for the "American experiment" to which he was now its elected leader. In his earned role to commandeer the empire, Biden implored that Capitol rioters "do not reflect a true America, do not represent who we are."[10] This, of course, asserted that being a real American is not in betraying the institutions that guarantee their way of life but rather in being a decent, sensible, democracy-respecting, faithful public who never would attempt such a thuggish breach of the social contract. For the rest of the world, viewing the Capitol events through Cavendish-colored lenses, it was clear that the United States had become something of a bruised banana. And as we know, a bruised banana is sweeter—that is to say, much funnier.

Chaotic Aggregates

Outside of the United States, from the former Third World, reactions to the Capitol Riot were humorous and echoed a "chickens always come home to roost" sentiment. Many underscored that the United States does not and has not practiced what it preaches for a very long time. The rise of Trump appeared not as a temporary aberration or a fleeting sentiment but rather as a fungal growth from within a rotten polity whose self-deluded view of its own glorious exceptional past had become a running joke, now a spectacular failure. In this view, the Capitol Riot, where Trump's "Stop the Steal" faithful sought to overturn the 2020 U.S. presidential election, provided unignorable evidence of the United States as a boastful yet fragile entity, mirroring its Trumpismo leadership. The event substantiated that its institutions are increasingly hollow and dysfunctional. Ironically, following this amusing line of thought, many in the underdeveloped world called for a UN peacekeeping mission to bring stability to a wracked United States, suggesting the United States was a failed state. The political cartoonist Patrick Gathara quipped that the "free world" must prevent Donald "Papa Don" Trump (referring to Haiti) from assuming totalitarian control of the nuclear-armed North American nation.[11] Uses of irony and comic critique led to a momentary inversion of global order and allowed for the historical victims of U.S. empire to blow off some steam. The riot created an opening for the othered world to interpret white backlash and use the same stereotyping language often projected onto them to, instead, unsettle U.S. hegemony.

In the chaotic wake of the riot and to Trump-era economic sanctions imposed on his country, the president of Zimbabwe tweeted, "Yesterday's events showed that the U.S. has no moral right to punish another nation under the guise of upholding democracy."[12] The global responses to January 6 often ranged from economic worry—what might this spell for international aid, for the U.S.-centered financial system, for global U.S. dependencies—to naming the hypocritical gangsterism foundational to U.S. self-mythology. The Kenyan press, too, reacted with the now infamous "WHO'S THE BANANA REPUBLIC NOW?" headline that pointed out the doublespeak of the U.S. political class. The Kenyan paper momentarily reversed the imperialist narrative by presuming the United States to be the disordered banana republic of its own imaginings, incapable of managing the peaceful transition of power. As an interregnal concept, the banana republic underscores the dysfunctions inflamed by the Trump period, the crisis yielded by a caudillo government unthinkable in the United States.[13] Tactfully, the headline utilized U.S. exceptionalism as a foil and spoke back to empire's power by redeploying the instruments designed to confine them, turning around a term habitually used to cast them as endemically corrupt and uncivilized. Even O. Henry, who pronounced in his short story "The Admiral," about the defective constitution of tropical persons: "The southern races are lacking in that particular kind of humour that finds entertainment in the defects and misfortunes bestowed by Nature."[14] O. Henry, it appears, underestimated the capacity of the banana people.

Surely for the Kenyans and the Colombians who were among the first to publish the ironic headline after Election Day 2020, they separately took up this simple line to underscore the United States' hypocrisy and its inability to resolve the Trumpian conundrum. Together, they spoke from a shared geohistorical and political location that resignified the term *banana republic* to accent its racialized, exploitative, and arrogant dimensions. By drawing on national memory, on stories of imperial adventurism that so profoundly impacted their histories, they leaned into stereotypes of Latin American and African politics to point out that they, the United States, are the prime mover in promoting corruption, corporate vampirism, economic dependency, and war, all across the world. Indeed, the satire crystallized the foundational role of the United States in birthing the banana republic as a sociohistorical, racial, and political form. Even if merely symbolic, a speaking back to the wretchedness of imperial colonialism and economic subservience, the ironic tone of these responses was like a sharp blade cutting deeply at empire's ego. Revising a term ordinarily used to signal a specific kind of racial backwardness, resource dependency, short termism, and democratic backsliding, it was now lodged against the U.S. political institutions that designed it and at the white supremacy that justified it. The Trumpian chaos of the Capital Riot became an opportune moment to voice this critique, to hold up a mirror to U.S. empire, so it could see that its dysfunction—that it tried to externalize with banana talk—was a homegrown byproduct of an overwrought, polarized, hollowed-out system.

Within U.S. common sense, the banana republic operates as a shorthand for the devolution of political culture and institutional decorum in the rest of the world, beyond U.S. jurisdictional boundaries. It is typically used to disparage the supposed instability of nonwhite governments, of kleptocratic leaders, even to express concerns about the "Latin Americanization" of U.S. politics. Florida and California, for instance, are often viewed in these terms due to the abundance of Latinx and migrant-origin voters who trigger nativists, feeding white resentment and rage.[15] This, in all, remains a great anxiety for the United States and leads political voices to reach for terms like *banana republic* to enlist racist ridicule as political commentary and analysis. Omar Encarnación, for instance, places Trump squarely in the caudillo tradition of Latin America, which has fed back into the Trumpification of Latin American politics as well.[16] Recall Governor Ron DeSantis's reaction to the FBI search at Trump's Mar-a-Lago mansion in August 2022, which also served as a fundraising pitch, where he exclaimed, "These are not actions indicative of leaders in a free republic. *This mirrors a Banana Republic*."[17] One editorial responded to DeSantis's remarks entertainingly with "it takes one to know one."[18] It appears that in moments of pressure to democratic institutions, where the wisdom of "politics as usual" is challenged, politicians waste no time resorting to racist, masculinist traditionalisms as per the banana republic.

Ridicule is cathartic, though in U.S. politics this often sustains what Raúl Pérez has called the "white schadenfreude," a racist pleasure that serves to make whiteness "a dominant and resistant racial order."[19] Here, the cheap stereotype of banana republic works similarly, but when unlatched from its chronology, it can be deployed to critique the United States of Trump, pointing its sharp edge against the white supremacist cultural compact that is U.S. democratic, neoliberal capitalism. "Common sense is a chaotic aggregate," writes Gramsci, where "one can find there anything that one likes."[20] As a commonsensical term, the *banana republic* has this discursive elasticity, which, when interpreted from the colored world, can signify history otherwise. It echoes not endemic dysfunction but instead the United States' unsatiable hunger for imperial dominion: of Operation PBFortune against the Guatemalan Revolution and 1954's coup against Arbenz or of the 1928 Banana Massacre in Colombia, of Zemurray's plot that placed Manuel Bonilla in the Honduran presidency, of various rogue militarisms and trade wars. Turning history on its head, Third Worldians thus relied on the double-edged racist ridicule found in the term to explain white insurrectionist behavior and as a framework to understand the political and racial animus, the hypocrisy at the heart of the U.S. polity, the constitutive fuel of the Capitol Riots.

As the Honduran journalist Telma Quiroz wrote, "Ex-President Bush's phrase reveals that (white) supremacist ideals are alive and well even among those that express disagreement with President Trump's actions and the vandalism of his followers."[21] Speaking as a citizen of the prototype banana republic, as if in step with the long history of resistance to banana imperialism that Kevin Coleman has revealed through the countervisuality of Central Americans, Quiroz underscored that the racist allegiance to using the term *banana republic* is not some party-specific misgiving but rather a shared value across the spectrum.[22] Quiroz asserted that it persists as a deep-seated racial epithet central to the functioning of U.S. nationalism. It is worth restating here that the term is still recognized among young Hondurans like Quiroz who remain clear-eyed on how this power-laden, racializing, and derogatory vocabulary remains operational. They see how gringos view themselves as inherently superior to others, subscribing to the United States' mythologized past and to an unending hegemonic future. Terms like *banana republic* mobilize the U.S.-centric view that places like Honduras are, as per Maritza Cárdenas, "incapable of achieving and reveling in the progress of modernity."[23]

For First World nations like the United States, whose identity is derived from unlinking themselves from the woes of lesser nations, the worst possible attribution is that of being a banana republic. This insulting, anachronistic, and degenerative term is not just schoolyard name-calling but is a political assessment of the United States. It suggests a country captured by caudillo corruption, sustained by an unsophisticated, brutish, social order, governed by retrograde social groups guided by nefarious external influences. Using it to categorize U.S. politics challenges the United States' self-perception as the luminous "city upon a hill," raising whether it remains equipped to lead the rest of the savage, godless, predemocratic world. Thus, rapidly leaning on this racially and politically loaded term, beyond it being imprecise, exposes members of the elected as having little grip on the political reality around them, prompting the facile return to descriptions like banana republic to assuage their own moral unease using a familiar, racist, classist, imperialist comfort.

Interregnum America

If *banana republic* is a prismatic, multipronged term that can help to decode interregnum politics, economics, culture, and racialization, as well as periodize the historical inequalities wrought by U.S. imperialism, then it, too, can assist in measuring empire's unfolding. The interregnum crystallized by the events of January 6, 2021, are "surprising" and "unpredictable" and reflect an accumulation of contradictions that the United States has generated in its march toward global hegemony.[24] From inside interregnum America, events like the Capitol Riots resemble past crises, from coups in the U.S. South to those of the Global South, prompted by unresolved contradictions putrefying in the social formation. The frenzied reach for ways to explain away the Capitol Riot by conjuring the banana republic appears as a monstrous, grotesque expression of this interregnum. By revivifying the banana republic to provide liberal narrativization to the shock, it instead floodlit the workings of a racial imperialist mythos, to the time of climate determinism, and underscored the ineptitude of U.S. leadership.[25] For some time now, the current state of affairs has been unable to chart a way out of the interregnum, of this historico-political stasis, and has in its place deepened it further. What was once a series of reliable dog whistles for consoling a white supremacist system in times of crisis, the invoking of the dividing line between the *civis* and the *barbaros* was, now in the wake of January 6, a hopeless and hapless attempt at a political resolution.

Unmistakably, the U.S. polity is in a deep interregnum. Its core values are in disarray, people worldwide are losing faith in U.S. leadership, and there are no serious political alternatives signaling a way forward. In one sense, the United States is living a moment of frustrated stasis that is enabling the toxic growths of authoritarian populism and militant white supremacy that brazenly express themselves in the public square. This is the condition of the interregnum: fragmented movements, sectorized struggle, planetary fatalism, being in a motionless time as we await the end of the world. But this is, perhaps, just the perception from within the United States; as for the rest of the middling planet, an interregnal period for the United States might indicate an opportunity for creative movements elsewhere, for fortifying counterhegemonic projects across the multiplying "blind spots" of racial imperialist power.[26] However, it may also be that January 6 was the highest expression of a revanchist, vengeful, conspiracist right that swelled in the interregnum, accelerated by the isolation of pandemic. Their coup against the transition of presidential power remains instructive, as insurrectionists sought to maintain a Trump-led status quo even if it meant, ironically, taking down the democratic institutions that enabled Trump's rise. Bruised bananas, while quickly ripening, also rot much faster.

As Jean Franco reminds us in *Cruel Modernity*, hypocrisy is a part of our shared historical tissue, where past violence becomes a latent, recurrent starting point, for the work of the present. Nation-states however, as thoroughly violent entities, renew their nationalisms, conceal cruelty, and discipline memory to reframe past violence as distant, external, and inapplicable to current concerns. In doing so, states promote progress from such episodes to cast themselves as newly illuminated, not delimited by crimes, injustices, and traumas of their pasts. The value-laden banana republic operates on this historical, moral, and political plane. The United States rewrites its nationalism repeatedly, through popular culture and vis-à-vis political discourse disseminated across media outlets as evident in postriot chatter. The terrain of culture becomes the battleground for reformulation, where national fictions are distilled into a rabid, unchallenged common sense.

This idea of Latin America—of which the banana republic is one enduring image—persists in the United States via active racialized discourses in institutional and fringe publics. These denigrative ideas work twofold: they promote a sense of national identity by relying on well-worn colonial tropes of enemy barbarism, externalizing internal dysfunction as if a result from outside forces or nefarious design. This was clear in the Capitol Riot, where occupiers were summoned to Washington by a conspiratorial ruse to defend electoral theft against Trump, driven by racial anxiety, anti-immigrant sentiment, the fear of Latin Americanization, and worries about the weakening of white American power (e.g., economic, social, cultural, in sexuality, and education). Secondly, such national fictions require for instability, underdevelopment, and insecurity to be racially codified as if endemic moral failings of Third World others. This permanent condition also deputizes imperial U.S. whiteness to assume leadership of nonwhite peoples, providing the divine blueprint for democracy. For the United States, Latin America remains a smattering of developing nations and banana republics, where its people are forever bound to a historical script written by U.S. imperialism, white supremacy, and a commonsense racism invented in the last two centuries.

One of the spooks of the American interregnum is the banana republic. It moves unchecked in political discourse, as a flexible, racially encoded term for understanding politics and international relations. It has been used to describe Pakistan, Uganda, Venezuela, the Philippines, India, and now the United States. The term's ideological circularity and reappearance in U.S. politics is a sign of interregnal times, whereby it provides no exit to political crisis but instead produces recursive calls for civility and traditionalism. Despite great uncertainty in the interregnum, in which critique must remain somewhat provisional, terms such as these effectively diagnose the depth of the crisis and, by exposing the hypocrisy of imperialism, underscore that hegemony is never complete.

NOTES

1. There is a vast critical literature on U.S. banana imperialism. See Striffler and Moberg, *Banana Wars*; Colby, *Business of Empire*; and Martin, *Banana Cowboys*.
2. Robinson, *Forgeries of Memory and Meaning*, 290–291.
3. Fraser, "Legitimation Crisis?"
4. Gramsci, *Selections*, 276.
5. Studies of voter behavior, electoral fraud, and on global trade imbalances have relied on the "banana republic" or the "banana state" as a heuristic. For a cultural history of U.S. bananas, see Soluri, *Banana Cultures*.
6. Wintrobe, "Tinpot and the Totalitarian."
7. Reading O. Henry, Townsend calls his work "banana republic realism" as it inaugurates a "realism" that still exists today, evident in how "pundits and politicos are now starting to fret that the U.S. (of all places) has become a banana republic." Townsend, "Money Mazes," 690.
8. King, "World Historical Novel," 128–129.
9. Some of the most widely circulated memes were gathered in this roundup, Mendes-Franco and Lewis, "'This Is the USA?'"
10. Meet The Press, "@JoeBiden."
11. Gathara, "Papa Don's Failed State."
12. President of Zimbabwe, "Last year."
13. For more, see Fleck, "Trump the Caudillo."
14. Henry, "Admiral," 134.
15. See the classic Wiarda, "Latin Americanization"; Bonilla-Silva and Dietrich, "Latin Americanization"; Beltrán, *Cruelty as Citizenship*.

16. Encarnación, "Trumpification."
17. DeSantis, "The raid of MAL."
18. "In a 'Banana Republic.'"
19. Pérez, *Souls of White Jokes*, 160.
20. Gramsci, *Selections*, 422.
21. Quiroz, "En 'república bananera.'"
22. Coleman, *Camera in the Garden*.
23. Cárdenas, *Constituting Central American-Americans*, 25.

24. Wolfgang Streeck writes of interregnums as a disruption in "cause" and "effect" that lead to unstable chains of *surprising events* in the place of predictable *structures*. See Streeck, "Return of the Repressed," 14–15.

25. In the twentieth century, climate determinists sought to prove the degeneration of races as a geographic phenomenon. See Huntington, *Civilization and Climate*, a fundamental text to human geography.

26. Maher, *Anticolonial Eruptions*. I draw out the meaning of the blind spot in Cuéllar, "Decolonial Groundwork."

BIBLIOGRAPHY

Beltrán, Cristina. *Cruelty as Citizenship: How Migrant Suffering Sustains White Supremacy*. Minneapolis: University of Minnesota Press, 2020.

Bonilla-Silva, Eduardo, and David R. Dietrich. "The Latin Americanization of US Race Relations: A New Pigmentocracy." In *Shades of Difference: Why Skin Color Matters*, edited by Evelyn Nakano Glenn. Palo Alto, CA: Stanford University Press, 2009.

Cárdenas, Maritza. *Constituting Central American-Americans: Transnational Identities and the Politics of Dislocation*. New Brunswick, NJ: Rutgers University Press, 2018.

Colby, Jason M. *The Business of Empire: United Fruit, Race, and US Expansion in Central America*. Ithaca, NY: Cornell University Press, 2013.

Coleman, Kevin. *A Camera in the Garden of Eden: The Self-Forging of a Banana Republic*. Austin: University of Texas Press, 2016.

Cuéllar, Jorge E. "Decolonial Groundwork: On Geo Maher's *Anticolonial Eruptions*." *NACLA*, April 29, 2022. https://nacla.org/anticolonial-eruptions-review.

DeSantis, Ron (@RonDeSantis). "The raid of MAL is another escalation in the weaponization of federal agencies against the Regime's political opponents." Twitter, August 8, 2022, 8:43 p.m. https://twitter.com/RonDeSantisFL/status/1556803433939755010.

Encarnación, Omar G. "The Trumpification of the Latin American Right." *Foreign Policy*, April 16, 2018. https://foreignpolicy.com/2018/04/16/the-trumpification-of-the-latin-american-right/.

Fleck, Micah J. "Trump the Caudillo: Tapping into Already-Existing Populist Unrest." In *The Anthropology of Donald Trump*, edited by Jack David Eller. London: Routledge, 2021.

Fraser, Nancy. "Legitimation Crisis? On the Political Contradictions of Financialized Capitalism." *Critical Historical Studies* 2, no. 2 (Fall 2015): 157–189.

Gathara, Patrick. "Papa Don's Failed State: The US as Seen from Kenya." *The Guardian*, January 9, 2021. https://www.theguardian.com/us-news/2021/jan/09/capitol-storming-us-failed-state-kenya-patrick-gathara.

Gramsci, Antonio. *Selections from the Prison Notebooks*. Edited by Quentin Hoare and Geoffrey Nowell-Smith. London: Lawrence & Wishart, 1971.

Henry, O. "The Admiral." In *Cabbages and Kings*. New York: Doubleday, Page & Company, 1904.

Huntington, Ellsworth. *Civilization and Climate*. New Haven, CT: Yale University Press, 1915.

"In a 'Banana Republic' It Takes One to Know One." *Sun Sentinel*, August 18, 2022. https://www.sun-sentinel.com/opinion/letters/fl-op-letters-desantis-trump-banana-republic-20220818-qkeobsleobhvjeyivqeilpdmim-story.html.

King, Edward. "The World Historical Novel." *New Left Review* 137 (September–October 2022): 128–129.

Maher, Geo. *Anticolonial Eruptions: Racial Hubris and the Cunning of Resistance*. Berkeley: University of California Press, 2022.

Martin, James W. *Banana Cowboys: The United Fruit Company and the Culture of Corporate Colonialism*. Albuquerque: University of New Mexico Press, 2018.

Meet The Press (@MeetThePress). "@JoeBiden: 'The scenes of chaos at the Capitol do not reflect a true America, do not represent who we are. What we're seeing is a small number of extremists dedicated to lawlessness.'" Twitter, January 6, 2021, 4:09 p.m. https://twitter.com/MeetThePress/status/1346926898429923329.

Mendes-Franco, Janine, and Emma Lewis. "'This Is the USA?' The Caribbean Reacts to the Capitol Protests." *Global Voices*, January 8, 2021. https://globalvoices.org/2021/01/08/this-is-the-usa-the-caribbean-reacts-to-the-capitol-protests/.

Pérez, Raúl. *The Souls of White Jokes: How Racist Humor Fuels White Supremacy*. Palo Alto, CA: Stanford University Press, 2022.

President of Zimbabwe (@edmnangagwa). "Last year, President Trump extended painful economic sanctions placed on Zimbabwe, citing concerns about Zimbabwe's democracy." Twitter, January 7, 2021, 8.42 a.m. https://twitter.com/edmnangagwa/status/1347176848694931457.

Quiroz, Telma. "En 'república bananera' convierten el Capitolio de EEUU." *Reportar sin miedo*, January 6, 2021. https://reportarsinmiedo.org/2021/01/06/el-capitolio-de-estados-unidos-convertido-en-una-republica-bananera/.

Robinson, Cedric. *Forgeries of Memory and Meaning: Blacks and the Regimes of Race in American Theater and Film before World War II*. Chapel Hill: University of North Carolina Press, 2007.

Soluri, John. *Banana Cultures: Agriculture, Consumption, and Environmental Change in Honduras and the United States*. Austin: University of Texas Press, 2005.

Streeck, Wolfgang. "The Return of the Repressed." *New Left Review* 104 (March–April 2017): 14–15.

Striffler, Steve, and Mark Moberg. *Banana Wars*. Durham, NC: Duke University Press, 2003.

Townsend, Sarah J. "Money Mazes, Media Machines, and Banana Republic Realisms." *American Literary History* 31, no. 4 (2019): 687–714.

Wiarda, Howard J. "The Latin Americanization of the United States." *New Scholar* 6 (1978): 51–86.

Wintrobe, Ronald. "The Tinpot and the Totalitarian: An Economic Theory of Dictatorship." *American Political Science Review* 84, no. 3 (September 1990): 849–872.

9

Mobile Privatization and the COVID-19 Pandemic

Charting the Interregnum

Andrew Ó Baoill and Brian Dolber

On March 19, 2020, Gavin Newsom of California became the first governor in the United States to issue a stay-at-home order to prevent the spread of the COVID-19 virus. While homes became offices, the luxuries and anxieties around working from home became fodder for think pieces.[1] In the meantime, reports predicted that the pandemic would breed a wave of automation, and the world of consumption, already transformed by Amazon's rapid home delivery, would become permanently relegated to the domestic sphere.[2]

Not all work, though, would be structured the same way. While white collar professionals could work from home with the assistance of digital technology, service sector workers faced mass layoffs. In the meantime, "essential workers"—health care providers, first responders, and grocery clerks—were compelled to labor in dangerous conditions. Such distinctions were laid bare when on the Memorial Day holiday, George Floyd, a Black COVID-positive security guard who had been laid off from his job at a bar, was murdered by Devin Chauvin, a white Minneapolis police officer. Using digital technologies as mobilization tools, protesters took to the streets in cities across the United States and the globe, demanding to "defund the police" and demonstrating that, even amid a pandemic in the digital age, public space still mattered.

Rather than reaffirming technological determinist predictions of a total movement toward the domestication of labor and the full enclosure of the commons, the COVID-19 pandemic has thrown preexisting shifts in societal relations into high relief, demonstrating how technological change operates in conjunction with the larger political economy to structure class formation. This essay puts these developments in historical perspective through the lens of Raymond Williams's notion of "mobile privatization."[3] Mobile privatization has not been a linear process; rather, it has been dialectical, contradictory, and experienced differently among different social groups at different times. While mobility and privacy are generally seen as marks of privilege, COVID-19 inverted that in significant ways.[4] Making sense of these inversions is critical to mapping the terrain on which we now struggle to build a new social order amid deep crisis.

We trace the evolution of mobile privatization from Williams's Keynesian era, where it was linked to the mass production of the automobile and broadcasting. These technologies allowed white middle-class consumers private access to the public, while bringing the public into private spaces. Under neoliberalism, logics of unpaid and mobile labor expanded while new technologies moved private consumption of cultural goods into the public realm. While the early years of the twenty-first century witnessed the decomposition of neoliberal common sense, the COVID-19 pandemic has exacerbated existing inequalities, tensions, and distortions in mobility and information flows. The raced and classed distinctions in how labor and mobility were experienced through the pandemic highlight the larger crisis within the neoliberal order and suggest the need and potential for intersectional organizing within civil society to build something new. By tracing out the historical shifts in mobile privatization within the U.S. context, we identify four areas—labor, surveillance, media fragmentation, and social protest—that may prove fruitful for building new social formations in our current interregnum.

A Brief History of Mobile Privatization

Raymond Williams introduced the concept of mobile privatization to explain broadcasting's mid-twentieth-century dominance, critically illuminating the interplay between capital, technological change, and personal agency.[5] For Williams, broadcasting's advent in the 1930s was associated with a period of social change and economic integration. As monopoly capitalism consolidated by the mid-twentieth century, relatively powerful trade unions, social welfare programs, and significant corporate taxes produced a "Great Compression," reducing wealth disparities that existed in earlier forms of capitalism.[6] A growing consumer class leveraged new technologies to cultivate a domestic space in which they were physically separated from the broader world, but they were increasingly dependent on their role in that world for the resources that enabled this domesticity. Broadcasting provided a conduit to the outside but also heralded possible threats to middle-class autonomy.

Through this framework, the concept of mobile privatization prompts a focus on the construction of and access to private and public spaces, and the choices made within systems of power, including the application of capital.

While Williams wrote within the context of this seemingly stable moment, he understood that this particular arrangement was not inevitable but contingent on structural and cultural factors, as "systems of mobility and transfer in production and communication... were at once incentives and responses within a phase of general social transformation."[7] In the United States, as the predominantly white postwar middle class could purchase the ability to move through coordinated, regulated public space with the automobile, others were excluded as race and class set the boundaries of participation, exemplified by the Federal Housing Authority's use of redlining and new highway systems that split neighborhoods and created segregated suburbs.[8]

Broadcasting was similarly contradictory.[9] While the medium brought a commercialized representation of the public into private homes, it also produced an audience commodity that performed the domestic labor of making advertising time valuable, compensated by the "free lunch" of programming. Broadcasters desired "audiences with predictable specifications which will pay attention in predictable numbers and at particular times to particular means of communication... in particular market areas."[10] Even at its height, the "mass society," then, was fragmented and segmented to meet the needs of capital, enabled and marked by forms of mobility (e.g., the development of the transistor radio in the 1940s; the rise of top 40 programming, aimed at the newly named consumer market of teenagers; and the later expansion of the FM band). Programming tended to reflect an imagined consumer class of white nuclear families offering "wages of whiteness" through media.[11] The Black freedom struggles that arose in the United States during the Keynesian era, then, were often articulated as demands for access to the realm of consumption, such as the Don't Buy Where You Can't Work campaign in the 1930s, the lunch counter sit-ins of the 1960s, and challenges over media representations and, in particular, broadcasting policies.[12]

Such fragmentation weakened the New Deal coalition, as the United States and other Western capitalist countries transitioned toward neoliberalism. Although this system did not solidify immediately in the United States, the ideological glue holding it together was mostly applied by the time of Reagan's election in 1980. While the political economy now depended on globalization for capital, labor, consumers, and the rapid circulation of value, brand culture reified an individualism perpetuated through reactionary social discourses around gender, race, and sexuality that emphasized the need for "individual responsibility."

Cable television began to divide audiences further than its free over-the-air counterpart, reflecting the ever-increasing individuation necessitated by new economic paradigms. New media technologies, such as the Sony Walkman, also reified neoliberalism's cultural ethos. As du Gay et al. argued, its "sleek high-tech [design] ... has become a sort of metaphor which stands for or represents a distinctively late-modern, technological culture or way of life." That way of life was centered on mobility, "being in two places at once, or doing two different things at once."[13] While broadcasting brought the public into the private sphere through a highly regulated infrastructure, the Walkman allowed for private consumption of cultural goods to happen in erstwhile public spaces and signaled a shift from segmented consumer cohorts to individualized consumption.

While the shift from analog to digital and the commercialization of the internet in the early 1990s amplified these trends, the neoliberal order came under increasing strain at the new millennium's dawn. On the one hand, media industries leveraged synergies and efficiencies in automation, convergence, and outsourcing that mirrored developments in other industries. These manifested in interlocking networks of influence, corporate board membership overlap, and the dominance of global media brands in an increasingly convergent environment driving the respatialization of media production and the instantiation of contingent labor and "flexibility."[14] On the other hand, as the dotcom bubble burst in 1998 highlighting the "new economy's" instability, a broad global justice movement with attendant independent media employed digital communication technologies to create a "globalization from below."[15]

By 2002, critics noted the rise of a "cyberteriat," a global precarious workforce dependent on and enabled by emerging information technologies.[16] The increasingly specific targeting of consumer segments had also begun to produce "filter bubbles," where fragmented publics shared their own sets of facts and ideological perspectives, harming political discourse and setting the stage for a "misinformation society."[17] While state-corporate power mobilized heightened fears of terrorism following the 9/11 attacks, stymying protest and critique against neoliberal regimes and their practices, new technologies produced and reproduced racial hierarchies through biometrics and predictive modeling, governing access to travel across borders and signaling Western imperialism's crisis.[18]

By the time of the 2008 global financial crisis, digital technologies were being integrated into the everyday patterns of consumption and labor. Smartphones and social networking sites like Facebook and Twitter enabled persistent mobile communication, allowing the user to be, presumably, anywhere, while engaging with the public (or at least some representation of it) everywhere. Movements such as the 2011 Arab Spring, #Occupy, and #BlackLivesMatter all made significant use of social media tools. While these technologies' efficacy to resist dominant structures has been hotly debated,[19] they have undeniably played a major role in mobilizing the production of value and the possibility for surveillance.[20]

Social networking sites and their advertising programs made everyday communication a productive economic activity.[21] A slew of new companies relied on digital AI technologies promising convenience for consumers and for workers made vulnerable by the dynamics of late neoliberalism, but more pertinently, by automating management, "gig companies" could circumvent labor laws as they colonized services such as transportation or delivery.[22] In this way, the workplace became dislocated, enabling production—as well as worker alienation—to take place anywhere and everywhere.[23]

Revisiting Mobile Privatization during COVID

Demonstrating a crack in the neoliberal consensus, a growing "techlash" over the last five years has reflected public frustrations with Silicon Valley's dominance in our economy and our everyday lives. But while left populists around the world, shaped by the post-2008 platform-connected struggles, developed policy proposals and campaign language aimed at Big Tech, the COVID-19 pandemic further solidified the centrality of platforms in our economy and culture. The pandemic "brought about a radical transformation of the space-time of everyday life," as workplaces, schools, and other public spaces shut down.[24] However, these dynamics were experienced differently across race and class lines.

Although platforms work to extend neoliberal logics, the pandemic also made clear that neoliberal authority has severely diminished, leaving us in an interregnum.[25] To chart the path forward, we need an analysis that enables the development of new political coalitions. We see the potential to suture together a "progressive populist" historical bloc, to borrow from Nancy Fraser, between professionals whose work has been domesticated and frontline workers who have assumed enormous risk.[26] While progressive neoliberalism, which Fraser identifies as the dominant ideology in the United States during prior decades, has left questions of class and economics off the table, the pandemic has helped to produce conditions that might engender a multiracial coalition of workers.

COVID-19 thus offers an opportunity to make visible issues of class mobility in two senses: issues of how we move physically in the world (e.g., as Uber passenger or driver) and the calcification of racialized class relations. Through this analysis, we point to some spaces for collective organizing that will be necessary to build a new commons and a new common sense for a post-neoliberal world. In the following areas, we see the potential for intersectional organizing.

Labor

As relatively privileged, quarantined workers relied more on broadband connections to work and study from home, it became clear that network architecture was designed to serve certain patterns of use. Sudden changes in behavior and usage levels challenged this, alongside broader questions of the contemporary digital divide. Working from home unexpectedly transferred certain costs—from toilet paper and energy costs to the physical working space itself—from employers to employees with the average employee investing $561 in equipment to enable working from home.[27] Working from home was significantly correlated with levels of formal educational attainment, and within that, benefits are greater for those on higher incomes, in large part due to the greater opportunity cost associated with time spent commuting.[28] There is a gendered element, too; women workers often juggled increased care responsibilities (including homeschooling for children) while adapting to a new working environment, resulting in "a powerful gendered perspective on the manifestation and experience of burnout during this atypical time."[29]

Unionization campaigns led by Amazon warehouse workers of color in Bessemer, Alabama, and Staten Island, New York, demonstrated how global labor and capital flows required mobile privatization for some while depriving others of mobility.[30] Labor shortages during 2021 in the United States raised the question of whether workers are willing to "go back to work" in unsafe, underpaid conditions among both white-collar professionals and service workers alike. Major strikes in the United States have occurred in industries including health care, food processing, manufacturing, higher education, and media production.[31] In this way, workers in various sectors of the economy who occupy different cultural milieus seem primed to take action and, potentially, begin forging bonds of solidarity.

Surveillance Technologies

Just as Williams noted that the same technologies that enabled greater privatized domesticity tied workers into systems of global capital, today's digital technologies that afford many professionals the opportunity to work from home also provide information about those workers and their work patterns to employers, platform providers, and others, extracting the raw materials of global informationalized capital. Technologies such as facial recognition and biometric systems also continue to be used as modes of surveillance and restraint as much as mobility. While existing surveillance infrastructures have been challenged in some contexts, there has also been an expansion of such tools into new domains, with the use of eye-tracking software to monitor "engagement" with computer-based homeschooling by pupils and students. In the workplace, technologies not only manage performance but identify employee emotion, geolocation, and professional reputation.[32] Schools and employers have required use of video-conferencing tools that mine user data, eliminating students' and workers' ability to provide meaningful consent, accentuating the impacts of race-based inequity and bias, and enabling "discriminatory outcomes and poor distributive justice in monitoring processes."[33]

Media Fragmentation

The balkanization of public space, driven by market segmentation and resulting in information bubbles, was made strikingly evident as the very reality of the pandemic was disputed by those in different information bubbles. While middle-class professionals sequestered in private spaces relied on global news and information flows to know when and how they might leave those spaces, the authoritative broadcast voices that once brought news reports into the home have been displaced by "cyber-cascades," where social media facilitate the rapid sharing of (mis/dis)information: rumors, memes, and claims of undetermined provenance.[34]

Such fragmentation means that we are not connecting to a single "mass media"—which would offer a way to leverage domesticity to forge nationwide allegiances—but instead to a disjointed set of interlocking realities, in which not only are we physically separated from our neighbors, but also our engagement with media serves to insulate us further.[35] This ecosystem led to the circulation of false news specifically around the coronavirus, creating alternate realities for how the pandemic was experienced based in algorithmic logics. College-educated progressives were left aghast at the rise of parallel information ecosystems, in which alienation and associated crises of legitimation manifest not just in ideologically distinct interpretations of meaning, but reports of verifiable data points are themselves increasingly subject to contestation and denial.[36] Skepticism of media reports are exacerbated as "news deserts" leave major gaps in trusted local sources, as 2,100 newspapers in 1,800 communities have closed since 2004. In April and May 2020, 30 papers closed or merged due to the pandemic's economic fallout.[37] In the meantime, the most vulnerable workers suffer as COVID spreads due to misinformation. Just as Williams had identified the significance of information flows for the dynamic interaction between domestic settings and engagement with the broader world, so too does this crisis in information and legitimation have an impact on public health and broader political engagement in the United States.[38] Simultaneously, this crisis also provides a site of contestation where diverse groups may organize together to build new, democratic media systems.

Private Mobilities, Public Protest, and Praxis

Exploitation of the data we shed by being in the world extends, of course, well beyond our role as workers to our personal time.[39] While social media amplify protests beyond physical boundaries and bypass institutional framing and gatekeeping, policing agencies leverage these same technologies and platforms as a means of surveillance and suppression.[40] These disciplinary tactics challenge our assumptions about the interplay of privacy, bodily integrity, and civil rights.[41]

In this context, the Black Lives Matter (BLM) protests that took place against the backdrop of the pandemic in the summer of 2020 illustrate the confluence of mobile privatization, protest, and praxis. Unlike antimask protests, the BLM actions have not constituted a rejection of quarantine and public-health recommendations but rather a counter-hegemonic response that asserts the urgency of tackling an epidemic of racist violence and impunity, and which sees risk both in protesting during the pandemic *and* in staying silent in the face of continued instances of violence against people of color.[42] For these protesters, the logics of "necessity" and personal safety are both multifaceted and in tension—is it safer to stay silent or to speak up? To stay at home or join others in protest? Simultaneously, it was widely noted that large numbers of white allies showed up for the first time, who had been increasingly following the news while quarantined and had more time to participate.

The BLM movement seeks, in important ways, to articulate and transform the racialized operation of mobility and privacy in the United States—the fact that, from George Floyd to Breonna Taylor, the dangers from police violence on the streets and in homes are an ever-present menace. That transformation accords with Harvey's call for a "right to the city" as "an active right to make the city different, to shape it more in accord with our heart's desire, and to re-make ourselves thereby in a different image."[43] If we might consider BLM actions as prefigurative of the desired social transformations, it is notable that while networked publics and hashtag activism are key to the tactics of the movement, at the core of the movement are bodies: those that lie silent in morgues, those that stand in protest, those for whom a better future—with vindicated rights to existence and mobility—is claimed.[44]

Conclusion

The mobile privatization framework has long been of value to cultural analysts, bringing together political economic sensibilities and a concern for lived experience and cultural practice. With this framework, Williams found a way to explore both the contradictions inherent in new relationships between public and private, and the role of capital in shaping these new affordances. Amid the erosion of hegemonic authority, the COVID-19 pandemic offers a different set of conditions for exploring these foundational issues of privilege, power, and society. Where mobility, by way of access to the emerging technology of the automobile, was a marker of privilege in the early twentieth century, during the pandemic privilege has been associated with the ability to work from home and to isolate oneself physically from the outside world. In part, this seems an extension of Williams's observation of the manner in which broadcasting connected the domestic sphere to the outside world. However, the risk of infection transferred explicitly to precarious frontline workers, such as those managed (and surveilled) by app-based delivery services, adds a rather pointed aspect to the analysis and a reminder of the persistence of materiality as a locus of power. Public health concerns have posed challenges for organizing groups, such as gig workers, during the pandemic and sometimes resulted in an irreducible tension between the risks of action and those of inaction, particularly when accounting for issues of race and class, as seen in the 2020 Black Lives Matter protests.

A key element of Williams's work was his repudiation of Marshall McLuhan's technological determinism. The response to the pandemic has revealed for all to see the impact of policy choices; of incentives and personal dealing; of racism, inequality, and profit motivation on outcomes. That assertion of the role of purposeful action in shaping our social structures bears within it a kernel of hope for the possibility of change. The fractures and tensions in our political and social systems exacerbated by the pandemic may open up a critical juncture, a moment when opportunities for radical systemic change arise and when, to borrow a phrase, another world is possible.[45] The upending of expectations and understandings has seen a dangerous explosion in conspiracy theories, as many are seduced by the promise of simplistic narratives and othered villains, falling down the rabbit hole offered by YouTube's recommendations engine or swayed by forwarded memes on WhatsApp. That poses both a challenge and an opportunity for critical educators and organizers, who may encounter newly receptive audiences for critical analysis and an appetite for transformative action.[46]

NOTES

1. Advani, "Awkward Lessons," 29; Ogletree, "Remote Schooling"; Segran, "These Kardashian-Approved"; Tschorn, "Pandemic Is Changing."
2. Brown, "Coronavirus Will Trigger."
3. Williams, *Television*.
4. Bauman, *Work, Consumerism*.
5. Williams, *Television*, 19.
6. Baran and Swezey, *Monopoly Capital*; Goldin and Margo, "Great Compression"; Piketty and Saez, "Income Inequality"; Krugman, "Confronting Inequality."

7. Williams, *Television*, 98.
8. Rothstein, *Color of Law*; Caro, *Power Broker*.
9. McGuigan and Moran, "Raymond Williams and Sociology."
10. Smythe, "On the Audience Commodity," 234.
11. Roediger, *Wages of Whiteness*.
12. Cohen, *Consumers' Republic*; Traci Parker, *Department Stores*; Perlman, *Public Interests*.
13. du Gay et al., *Doing Cultural Studies*, 4.
14. McChesney, *Rich Media, Poor Democracy*; Bagdikian, *New Media Monopoly*; Miller and Leger, "Runaway Production"; Castells, *Rise of the Network*, 289.
15. Crain, "Financial Markets"; Klein, *No Logo*; Wolfson, *Digital Rebellion*.
16. Huws, *Making of a Cyberteriat*.
17. Brock and Robin-Havt, *Fox Effect*; Gitlin, *Media Unlimited*; Pickard, "Big Picture"; Pariser, *Filter Bubble*; Sunstein, *Republic.com*.
18. Gates, *Our Biometric Future*; Noble, *Algorithms of Oppression*.
19. Castells, *Networks of Outrage*; Gladwell, *David and Goliath*; Kellner, "Media Spectacle"; Shirky, "Political Power"; Tufekci, *Twitter and Tear Gas*.
20. Zuboff, *Age of Surveillance Capitalism*.
21. Crain, "Financial Markets"; Crain and Nadler, "Political Manipulation."
22. Cant, *Riding for Deliveroo*; Dolber, "Precarity and Solidarity."
23. Attoh, Wells, and Cullen, "We're Building Their Data."
24. Dyer-Witheford, "Left Populism"; Gilbert and Williams, *Hegemony Now*; Fuchs, "Everyday Life."
25. Gilbert and Williams, 204–207.
26. Fraser, "From Progressive Neoliberalism."
27. Barrero, Bloom, and Davis, *Why Working*, 3.
28. Barrero, Bloom, and Davis.
29. Aldossari and Chaudhry, "Women and Burnout."
30. Cohen, "Amazon Retaliated"; Sainato, "Retail Workers at Amazon."
31. Chang, Marquez Janse, and Dorning, "Striketober."
32. Ball, *Electronic Monitoring*, 6.
33. Campaign for a Commercial-Free Childhood and Center for Digital Democracy, "Re: Request"; Lorenz, Griffith, and Isaac, "We Live in Zoom"; Perry and Lee, "AI Is Coming," 8.
34. Sunstein, *Republic.com 2.0*.
35. Pariser, *Filter Bubble*.
36. Fuchs, "Coronavirus Capitalism."
37. Abernathy, *News Deserts*.
38. Williams, *Television*.
39. Fuchs, "Dallas Smythe Today."
40. Tufekci, *Twitter and Tear Gas*.
41. Electronic Frontier Foundation, "Attending a Protest."
42. Carroll, "Hegemony, Counter-Hegemony, Anti-Hegemony."
43. Harvey, "Right to the City," 941.
44. Castells, *Rise of the Network*; Castells, *Networks of Outrage*; Tufekci, *Twitter and Tear Gas*; Yang, "Narrative Agency."
45. McChesney, *Communication Revolution*.
46. Dolber and Ó Baoill, "Pressing Pause."

BIBLIOGRAPHY

Abernathy, Penelope Muse. *News Deserts and Ghost Newspapers: Will Local News Survive?* University of North Carolina Hussman School of Journalism and Media, 2020. https://www.usnewsdeserts.com/reports/news-deserts-and-ghost-newspapers-will-local-news-survive/.

Advani, Shruti. "The Awkward Lessons of My Luxury Lockdown in Kensington." *Financial Times*, June 26, 2020, 29. https://www.proquest.com/docview/2427191640.

Aldossari, Maryam, and Sara Chaudhry. "Women and Burnout in the Context of a Pandemic." *Gender, Work and Organization* 28 no. 2 (2020): 826–834. https://doi.org/10.1111/gwao.12567

Attoh, Kafui, Katie Wells, and Declan Cullen. "'We're Building Their Data': Labor, Alienation, and Idiocy in the Smart City." *Environment and Planning D: Society and Space* 37, no. 6 (December 2019): 1007–1024. https://doi.org/10.1177/0263775819856626.

Bagdikian, Benjamin H. *The New Media Monopoly*. Boston: Beacon, 2004.

Ball, Kirstie. *Electronic Monitoring and Surveillance in the Workplace: Literature Review and Policy Recommendations*. Luxembourg: Publications Office of the European Union, 2021. https://doi.org/10.2760/5137.

Baran, Paul, and Paul Swezey. *Monopoly Capital*. New York: Monthly Review, 1966.

Barrero, Jose Maria, Nicholas Bloom, and Steven J. Davis. *Why Working from Home Will Stick*. Cambridge, MA: National Bureau of Economic Research, 2021. https://doi.org/10.3386/w28731.

Bauman, Zygmunt. *Work, Consumerism, and the New Poor*. New York: McGraw-Hill Education, 2004.

Brock, David, and Ari Robin-Havt. *The Fox Effect: How Roger Ailes Turned a Network into a Propaganda Machine*. New York: Anchor, 2012.

Brown, Jeffrey. "Coronavirus Will Trigger a Superspread of Automation." *Brink*, June 1, 2020. https://www.brinknews.com/how-can-automation-accelerate-economic-recovery-from-coronavirus/.

Campaign for a Commercial-Free Childhood and Center for Digital Democracy. "Re: Request for Public Comment on the Federal Trade Commission's Implementation of the Children's Online Privacy Protection Rule." Campaign for a Commercial-free Childhood, March 25, 2020. https://commercialfreechildhood.org/wp-content/uploads/2020/03/6B-Letter-3.25.20.pdf.

Cant, Callum. *Riding for Deliveroo: Resistance in the New Economy*. Medford, MA: John Wiley & Sons, 2019.

Caro, Robert. *The Power Broker: Robert Moses and the Fall of New York*. New York: Vintage, 1974.

Carroll, William K. "Hegemony, Counter-Hegemony, Anti-Hegemony." *Socialist Studies / Études Socialistes* 2 (Fall 2006): 9–43.

Castells, Manuel. *Networks of Outrage and Hope: Social Movements in the Internet Age*. Malden, MA: John Wiley & Sons, 2015.

———. *The Rise of the Network Society*. 2nd ed. Vol. 2 of *The Information Age: Economy, Society, and Culture*. Malden, MA: Wiley-Blackwell, 2010.

Chang, A., A. Marquez Janse, and C. Dorning. "'Striketober' Could Have Lasting Impact on Labor." NPR, October 28, 2021. https://www.npr.org/2021/10/28/1050177227/striketober-could-have-lasting-impact-on-labor.

Cohen, Lizabeth. *Consumers' Republic: The Politics of Mass Consumption in Postwar America*. New York: Knopf, 2003.

Cohen, Rachel M. "Amazon Retaliated against Chicago Workers Following Spring Covid-19 Protests, NLRB Finds." *The Intercept*, March 17, 2021. https://theintercept.com/2021/03/17/amazon-covid-chicago-nlrb-strike/.

Crain, Matt. "Financial Markets and Online Advertising: Reevaluating the Dotcom Investment Bubble." *Information, Communication, and Society* 17 no. 3 (2014): 371–384.

Crain, Matt, and Anthony Nadler. "Political Manipulation and Internet Advertising Infrastructure." *Journal of Information Policy* 9 (2019): 370–410.

Dolber, Brian. "Precarity and Solidarity at Neoliberalism's Twilight: The Potentials of Transnational Production Auto-ethnography." *Cultural Studies ↔ Critical Methodologies* 20, no. 4 (2019): 311–321.

Dolber, Brian, and Andrew Ó Baoill. "Pressing Pause: Critical Reflections from the History of Media Studies." *tripleC: Communication, Capitalism, and Critique* 16, no. 1 (2018): 264–279. https://doi.org/10.31269/triplec.v16i1.927.

du Gay, Paul, Stuart Hall, Linda Janes, Anders K. Madsen, Hugh MacKay, and Keith Negus. *Doing Cultural Studies: The Story of the Sony Walkman*. 2nd ed. London: SAGE, 2013.

Dyer-Witheford, Nick. "Left Populism and Platform Capitalism." *tripleC: Communication, Capitalism, and Critique* 18, no. 1 (2020). https://doi.org/10.31269/triplec.v18i1.1130.

Electronic Frontier Foundation. "Attending a Protest." *Surveillance Self-Defense*, 2020. https://ssd.eff.org/en/module/attending-protest.

Fraser, Nancy. "From Progressive Neoliberalism to Trump—and Beyond." *American Affairs* 1, no. 4 (Winter 2017): 46–64. https://americanaffairsjournal.org/2017/11/progressive-neoliberalism-trump-beyond/.

Fuchs, Christian. "Dallas Smythe Today—the Audience Commodity, the Digital Labour Debate, Marxist Political Economy, and Critical Theory." *tripleC: Communication, Capitalism, and Critique* 10, no. 2 (2012): 692–740. https://doi.org/10.31269/triplec.v10i2.443.

———. "Everyday Life and Everyday Communication in Coronavirus Capitalism." *tripleC: Communication, Capitalism, and Critique* 18, no. 1 (2020): 375–399. https://doi.org/10.31269/triplec.v18i1.1167.

Fukuyama, Francis. "The End of History?" *National Interest* 16 (1989): 3–18.

Gates, Kelly A. *Our Biometric Future: Facial Recognition Technology and the Culture of Surveillance*. New York: NYU Press, 2011.

Gilbert, Jeremy, and Alex Williams. *Hegemony Now: How Big Tech and Wall Street Won the World (and How We Win It Back)*. New York: Verso, 2022.

Gitlin, Todd. *Media Unlimited: How the Torrent of Images and Sounds Overwhelms Our Lives*. New York: Metropolitan Books, 2001.

Gladwell, Malcolm. *David and Goliath: Underdogs, Misfits, and the Art of Battling Giants*. New York: Little, Brown, 2013.

Goldin, Claudia, and Robert A. Margo. "The Great Compression: The Wage Structure in the United States at Mid-Century." *Quarterly Journal of Economics* 107, no. 1 (1992): 1–34.

Goode, Lauren. "The iPhone's Face ID Will Soon Work with a Mask—if You Have an Apple Watch." *Wired*, February 2, 2021. https://www.wired.com/story/iphone-face-id-mask-ios-beta/.

Harvey, David. "The Right to the City." *International Journal of Urban and Regional Research* 27, no. 4 (December 2003): 939–941.

Huws, Ursula. *The Making of a Cyberteriat: Virtual Work in a Real World*. New York: Monthly Review, 2002.

Kellner, Douglas. "Media Spectacle, Insurrection, and the Crisis of Neoliberalism from the Arab Uprisings to Occupy Everywhere!" *International Studies in Sociology of Education* 23, no. 3 (2013): 251–272.

Klein, Naomi. *No Logo*. New York: Picador, 2000.

Krugman, Paul. "Confronting Inequality." In *They Say / I Say: The Moves that Matter in Academic Writing with Readings*, edited by Gerald Graff and Cathy Birkenstein, 586–603. New York: W. W. Norton, 2007.

Lorenz, Taylor, Erin Griffith, and Mike Isaac. "We Live in Zoom Now." *New York Times*, March 17, 2020. https://www.nytimes.com/2020/03/17/style/zoom-parties-coronavirus-memes.html.

McChesney, Robert W. *Communication Revolution: Critical Junctures and the Future of Media*. New York: New Press, 2007.

———. *Rich Media, Poor Democracy: Communication Politics in Dubious Times*. Urbana: University of Illinois Press, 1999.

McGuigan, Jim, and Marie Moran. 2014. "Raymond Williams and Sociology." *Sociological Review* 62, no. 1 (2014): 167–188.

Miller, Toby, and Marie C. Leger. "Runaway Production, Runaway Consumption, Runaway Citizenship: The New International Division of Cultural Labor." *Emergences: Journal for the Study of Media and Composite Cultures* 11, no. 1 (2001): 89–115.

Noble, Safiya U. *Algorithms of Oppression: How Search Engines Reinforce Racism*. New York: NYU Press, 2018.

Ogletree, Kelsey. "Remote Schooling Is the New First-Class Hotel Perk." *Wall Street Journal*, October 8, 2020. https://www.wsj.com/articles/remote-schooling-is-the-new-first-class-hotel-perk-11602172183.

Pariser, Eli. *The Filter Bubble: What the Internet Is Hiding from You*. London: Penguin, 2011.

Parker, Traci. *Department Stores and the Black Freedom Movement: Workers, Consumers, and Civil Rights from the 1930s to the 1980s*. Durham: University of North Carolina Press, 2019.

Perlman, Allison. *Public Interests: Media Advocacy and Struggles over U.S. Television*. New Brunswick, NJ: Rutgers University Press, 2016.

Perry, Andre M., and Nicol Turner Lee. "AI Is Coming to Schools, and if We're Not Careful, so Will Its Biases." Brookings Institution, September 26, 2019. https://www.brookings.edu/blog/the-avenue/2019/09/26/ai-is-coming-to-schools-and-if-were-not-careful-so-will-its-biases/.

Pickard, Victor. "The Big Picture: Misinformation Society." Public Books, November 28, 2017. https://www.publicbooks.org/the-big-picture-misinformation-society/.

Piketty, Thomas, and Emmanuel Saez. "Income Inequality in the United States, 1913–1998." *Quarterly Journal of Economics* 118, no. 1 (2003): 1–41.

Roediger, David. *The Wages of Whiteness: Race and the Making of the American Working Class*. New York: Verso, 1999.

Rothstein, Richard. *The Color of Law: A Forgotten History of How Our Government Segregated America*. New York: Liveright, 2018.

Sainato, Michael. "Retail Workers at Amazon and Whole Foods Coordinate Sick-Out to Protest Covid-19 Conditions." *The Guardian*, May 1, 2020. https://www.theguardian.com/world/2020/may/01/retail-workers-at-amazon-and-whole-foods-coordinate-sick-out-to-protest-covid-19-conditions.

Segran, Elizabeth. "These Kardashian-Approved Survival Kits Are Designed for Anti-Preppers." Fast Company, September 3, 2020. https://www.fastcompany.com/90472865/these-kardashian-approved-survival-kits-are-designed-for-anti-preppers.

Shirky, Clay. "The Political Power of Social Media: Technology, the Public Sphere, and Political Change." *Foreign Affairs* 90, no. 1 (2011): 28–41.

Smythe, Dallas W. "On the Audience Commodity and Its Work." In *Media and Cultural Studies: Keyworks*, edited by Meenakshi Gigi Durham and Douglas M. Kellner, 230–256. Malden, MA: Wiley, 2012.

Sunstein, Cass R. *Republic.com*. Princeton, NJ: Princeton University Press, 2001.

———. *Republic.com 2.0*. Princeton, NJ: Princeton University Press, 2007.

Swauger, Shea. "Software that Monitors Students during Tests Perpetuates Inequality and Violates Their Privacy." *MIT Technology Review*, August 7, 2020. https://www.technologyreview.com/2020/08/07/1006132/software-algorithms-proctoring-online-tests-ai-ethics/.

Tschorn, Adam. "The Pandemic Is Changing the Future of Fashion and Shopping. Why That's a Good Thing." *LA Times*, September 4, 2020. https://www.latimes.com/lifestyle/story/2020-09-04/covid-19-pandemic-sped-up-beauty-fashion-trends.

Tufekci, Zeynep. *Twitter and Tear Gas: The Power and Fragility of Networked Protest*. New Haven, CT: Yale University Press, 2017.

Williams, Raymond. *Television: Technology and Cultural Form*. London: Routledge, 2004.

Wolfson, Todd. *Digital Rebellion: The Birth of the Cyberleft*. Champaign: University of Illinois Press, 2014.

Yang, Guobin. "Narrative Agency in Hashtag Activism: The Case of #BlackLivesMatter." *Media and Communication* 4, no. 4 (2016): 13–17. https://doi.org/10.17645/mac.v4i4.692.

Zuboff, Shoshana. *The Age of Surveillance Capitalism: The Fight for a Human Future at the New Frontier of Power*. London: Profile Books, 2019.

Perils of the Interregnum

10

Reforming White Supremacy

The Comparative Grammars of Counterextremism

Najwa Mayer

What if the crowds who attacked the U.S. Capitol on January 6, 2021, were not predominantly white and Christian but rather Black and/or Muslim? Variations of this question appeared across op-eds, social media, and counterextremism analyses after January 6.[1] Recounting an attempted government takeover consecrated by white supremacy, Far Right politics, and Christian nationalism, these analyses conjured the specters of racial and religious Others as analogues for how white and Christian violence against the U.S. state could be imagined and managed. Some understandably used these comparisons to implicate racist disparities in U.S. policing. In an era when militarized counterinsurgency tactics inform local policing against Black, brown, and poor people, U.S. security response to the Capitol was strikingly slow and limited, if not outright complicit in the violence.[2] Yet others used analogy as a kind of liberal secular reasoning to synonymize different forms of political violence—whether committed by white Christian, Muslim, or Black people (of any religion)—within dehistoricized, ideological frameworks of "extremism," equally transliterated as racism, religiosity, and hate.

Analogy offers wide-ranging political functions, including critique. As a rhetorical device analogy is not simply comparative but, presumably, clarifying. Rather than only offer similarity, as might a metaphor or simile, an analogy proposes explanation through strategic comparison. For instance, in political critique, anticolonial social movements across Palestine and South Africa aligned by analogizing apartheid as a racially stratified and segregated political structure, with varied localized effects.[3] In the rhetoric of policing, on the other hand, analogy may rationalize epistemes of criminality or subjectivities exceeding state protection by drawing expressive, *rather than structural*, comparisons between distinct and possibly unequitable phenomena—thereby reinforcing the explanatory authority of the police and state. In the latter case, literary scholars have long drawn relation between the production of narrative, knowledge, and (carceral, colonial) power.

Analogical analyses of extremism not only proliferated in the popular sphere after January 6 but also among security professionals, which include academic, state, and private counterextremism and counterterrorism specialists. Following Donald Trump's successful and explicitly white Christian nationalist presidential campaign in 2016, security professionals increasingly have adapted domestic terrorism policies to better incorporate white supremacists within the criminal psychology of "extremism" and into the legal subject of the "terrorist," which heretofore overwhelmingly figured Muslims. Seeking to resuscitate a failed liberal order wherein the state's foundational white Christian nationalism is its emergency, these analyses attempt to reform the state and whiteness itself by expanding the (always-already racialized) repertoires of securitization.

The mass industrialization of U.S. and transnational counterextremism and counterterrorism "expertise" in the late twentieth and early twenty-first centuries is an ideological product of profitable policing, carceral, and defense industries.[4] These disciplines produce not only capacious criminal categories but also interpretive grammars, which journalism and popular culture reproduce. Their narrative politics—formal tools like language, tropes, motifs, and so on—help systematize and codify two historically flexible categories of criminalization. With their state, academic, and private sector growth following the September 11, 2001, attacks in the United States, counterextremism and counterterrorism's knowledge disciplines and security arms formalized a racialized Muslim archetype—which they analogically modeled on longer U.S. state histories of surveilling Black (including Black Muslim) political dissidents as well as Palestinians and Palestine activism[5]—through predominantly studying and policing so-called radical Islam. "Muslim," as a racially fungible category (albeit overwhelmingly Black or brown), served as both template and synonym for "extremist" and "terrorist" within security and popular discourse in the United States since at least the twentieth century, with longer colonial histories.[6] Despite unprecedented inflation and financing of counterterrorism and counterextremism enforcement, the Department of Homeland Security (DHS)—which formed after 9/11—reported between 2019 and 2021 that white supremacist violence represents the gravest domestic threat to the United States.[7] Officials added that white supremacists permeate the U.S. military, and federal agencies are underprepared.[8]

Notwithstanding their unconvincing characterization of white supremacy as "infiltrating" rather than historically structuring U.S. militarism, this self-admission evidences homeland security as a foundationally racial project.

Counterextremist specialists mobilize extremism as a seemingly "neutral" genre to narrate various political violences, regardless of context or relationship to state power, through shared symptomatic tropes.[9] Yet, even as counterextremism targets white supremacists, the epistemological and racial imprint of "radical Islam" in the field apparently sustains its grammar. Following the Capitol attacks, counterextremist analyses have repeatedly invoked "Islamism"[10] as a generic model with which to formally measure other extremisms.[11] Counterextremism's grammar, influenced by its highly symptomatic methodologies and its emphasis on Islam, mobilize analogy as an epistemic and security tool. Lost in analogy is the ongoing state and imperial structures that empower and institutionalize white supremacy and Christian hegemony in the United States. When counterextremist analyses diagnose white Christian violence in relation to prefigured grammars of extremism qua "Islamism," they manage certain expressions of white power while disguising others. Further, they render white supremacy and Christian nationalism as hateful ideologies rather than racial-secular structures, the violence of which is only perceived "extreme" when directed at the state and not by it.

I begin this chapter by situating the entwined racial and religious foundations of the U.S. Capitol attacks, while challenging news media depictions of "white Christian nationalism" as a moment of political crisis rather than a persistent structure of white supremacy and Christian hegemony enfolded within the liberal secular state. I then consider how analogies of political violence operate in both popular and security analyses of the attacks. I focus on how counterextremism specialists analogize white Christian nationalism, and white supremacy broadly, with "Islamism," taking post–January 6 analyses published in mainstream media as case studies. By analyzing mainstream publications (while drawing on academic literatures as secondary sources), I reflect on the popularization of counterextremism's grammars—from academic, government, and state security documents to quotidian discourse—producing a culture of counterextremism. I contextualize counterextremism's comparative grammars and its attempted reformation of white supremacy within the security state's liberal modes of crisis reform, which operate through exceptional yet perpetual logics of managing crisis. In the twenty-first century, these securitized reforms are produced at once through institutions of policing, militarism, and post-civil-rights laws' racial liberalism—what Dylan Rodriguez calls "white reconstruction" as counterinsurgent reforms to white supremacy, what Junaid Rana terms as the "racial infrastructure of the terror-industrial complex," and extending from Nikhil Pal Singh's notion of a "long war" against racialized domestic communities.[12] Within these contexts, liberal modes of reparative security reckon with a seeming ideological interregnum, wherein the foundations of the liberal U.S. state—whiteness and Christianity—are its crises. Yet media and expert analyses that diagnose, renounce, or criminalize white supremacy and Christian nationalism as extremist and analogically abject them in relation to Islam ultimately disguise systemic white power as "secular," "moderate," and "mundane."

Race, Religion, and the U.S. Capitol Attacks: White Christian Nationalism as Crisis vs. Structure

Following Donald Trump's reelection defeat in the 2020 presidential election, thousands of his supporters traveled to the U.S. Capitol building in Washington, DC, on January 6, 2021. Their apparent objective was to prevent a joint session of Congress from counting the electoral college votes that would affirm president-elect Joseph Biden's victory. Their charge to keep Trump in power was, according to participants, delivered by Trump himself.[13] Over two thousand individuals entered the Capitol building, some with weapons, overrunning police and causing hundreds of injuries. Five lost their lives in association with the attacks. Yet news media noted that Trump and other state officials did not immediately increase policing nor deploy the National Guard in response to the violence, enabling the crowd's temporary takeover of government offices.[14]

In addition to a failed coup, the crowds also incorporated traditional forms of right-wing political protest, proclaiming issues like border control as well as a host of planned and spontaneous performances of nationalist grievance steeped in rhetorical and visual cultures of Christian whiteness. Journalists and scholars predominantly mediated the Capitol attacks through the relatively broad formation "white Christian nationalism"—as white Christian supremacism articulated through the nation-state project—evidenced by the symbols worn or carried by dominantly white participants as well as their own racial and religious assertions.[15] Demographically, the crowds substantially comprised white men, many brandishing insignia like swastikas, Confederate flags, as well as logos affiliated with white nationalist organizations like the Oath Keepers and Proud Boys, both of which also mobilize Christian symbology.[16] Protest signs read "Proud American Christian" and "No Matter Who Is President, Jesus Is King." Alongside U.S. flags, individuals bore Bibles and crosses while some reenacted Biblical scenes like the siege of Jericho,[17] thereby performatively mandating their attack *not* as a coup d'état but rather as national order restored by two senses of sovereign authority: white [heteromasculine] American citizenship and God's will.

While Christian symbolism was certainly ubiquitous, the ritualistic breadth exhibited on January 6 demonstrates the plural formations of white power, Christian nationalisms, and racialized fascisms invested in and expressed through the nation-state. Even as nonwhite participants were underrepresented at this event, their limited presence and Trump's growing popularity with a multi-racial right extend what Cheryl Harris termed the "property of whiteness."[18] In terms of religious demographics, a wide spectrum of denominations took part, including reports of Evangelical, Protestant, Catholic, Mormon, Unitarian, and atheist participants.[19] Crusader imagery and costumes were prevalent, which is consistent with their war-on-terror era rise within Euro-American popular cultures—harkening an imagined resurrection of imperial Christendom against Islam as a universal threat.[20] A large showing of the Far Right conspiratorial movement QAnon demonstrated their own religious heterogeneity. Studies suggest that QAnon affiliates subscribe to several religious traditions from Christian denominations to neopagan customs, yet a concerted majority (72 percent) agree that Islam is uniquely "at odds with American values and way of life."[21]

Global Far Right movements also constellated at the Capitol through much fewer albeit discernible religious, ethnic, and nationalist symbols like that of Israeli and Indian flags,[22] invoking political alliances between Zionist, Hindutva, and white Christian supremacist movements in this century. Although often regarded as a conservative isolationist, Trump regularly celebrated and empowered the ethno-religious supremacist leadership of both India and Israel (which are not new nor exclusively conservative U.S. foreign policy positions but rather consistent ones).[23] Following Alyosha Goldstein and Simón Ventura Trujillo, we may disabuse analogy by understanding how several contemporary fascistic nationalisms in liberal democracies, whether through authoritarian state rule or extralegal actors, respond to the material effects of the interbedded crises of capitalism *and* imperialism within global relations of labor, property, and militarism[24]—most apparently, as in the cases of the United States, Israel, and India, through ethno-racial, religious, and gendered-sexual control domestically as well as colonial extractions internationally. Religious cosmologies may also be conscripted toward providing a telos for not only nationalized ethno-supremacism but also for social relations among ethno-supremacist states.

Whether racialized nationalisms and fascisms reflect liberalism's points of crises or inevitable progressions, it is clear that religion consigns meaning to white power in the United States. Kathryn Gin Lum describes the production and protection of whiteness as a Christian formation and the racial Other as a "heathen inheritance" within U.S. history. Modern, secular conceptions of race did not entirely replace ideas of religious difference; rather, religion lingers within the construction of race.[25] Thus, when white protesters at the Capitol bore signs reading, "Proud American Christian,"[26] the subtextual whiteness of "American" and "Christian" coconstitute both the centers ("truths") and boundaries of race, religion, and nation. Under liberal statehood, U.S. secularism also regulates rather than protects difference, with a majoritarian conception of religion—marked by dominantly white forms of Christianity—categorically formed within secular rule. In effect, exercises of "religious freedom" in legal and national conventions are contingent on proximities to whiteness while religious legibility is associated with and historically disciplined into Protestant norms.[27]

Racial and religious difference produce not only the boundaries of U.S. nationalism and secularism but also the effects of state securitization. Policing and carceral institutions emerged to protect the property, including enslaved human property, of white (dominantly Christian, upper-class) Americans.[28] Local and federal policing regularly engage racial and religious profiling, disproportionately against nonwhite, non-Christian communities.[29] Indeed, the congressional report on the Capitol attacks underplayed the largely white supremacist, Christian, and heteropatriarchal claims of the event;[30] the report instead named "Trumpism" as its pretext, thereby revealing another racialized imbalance in which political violence is rendered a pathology of religious culture (as in the case of "Islamic terrorism") within secular governance. Similarly, the Department of Defense's 2021 *Report on Countering Extremist Activity within the Department of Defense* signaled white supremacist groups as the most significant domestic violence threats yet avoided naming Christianity,[31] in stark contrast to their explicit management of Islam within domestic and imperial modes of secular rule.

From the settler-colonial, anti-Black, and Christian formations of the secular liberal republic to the neoliberal, racialized security state, a persistent, albeit disavowed, difference emerges through the violent enforcement of liberal ideologies like equality, freedom, rights, and secularism.[32] Many scholars show that while Christian ideologies, Enlightenment-era secular philosophies, and white Europeanness as human/ism undergird Western liberal modernity, Blackness and Islam historically constituted their boundaries.[33] In the United States, the discursive specters of Islam and Blackness haunted the foundational ideologies of nation building and liberal republicanism, forging early constitutional questions over issues like citizenship bound by whiteness and anxieties over executive governance being usurped by Muslims or other non-Christians.[34] This discursive legacy lingers today when, to make sense of liberalism's dilemma in the Capitol attack, some sought conjectural analysis not through U.S. liberalism's ideological continuities—the white Christian nationalisms on display—but rather through the racial and religious limits of Western liberalism itself: Blackness and Islam.

"What if . . .": Speculative Analogy and Liberal Critique

"What if the rioters who breached the U.S. Capitol were Black?" Solomon Jones conjectured for a Philadelphia PBS station.[35] "What if the crowd who swarmed the U.S. Capitol was Black or Muslim?" Heidi Stevens asked for the *Chicago Tribune*.[36] "If those were Muslims who waged that attack, the result would've been vastly different," Dean Obeidallah is quoted by Hannah Allam in the *Washington Post*.[37] "If rioters were Black, 'hundreds' would have been killed," Nandita Bose and Makini Brice reported for Reuters.[38] Variations of these speculative analyses across news and social media in the aftermath of the U.S. Capitol attacks implicated the uneven policing of political violence committed by white Christian actors. Unquestionably, not only was the attack's securitization slow and restrained, but some Capitol police officers facilitated the siege. Analogy, thus, operates critically in these popular analyses, toward exposing unequitable punitive systems. Speculative analogy is perhaps also redundant, though, given Black and brown people actually and continually face police violence in the United States.

While certainly ongoing U.S. histories of racialized state security confirm the disproportionate criminalization of nonwhite peoples by police and military as well as white Christian vigilante violence against Black, Indigenous, and immigrant communities, one may also attribute the preponderance of these analyses across media to recent stark conjunctures. First, the U.S. public witnessed overwhelming, weaponized escalations of (historically consistent) police violence against BLM protests across the country within the year before the Capitol attacks, following the 2020 police murder of George Floyd.[39] Second, police response to the Capitol was slow and limited while prosecution of those arrested was measured by (white) citizenship protections. In contrast, militarized counterinsurgency tactics inform contemporary domestic policing, disproportionately against Black and brown communities, while post-9/11 counterterrorism policies habituate wartime practices like indefinite detention, including against some U.S. citizens, often Muslims.[40] Third, the imagined fortress of the U.S. security state, symbolized at the Capitol's legislative center, was quite quickly breached by armed nonstate actors.

Stevens's op-ed captures a sense of indignant shock following the seeming fissures of the security state: "How were armed insurgents allowed to breach the U.S. Capitol, forcing the evacuation of the United States Congress? How are we seeing photos of a man sitting in Nancy Pelosi's desk, with access to the emails still on her screen? How did it get to that point? And would it have, had the group been made up of people of color?"[41] This unnerved prose of serial *hows* suggests an interregnal break in the imaginary of the contemporary security state that, particularly since 9/11, resulted in the most funded defense infrastructure in U.S. history. Yet Stevens's culminating analogical question suspends disbelief and rupture, offering in it an answer: "And would it have, had the group been made up of people of color?" No, and not simply because policing is racist in the United States, as the op-ed concludes, but also because this prose implies there is something amiss in the political rationalism of statehood—that is, its monopoly on the legitimate use of violence—when *certain* "armed insurgents [are] allowed to breach the U.S. Capitol." Surely, many Americans expressed a similar sense of surprise, which one may recognize as false consciousness or white privilege, yet we may also contextualize within the ubiquitous structures, performances, and rhetorics of security that saturate U.S. public life.

These popular analyses simultaneously impart a banal awareness of a racially protected class of vigilante violence in the United States coupled with an unnerved sense of the security state's diminished sovereignty. This conjuncture recalls what Inderpal Grewal describes as an advanced stage of neoliberalism wherein an exceptionalized class of white Christian citizens recuperate the U.S. security state's waning power equally through their vigilante militarism and selective humanitarianism—implicitly authorized by the state.[42] Yet, in this case, the perceived "crisis" is less the protesters' exercise of exceptionalized white sovereignty but rather that their violence is momentarily directed at the very state that produced their conditions of possibility.

Despite these op-eds' accurate critiques of racialized punitive systems in the United States, their speculative analogies about white political violence often proceed either explicitly or implicitly toward a common conclusion: they advocate resolving the inequalities of policing and law through more equitable distributions, which, if even inadvertently, implicates police expansion. They, thus, reproduce what the abolitionist activists Mariame Kaba and Andrea Ritchie describe as a reformist and legitimating ideology of policing, which implies that policing is failing rather than perfectly functioning as a racial technology.[43] Through such reformist critiques, news and social media analyzed two subjects—terrorism and extremism—with a particularly liberal ethos of multiculturalism and secularity. The colloquialization of these security categories emerges from this century's mass industrialization of two disciplines: counterextremism and counterterrorism.

Displacing White Supremacy in the Comparative Grammars and Cultures of Counterextremism

While scholars generally trace the U.S. state's officiation of counterterrorism and counterextremism as security disciplines to the twentieth century, the circulation and policing of subjectivities like "terrorist," "extremist," and "radical" have longer colonial histories.[44] Counterextremism and counterterrorism as sites of "expertise" proliferated after 9/11 through government and commercial sector careers, academic literature, surveillance, and policing. The DHS offered multimillion-dollar grants for post-9/11 Countering Violent Extremism projects, effectively bankrolling the genres and their pre/occupations.[45] Security experts themselves admit that the study and policing of Islam in the age of the global war on terror saturated these fields.[46]

Following scholarship on the dangerously capacious logics of counterextremism and counterterrorism as policing disciplines,[47] I focus on the racial and security work of their narrative forms with analogy as one case study. Post–January 6 counterextremism analyses levy analogy in a moment when the field faces its own epistemological and security crisis: that is, how to resolve the subjects of "extremism" and "terrorism" in security enforcement (which dominantly targeted Muslims in the post-9/11 age but also included categories like "Black identity extremists") with the predominant agents of nonstate political violence in the contemporary United States (white supremacists). Counterextremist analysts employ analogy, a formal technology with political stakes, as an epistemology of policing when comparing distinct kinds of violence by how similarly they are expressed within an ideological grammar of extremism rather than by their different, or often disparate, political and historical contexts.

Counterextremism's grammar relies on symptomatic tropes of extremism via expressions like hate, (nonstate) violence, excessive belief, and disinformation. Given that Muslims comprised the most-studied models of counterextremism and counterterrorism, proceeding from longer histories of policing arms containing Palestinian and Black political dissidents (including Black Muslims), the fields not only systematize a bias in enforcement but also generically produce Muslim, Palestinian, and Black actors as extremism's prototypical subjects. In the aftermaths of the Donald Trump presidency and Capitol attacks, counterextremist specialists more frequently channel funding and thinking toward white supremacists, while deploying extremism as a genre to narrate and analogize various nonstate violence, regardless of context or relationship to state power, through signifying themes. For instance, they ideologically relate "extremism" with hate and excessive belief, while defining "radicalization" as the process through which one becomes extreme by absorbing ideas within mediated (dis)information networks. Counterextremist specialists thus may characterize white supremacy as an ideology[48] or set of "beliefs" in the same genre as "Islamist terrorism," "the radical left," and "animal rights activism."[49] In this paradigm, they conceptualize white supremacy symptomatically rather than structurally—thereby formalizing it within a pathological and individually policeable grammar of extremism while absenting it, or at best peripheralizing it, from state or state-sanctioned racial governance.

Narrating white Christian supremacy as extremism does not absolve the category's racist tropes. Rather, the analogies invoked by counterextremism experts often reify an associative link between the genre's tropes and its overdetermined subject (Islam). In other words, analogy interpellates "Islamism" as a generic model for white violence—sometimes explicitly. In *Foreign Policy*, Rita Katz, director of the counterterrorism organization SITE Intelligence Group, claims, "White supremacist terrorists have taken a page from the Islamic State's playbook—discarding concerns about image and embracing shocking displays of public violence."[50] Analogy apparently substitutes historical contexts when Katz describes recent white supremacist vigilante violence in the United States as "just like" Islamic State tactics of unabashed violence and hate. Ironically, the white supremacists Katz names, such as Brenton Tarrant, who murdered fifty-one Muslims in New Zealand mosques, take inspiration from the tenth- through thirteenth-century European Crusades, white supremacist states like Nazi Germany, and "white replacement theories"[51] (which she cites yet dismisses in her analogy) that are central to current state-aligned anti-immigration movements in Europe and North America. Katz does not situate these Western state and Christian imperial histories as centuries-long foundations for contemporary white supremacist violence; rather, she suggests they imitate the two-decade-old Islamic State. By equating expressive features of violence with the generic subject of terrorist/extremist, she portrays violent symptoms as operating within an equivalent landscape of power and ideology. Consequently, Katz erases U.S. imperialism's own violent role in producing the Islamic State,[52] uproots Western histories of white supremacy onto Islamic geopolitics, and analogizes distinct political formations as equivalent pathologies of violence.

The discursive transliteration of symptoms with political movements is common in security, academic, and journalistic narratives of counterextremism. The national security reporter Jim Sciutto argues, "The Capitol rioters speak just like the Islamist terrorists I reported on.... Followers of both are drawn to a cause greater than themselves that gives them a shared identity and a mission to correct perceived wrongs, by whatever means necessary. At the core of this cause is a profound sense of victimization and humiliation."[53] Here, analogy equates divergent political movements by way of commonly politicized emotions. For example, shared identity/mission and sense of victimization are not reducible to Far Right movements but generative tropes in most populist politics (violent and nonviolent) as well as within state narratives of nationalism. Sciutto not only dehistoricizes the formations of each political violence but also discounts the constructive role of white supremacy within Western imperial projects that contributed to the emergence of militant nonstate "Islamist" movements.

In academic counterextremism, scholars may also transliterate racism with religiosity through symptomatic motifs—reducing racism as bad belief rather than an organizing system of power. In 2021, the George Washington University Program on Extremism published the report *Rise of the Reactionaries: Comparing the Ideologies of Salafi-Jihadism and White Supremacist Extremism*. They measure white supremacist racism against a politicized religious tradition, suggesting that an ideological excess violently reproduces both. While the report takes greater care to consider the historical developments and, at times, political relationships between both (i.e., considering how European colonialism produced conditions for what they term "Salafi-Jihadism"), a formulaic diagnostic of extremism eclipses these nuances through broad expressive motifs. The report analogizes reactionary Salafism and white supremacy via "overlaps" in "chauvinist collective identity, conspiracism, antisemitism, necessity and legitimacy of violence, and utopianism."[54] Again, these are common tropes and affects among not only many political movements but also ideologies of (violent) nation-states. One could easily trace each of these examples—from chauvinism and antisemitism to violence and utopianism—to historical and ongoing popular narratives of U.S. nationalism. Indeed, the counterextremism genre produces extremism as a criterion that disciplines *certain nonstate* political violence.[55] Thus, it not only reduces political violence to individual or social ills rather than structural features of nation-states; it also distinguishes extremist violence from the presumably reasonable violence of (racial) states.

Notably, such discourses of comparative counterextremism and liberal reform are not superficially "colorblind," as some observe in other (particularly European) counterextremism analyses.[56] Mirroring common U.S. rhetorics of multicultural liberalism, these journalists and academics apparently see differences among the Islamic State, Salafism, and white supremacism. Rather, they conflate political violences through the ideologization of racial and religious "extremisms" as equal products of hate or other emotions/symptoms. These distinctions are instrumental to their conflation because their assembling as bad ideologies renders them depoliticized and dehistoricized not only individually but in relation. "Extremism" itself, or the inability to reform and moderate, becomes the core problem and not, for instance, the fact that U.S. legal, civic, and social institutions routinize white supremacy[57]—the perceived loss of which is the object of white Christian nationalist violence. Reform and moderation also relate to the performance of secularism so counterextremist policing emerges as a liberal form of both secularism and multiculturalism.

Some counterextremism experts like Cynthia Miller Idriss attempt to nuance the term extremism by, importantly, challenging fringe treatments of Far Right violence. In *Foreign Policy*'s "How Extremism Went Mainstream," she argues traditional counterextremism models fail to describe the Capitol attacks because "the majority of the rioters were hitherto ordinary Americans who had only recently embraced radical ideas. Their pathways to political violence did not involve a clearly defined ideology or an affiliation with particular groups but instead were shaped by a propaganda campaign that engulfed the full spectrum of right-wing politics."[58] Despite these contradictions to the field's definitions, she preserves the categorical promise of extremism to mark many antagonistic subjects of liberal rule by tracing its popular dispersions. Even in demarcating a popularized grammar of extremism, which her books more subtly develop and relate to historical geopolitics,[59] the imprecise logics of counterextremism remain. To illustrate, she distinguishes "ordinary Americans" susceptible to highly mediated right-wing ideologies that "shaped" their extremism from those (extraordinary?) extremists who (more willfully, inherently?) pursue organized or "clearly defined" political violence. In effect, she identifies a culture of extremism and produces a culture of counterextremism as antidote. Counterextremism's imprecision and cultural optic may vanish unequal political contexts, enabling a host of racial subtexts to take root. Further, if white racial extremists are the identified problem, then what about the structuralized white supremacy that produces "mundane" state violence via policing, income inequality, border enforcement, militarism, health care discrimination, and more? Such presumably "moderate," state-sanctioned white supremacy not only substantiates nonstate white-power groups' racial claims but is also institutionally sustained through the full spectrum of liberal, centrist, and right-wing politics by "ordinary Americans." When distinguishing or even weeding out white extremists, counterextremism does not eliminate or challenge systemic white supremacy but rather reforms it.

Miller Idriss adds that a hypermediated process of political radicalization sutures unlikely support between the U.S. Christian Far Right and Taliban or right-wing and left-wing antigovernment militias. Certainly, incongruous and transnational relations do form between Far Right social and state movements. But characterizing them as similar kinds of extremism obscures more than it clarifies. For instance, U.S. imperialist interventions, under administrations summoning both liberal and right-wing ideologies, contributed directly to forming the Taliban. Further, at the Capitol attacks, Israeli, Indian, and U.S. flags waved in unison, signaling a rise in political alliances between Zionist, Hindutva, and white Christian supremacist movements. All three securitized states entwine state-sanctioned Islamophobia, institutionalized ethno-religious supremacy, practices of territorial colonization, and war-on-terror military collaborations[60]—demonstrating that religio-racialized nationalisms are not isolationist nor politically partisan (liberal vs. conservative) but imperial and systemic. Comparative extremism as a genre occludes the resonances between state and popular Far Right interests. We must situate such resonances historically *and* understand their geopolitical specificity. For instance, other scholars systemically contextualize growing Far Right movements in relation to "reactionary democracy's" entrenchments in liberal institutions[61] or via fascism as a convergence of authoritarian state and extralegal racialized nationalisms responding to global destabilizations wrought by capitalism and imperialism.[62]

Liberal efforts to recuperate counterextremism, alongside several recent, unsuccessful[63] police reform initiatives, still codify and sustain the very inequality of policing that they claim to remedy. Activists long critiqued the formal imprecision of "terrorism" and "extremism" in law and policing because the state may criminalize a host of protest traditions or dissident figures under these widely interpretive terms, while also tempering any political expression that misaligns with state power.[64] Post-9/11 counterterrorism enforcement indicted Muslims who challenged war-on-terror policies, surveilled BLM activists as "Black identity extremists," and charged Indigenous protesters who objected to the state's environmental encroachments.[65] Meanwhile, some holistic counterextremist specialists propose "inoculating" against extremism[66] as a generic problem—encompassing white Christian nationalists, Islamists, radical leftists, and so on—through secular multicultural models of mental health, following European countries. In her study of the historical discourse of terrorism as an "epidemic," Anjuli Raza-Kolb notes that using disease rhetorics and methods to contain national security threats, particularly against nonwhite people, has long racial-colonial histories.[67] Relatedly, activists warn that even if therapists identify the white Christian Far Right as extremists, they may rely on these racial-colonial histories when interpreting other behaviors/bodies as "radical."[68] Tarek Younis's research on anti-Muslim surveillance in U.K.-based mental health industries provides similar lessons, revealing that while many presume psychology, mental health, and counterextremist programs to be apolitical secular sciences, they are produced within political, economic, and defense infrastructures. Under the multinational war on terror, defense industries commodified and sold counterextremist psychological formulas, using Muslims as their subject populations.[69]

Ultimately, when policing's academic, social, and carceral infrastructures narrate and discipline nonstate white Christian political violence through comparative grammars of extremism, a reformed white supremacy persists—further legitimated—as "rational," racial statehood. If the Capitol attacks represent an interregnal dilemma, wherein the U.S. state's formative whiteness and Christianity are its crises, then securitizing white Christian nationalism as "extremism" sustains U.S. liberalism's aporia.

ACKNOWLEDGEMENTS

I thank Inderpal Grewal and Kayla Renee Wheeler for comments on earlier drafts, as well as the reviewers and editors of *Cultural Studies in the Interregnum* for their revisions. This chapter builds on a short-form essay published in *The Immanent Frame* (November 2023) with editorial support from Mona Oraby.

NOTES

1. See, for instance, Jones, "What if the Rioters"; Stevens, "What if Crowd"; Allam, "Welcome to Our World"; Bose and Brice, "If Rioters Were Black"; Cullors, "If it Were Black"; Armstrong, "Imagine"; Blair, "What if the Capitol."
2. Mazzetti and Haberman, "Why Did It Take."
3. Some argue analogy has a limit here too: Qutami, "Moving Beyond."
4. Stampnitsky, *Disciplining Terror*; Walker, *Emergence of "Extremism"*; Kundnani, *Muslims Are Coming!*
5. Li, "Anti-Palestinian at the Core."
6. Nguyen, *Suspect Communities*; Daulatzai and Rana, *With Stones*; Daulatzai, *Black Star Crescent Moon*.
7. Department of Defense, *Report*.
8. Donnelly, "Pentagon Report"; *Capitol Insurrection: Unexplained Delays and Unanswered Questions*.
9. "Terrorist" produces a similar function: Husain, "Deracialization, Dissent, and Terrorism."
10. I use quotations around "Islamism" because, much like "jihadism," its deployment in state security discourse is ill-defined, broad, and bereft of indigenous contexts, while potentially encapsulating any and all political Islams—statist and nonstate, authoritarian and decolonial, and so on—in its capture. Qureshi, "Case against 'Islamism'"; Li, *Universal Enemy*.
11. See, for instance, Meleagrou-Hitchens, Crawford, and Wutke, *Rise of the Reactionaries*; Idriss, "How Extremism Went Mainstream"; Katz, "How 'Screw Your Optics.'"
12. Rana, "Racial Infrastructure"; Rodriguez, *White Reconstruction*; Singh, *Race and America's Long War*.
13. Rodriguez-Delgado, "Trump Asked Us."
14. See note 2.
15. Jenkins, "How the Capitol Attacks"; Blake, "An 'Imposter Christianity'"; Gorski, "White Christian Nationalism."
16. Simon and Sidner, "Decoding the Extremist Symbols."
17. Jones, "Taking the White Christian."
18. Harris, "Whiteness as Property."
19. See note 15.
20. Razack, *Nothing*.
21. Jenkins, "Study."
22. Rose, "Many Flags."
23. Walia, *Border and Rule*; Essa, *Hostile Homelands*.

24. Goldstein and Trujillo, *For Antifascist Futures*.
25. Lum, *Heathen*.
26. Jenkins, "How the Capitol."
27. Wenger, *Religious Freedom*.
28. Hinton and Cook, "Mass Criminalization."
29. Johnson and Weitzman, *FBI and Religion*.
30. Dalsheim and Starrett, "Christian Nationalism Is Downplayed."
31. Department of Defense, *Report*.
32. Lowe, *Intimacies of Four Continents*.
33. Wynter, "Unsettling the Coloniality"; Hesse, "Racialized Modernity"; Mills, *Racial Contract*.
34. Marr, *Cultural Roots*.
35. Jones, "What if the Rioters."
36. Stevens, "What if Crowd."
37. Allam, "Welcome."
38. Bose and Brice, "If Rioters Were Black."
39. Dessem, "Police Erupt in Violence."
40. Rodriguez, *White Reconstruction*; Besteman et al., "Human Rights."
41. Stevens, "What if Crowd."
42. Grewal, *Saving the Security State*.
43. Kaba and Ritchie, *No More Police*.
44. See note 4. Ho-Jung, *Menace to Empire*; Raza-Kolb, *Epidemic Empire*.
45. Department of Homeland Security, "DHS Countering Violent Extremism."
46. Reitman, "U.S. Law Enforcement Failed."
47. In addition to other citations in this chapter, see the work of Sohail Daulatzai, Junaid Rana, Lisa Stampnitsky, Darryl Li, Silva Kumarini, Sahar Selod, Arun Kundnani, Nicole Nguyen, Tarek Younis, Maha Hilal, and Atiya Husain, among others.
48. Doxsee et al., "Pushed to Extremes."
49. Washington Journal, "Cynthia Miller Idriss."
50. Katz, "How 'Screw Your Optics.'"
51. Gelineau, "Mosque Shooter."
52. Gopal, "Roots of ISIS."
53. Sciutto, "Capitol Rioters."
54. Meleagrou-Hitchens, Crawford, and Wutke, *Rise of the Reactionaries*.
55. Stampnitsky, *Disciplining Terror*.
56. Younis, *Muslim, State and Mind*.
57. Harris, "Whiteness as Property"; Lipsitz, *Possessive Investment in Whiteness*.
58. Miller Idriss, "How Extremism Went Mainstream."
59. Among her books about extremism, Miller Idriss's U.S.-based *Hate in the Homeland* expands the main points of the aforementioned article while providing a more nuanced account of how racist ideologies circulate via mediated networks. She also importantly situates white extremism within U.S. histories of systemic racism. Yet, in sustaining extremism as an epistemological and policing tool, her analysis of racism remains wedded to an individually pathologizing heuristic central to liberal multicultural modes of state securitization. Even the rhetoric of "hate" reinforces the individualization of structural racism and the seeming neutrality of carceral power—a point critical race scholars have critiqued for several decades.
60. See note 23.
61. Mondon and Winter, *Reactionary Democracy*.

62. Goldstein and Trujillo, *For Antifascist Futures*.
63. Chow, "People Expected Police Behavior."
64. In the U.S. context, see Patel, "We Don't Need More"; Health Justice Team, "CVE in Healthcare."
65. Lubin, *Never-Ending War on Terror*; Auston, "Prayer, Protest"; Barker, *Red Scare*.
66. Green, "How Inoculating Americans."
67. Raza-Kolb, *Epidemic Empire*.
68. See note 64.
69. Younis, *Muslim, State and Mind*.

BIBLIOGRAPHY

Allam, Hannah. "Welcome to Our World." *Washington Post*, November 30, 2021, https://www.washingtonpost.com/national-security/capitol-riot-muslims-reaction/2021/11/29/bd5a454e-43c8-11ec-8534-ec852a55e0e6_story.html.

Armstrong, Jenice. "Imagine What Would Have Happened if the Rioters Who Stormed the Capitol Had Been Black." *Philadelphia Inquirer*, January 7, 2021, https://www.inquirer.com/opinion/trump-capitol-riot-mob-black-lives-matter-jenice-armstrong-20210107.html.

Auston, Donna. "Prayer, Protest, and Police Brutality." *Transforming Anthropology* 25 (June 2017): 11–22.

Barker, Joanne. *Red Scare: The State's Indigenous Terrorist*. Berkeley: University of California Press, 2021.

Besteman, Catherine, et al. "Human Rights and Civil Liberties," Brown University, Watson Institute for International and Public Affairs, Costs of War, June 2021. https://watson.brown.edu/costsofwar/costs/social/rights.

Blair, Olivia. "What if the Capital Rioters Were Black?" *Elle*, January 7, 2021. https://www.elle.com/uk/life-and-culture/a35149462/capitol-riots-trump-black-lives-matter-police.

Blake, John. "An 'Imposter Christianity' Is Threatening American Democracy." CNN, July 24, 2022. https://www.cnn.com/2022/07/24/us/white-christian-nationalism-blake-cec/index.html.

Bose, Nandita, and Makini Brice. "If Rioters Were Black, 'Hundreds' Would Have Been Killed." Reuters, January 8, 2021. https://www.reuters.com/article/us-usa-election-inequality/if-rioters-were-black-hundreds-would-have-been-killed-washington-reflects-on-capitol-rampage-idUSKBN29D1HM.

"The Capitol Insurrection: Unexplained Delays and Unanswered Questions; Hearing before the Committee on Oversight and Reform, House of Representatives, 107th Cong." May 12, 2021.

Chow, Andrew. "People Expected Police Behavior to Change after George Floyd's Murder." *Time*, May 13, 2021. https://time.com/6046645/police-killings-2021/.

Cullors, Patrisse. "'If It Were Black People' at Capitol, 'It Would Have Been a Massacre,'" *Good Morning America*, January 7, 2021. https://www.goodmorningamerica.com/gma3/video/black-people-capitol-massacre-blm-founder-75111587.

Dalsheim, Joyce, and Gregory Starrett. "Christian Nationalism Is Downplayed in the Jan. 6 Report and Collective Memory." *The Conversation*, September 6, 2022. https://theconversation.com/christian-nationalism-is-downplayed-in-the-jan-6-report-and-collective-memory-189440.

Daulatzai, Sohail. *Black Star Crescent Moon: The Muslim International and Black Freedom beyond America*. Minneapolis: University of Minnesota Press, 2012.

Daulatzai, Sohail, and Junaid Rana, eds. *With Stones in Our Hands: Writings on Muslims, Racism, and Empire*. Minneapolis: University of Minnesota Press, 2018.

Department of Defense. *Report on Countering Extremist Activity within the Department of Defense*. December 2021, https://media.defense.gov/2021/Dec/20/2002912573/-1/-1/0/REPORT-ON-COUNTERING-EXTREMIST-ACTIVITY-WITHIN-THE-DEPARTMENT-OF-DEFENSE.PDF.

Department of Homeland Security. "DHS Countering Violent Extremism Grants." DHS.gov, Archived Content, updated February 22, 2021. https://www.dhs.gov/cvegrants.

Dessem, Matthew. "Police Erupt in Violence Nationwide." *Slate*, May 31, 2020. https://slate.com/news-and-politics/2020/05/george-floyd-protests-police-violence.html.

Donnelly, John. "Pentagon Report Reveals Inroads White Supremacists Have Made in Military." Roll Call, February 16, 2021. https://rollcall.com/2021/02/16/pentagon-report-reveals-inroads-white-supremacists-have-made-in-military.

Doxsee, Catrina, Seth Jones, Jared Thompson, Kateryna Halstead, and Grace Hwang. "Pushed to Extremes: Domestic Terrorism amid Polarization and Protest." Center for Strategic and International Studies, May 17, 2022. https://www.csis.org/analysis/pushed-extremes-domestic-terrorism-amid-polarization-and-protest.

Essa, Azad. *Hostile Homelands: The New Alliance between India and Israel*. London: Pluto, 2023.

Gelineau, Kristen. "Mosque Shooter a White Nationalist Seeking Revenge." AP News, March 15, 2019. https://apnews.com/article/immigration-shootings-ap-top-news-international-news-australia-1e19fefcb2e948a1bf7ce63429bc186e.

Goldstein, Alyosha, and Simón Ventura Trujillo, eds. *For Antifascist Futures: Against the Violence of Imperial Crisis*. Brooklyn: Common Notions, 2022.

Gopal, Anand. "The Roots of ISIS: Imperialism, Class, and Islamic Fundamentalism." *International Socialist Review* 102 (June 2016). http://isreview.org/issue/102/roots-isis.

Gorski, Philip. "White Christian Nationalism: What It Is and Where It's Going." Political Theology Network, October 13, 2022. https://politicaltheology.com/white-christian-nationalism-what-it-is-and-where-its-going.

Green, Zachary. "How Inoculating Americans against Radicalization Can Fight Domestic Terrorism." PBS, June 27, 2021. https://www.pbs.org/newshour/show/how-inoculating-americans-against-radicalization-can-fight-domestic-terrorism.

Grewal, Inderpal. *Saving the Security State*. Durham, NC: Duke University Press, 2017.

Harris, Cheryl. "Whiteness as Property." *Harvard Law Review* 106, no. 8 (June 1993): 1707–1791.

Health Justice Team. "CVE in Healthcare and Counseling." Muslim Justice League. Accessed October 16, 2024. https://muslimjusticeleague.org/for-health-care-professionals/.

Hesse, Barnor. "Racialized Modernity: An Analytics of White Mythologies." *Ethnic and Racial Studies* 30, no. 4 (2007): 643–663.

Hinton, Elizabeth, and DeAnza Cook. "The Mass Criminalization of Black Americans: A Historical Overview." *Annual Review of Criminology* 4 (January 2021): 261–286.

Ho-Jung, Moon. *Menace to Empire: Anticolonial Solidarities and the Transpacific Origins of the US Security State*. Berkeley: University of California Press, 2022.

Husain, Atiya. "Deracialization, Dissent, and Terrorism in the FBI's Most Wanted Program." *Sociology of Race and Ethnicity* 7, no. 2 (April 2021): 208–225.

Idriss, Cynthia Miller. "How Extremism Went Mainstream." *Foreign Policy*, January 3, 2022. https://www.foreignaffairs.com/articles/united-states/2022-01-03/how-extremism-went-mainstream.

Jenkins, Jack. "How the Capitol Attacks Helped Spread Christian Nationalism." *Washington Post*, January 26, 2022. https://www.washingtonpost.com/religion/2022/01/26/christian-nationalism-jan-6-extreme-right.

———. "Study: QAnon Draws from Several Faith Groups." Religion News Service, February 24, 2022. https://religionnews.com/2022/02/24/study-qanon-draws-from-several-faith-groups-numbers-more-than-40-million.

Johnson, Sylvester, and Steven Weitzman, eds. *The FBI and Religion*. Berkeley: University of California Press, 2017.

Jones, Robert. "Taking the White Christian Nationalist Symbols at the Capitol Riot Seriously." Religion News Service, January 7, 2021. https://religionnews.com/2021/01/07/taking-the-white-christian-nationalist-symbols-at-the-capitol-riot-seriously.

Jones, Solomon. "What if the Rioters Who Breached the US Capitol Were Black?" WHYY PBS, January 7, 2021. https://whyy.org/articles/what-if-the-rioters-who-breached-the-us-capitol-were-black.

Kaba, Mariame, and Andrea Ritchie. *No More Police*. New York: New Press, 2022.

Katz, Rita. "How 'Screw Your Optics' Became a Far-Right Rallying Cry." *Foreign Policy*, October 23, 2022. https://foreignpolicy.com/2022/10/23/far-right-terrorism-white-supremacy-islamic-state.

Kundnani, Arun. *The Muslims Are Coming! Islamophobia, Extremism, and the Domestic War on Terror*. Brooklyn: Verso, 2014.

Li, Darryl. "Anti-Palestinian at the Core: The Origins and Growing Dangers of U.S. Antiterrorism Law." Palestine Legal and Center for Constitutional Rights, February 20, 2024. https://ccrjustice.org/sites/default/files/attach/2024/02/Anti-Palestinian%20at%20the%20Core_White%20Paper_0.pdf.

———. *The Universal Enemy*. Redwood City, CA: Stanford University Press, 2019.

Lipsitz, George. *The Possessive Investment in Whiteness*. Philadelphia: Temple University Press, 2018.

Lowe, Lisa. *The Intimacies of Four Continents*. Durham, NC: Duke University Press, 2015.

Lubin, Alex. *Never-Ending War on Terror*. Berkeley: University of California Press, 2021.

Lum, Kathryn Gin. *Heathen: Religion and Race in American History*. Cambridge, MA: Harvard University Press, 2022.

Marr, Timothy. *The Cultural Roots of American Islamicism*. Cambridge: Cambridge University Press, 2006.

Mazzetti, Mark, and Maggie Haberman. "Why Did It Take So Long to Deploy the National Guard?" *New York Times*, July 21, 2022, https://www.nytimes.com/2022/07/21/us/politics/national-guard-january-6-riot.html.

Meleagrou-Hitchens, Alexander, Blyth Crawford, and Valentin Wutke. *Rise of the Reactionaries: Comparing the Ideologies of Salafi-Jihadism and White Supremacist Extremism*. Washington, DC: George Washington University, 2021.

Mills, Charles. *The Racial Contract*. Ithaca, NY: Cornell University Press, 1997.

Mondon, Aurelien, and Aaron Winter. *Reactionary Democracy: How Racism and the Populist Far Right Became Mainstream*. New York: Verso, 2020.

Nguyen, Nicole. *Suspect Communities: Anti-Muslim Racism and the Domestic War on Terror*. Minneapolis: University of Minnesota Press, 2019.

Patel, Faiza. "We Don't Need More Terrorism Laws after the Capitol Riot." *Newsweek*, February 14, 2021. https://www.newsweek.com/we-dont-need-more-terrorism-laws-after-capitol-riot-just-look-our-9-11-mistakes-opinion-1568327.

Qureshi, Asim. "The Case against 'Islamism.'" Ummatics, October 22, 2022. https://ummatics.org/the-case-against-islamism/.

Qutami, Loubna. "Moving beyond the Apartheid Analogy in Palestine and South Africa." MERIP, February 3, 2020. https://merip.org/2020/02/moving-beyond-the-apartheid-analogy-in-palestine-and-south-africa-trump.

Rana, Junaid. "The Racial Infrastructure of the Terror-Industrial Complex." *Social Text* 34, no. 4 (December 2016): 111–138.

Razack, Sherene. *Nothing Has to Make Sense: Upholding White Supremacy through Anti-Muslim Racism.* Minneapolis: University of Minnesota Press, 2022.

Raza-Kolb, Anjuli. *Epidemic Empire: Colonialism, Contagion, and Terror, 1817–2020.* Chicago: University of Chicago Press, 2021.

Reitman, Janet. "U.S. Law Enforcement Failed to See the Threat of White Nationalism." *New York Times*, November 3, 2018. https://www.nytimes.com/2018/11/03/magazine/FBI-charlottesville-white-nationalism-far-right.html.

Rodriguez, Dylan. *White Reconstruction: Domestic Warfare and the Logics of Genocide.* New York: Fordham University Press, 2020.

Rodriguez-Delgado, Cresencio. "Trump Asked Us to Come." PBS, January 9, 2022. https://www.pbs.org/newshour/politics/watch-trump-asked-us-to-come-rioters-said-during-jan-6-attack.

Rose, Emma. "The Many Flags that Flew during the US Capitol's Storming." *The Wire*, January 15, 2021. https://thewire.in/world/us-capitol-storming-flag-india-militia-groups-nationalism.

Sciutto, Jim. "The Capitol Rioters Speak Just Like the Islamist Terrorists I Reported On." *Washington Post*, February 19, 2021. https://www.washingtonpost.com/outlook/capitol-riot-terrorism-islam-violence/2021/02/19/6d4b499a-7222-11eb-85fa-e0ccb3660358_story.html.

Simon, Mallory, and Sara Sidner. "Decoding the Extremist Symbols and Groups at the Capitol Hill Insurrection." CNN, January 11, 2021. https://www.cnn.com/2021/01/09/us/capitol-hill-insurrection-extremist-flags-soh/index.html.

Singh, Nikhil Pal. *Race and America's Long War.* Berkeley: University of California Press, 2017.

Stampnitsky, Lisa. *Disciplining Terror: How Experts Invented "Terrorism."* Cambridge: Cambridge University Press, 2013.

Stevens, Heidi. "What if Crowd Who Swarmed the US Capitol Was Black or Muslim?" *Chicago Tribune*, January 6, 2021. https://www.chicagotribune.com/columns/heidi-stevens/ct-heidi-stevens-trump-supporters-mob-capitol-double-standard-0106-20210106-njqyjby45vhx3b3twsem4d257a-story.html.

Walia, Harsha. *Border and Rule: Global Migration, Capitalism, and the Rise of Racist Nationalism.* Chicago: Haymarket Books, 2021.

Walker, Rob Faure. *The Emergence of "Extremism."* London: Bloomsbury, 2021.

Washington Journal. "Cynthia Miller Idriss on White Supremacy." C-SPAN, August 8, 2019. https://www.c-span.org/video/?463301-3/cynthia-miller-idriss-white-supremacy.

Wenger, Tisa. *Religious Freedom: The Contested History of an American Ideal.* Chapel Hill: University of North Carolina Press, 2017.

Wynter, Sylvia. "Unsettling the Coloniality of Being/Power/Truth/Freedom." *New Centennial Review* 3 (2003): 257–337.

Younis, Tarek. *The Muslim, State and Mind.* London: SAGE, 2022.

11

The Sea Birds, Still

Spirit Work and Structural Adjustment

James Bliss

> Where are the evolved, poised-for-light adepts who will assume the task of administering power in a human interest, of redefining power as being not the privilege or class right to define, deform, and dominate, but as the human responsibility to define, transform, and develop?
>
> —Toni Cade Bambara[1]

In the interval between the publication of *The Sea Birds Are Still Alive* (1977) and the appearance of *The Salt Eaters* (1980), Toni Cade Bambara discussed the challenges of living through "periods of high conflict and low consciousness."[2] It was an interregnum that many call "post-civil rights," though Bambara insisted the moment was not post- anything. "I often read in reviews that my stories are set in the sixties and are nostalgic and reminiscent of days when revolutions were believed in. News to me."[3] Moving from her second collection of short stories to her first novel, Bambara began from the observation that "not since the maroon experience of Toussaint [Louverture]'s era have psychic technicians and spiritual folk (medicine people) and guerillas (warriors) merged. It is a wasteful and dangerous split."[4] The following vignettes weave through stories from *Sea Birds* and then to *The Salt Eaters* to track how Bambara constructs worlds where resistance to anti-Blackness, capitalism, and colonialism traverse the spiritual and the political.

For Bambara, there is no singular outside to anti-Blackness, capital, and the settler state. Bambara's stories travel across intersecting and disconnected terrains of struggle—a drive across town, a walk through a snowstorm, a boat ride across the bay, hidden in a bathtub, sitting on the healer's stool. I read these moments in Bambara's work as elements in a Black feminist critique of violence during a period that anticipated the fascisms and nationalisms, the ecological and economic calamities, and the apocalyptic nihilism of white culture in the United States that mark our present. Bambara's is a feminist Black radicalism that links the workings of the spirit and the work of militant struggle. Along the way, I link these moments in Bambara's oeuvre to the beginnings of an account of the financialization of racial capitalism, as one name for the interregnum that we inhabit and Bambara anticipated.

Neoliberalism is one name for a historically specific set of attempts to resolve the contradictions of racial capitalism. By the 1970s, those contradictions had grown to a point of crisis, and that moment is written into Bambara's second collection of stories and her first novel. In the present, those crises and the attempts to resolve them have metastasized as an interregnum where the old world cannot keep going and a new world cannot be imagined—caught between the old overdeterminations and the indeterminacy of our inarticulate longing for a revolutionary otherwise. In this new point of crisis, it may be that our best understandings of neoliberalism missed the mark. The present chapter outlines the current interregnum through histories of structural adjustment and financialization that are also attentive to the structuring force of anti-Blackness. Drawing attention to the financialization of racial capitalism, coterminous with but not identical to the project of neoliberalism, illuminates aspects of the interregnum that have evaded the contemporary project of cultural studies.

A Drive across Town

In "The Apprentice," Bambara's narrator is shadowing a more seasoned community worker, Naomi. Bambara plays the two off each other. Her narrator is caught on some edge of exhaustion while Naomi appears to us as indefatigable. The speaking voice of the text is trying her best, trying not to give in to cynicism, sarcasm, and defeatism: "Naomi assumes everybody wakes up each morning plotting out exactly what to do to hasten the revolution."[5] To the extent that we only experience the narrator's interiority, to the extent that Naomi is pure surface, "The Apprentice" is a story about the vicissitudes of living a politics—the anxiety and exhaustion of working to make revolution irresistible. "But for all my hollerin," the story's voice offers, "I love the sister and am always refreshed, coming off work, to see her car idling at the curb, ready to make the rounds, keep this committee in touch with that project in touch with thusnsuch organization in touch with the whatchamacallit league" (28).

The action of the story follows just such a day of making the rounds: meeting with the old folks at the retirement home, stopping to talk with Edward Decker from the Brothers of Canaan Lodge (the sort of petit bourgeois local elite that made revolutionary struggle possible and made postrevolutionary life so vexed), intervening on a traffic cop harassing a Black motorist, and ending at a drive-up restaurant caught in a confluence of late night rushes. All along the way, the story's voice returns to the soreness in her feet and legs, the exhaustion burning behind her eyes, and these bodily and affective tensions release themselves in the odd sarcastic remark, for which Naomi is not at all the audience. "My work attitude ain't too progressive, I've been told more than once at the group criticism sessions." She goes on, "I am negative. I guess that's why I've been teamed with Naomi. She views everything and everybody as potentially good, as a possible hastener of the moment, an usherer in of the new day. Examines everybody in terms of their input to making revolution an irresistible certainty" (32–33).

"Easy for Naomi—hell, she'd been to countries where ordinary folk had done it, had stood up and flexed their knees, and in that simple gesture toppled the whole johnson built on their backs, feeding off their backs, breaking their backs for generations after generation" (33). Sure, Naomi can see the society to come. She'd been to the liberated countries and seen the liberated people. She'd seen newly burnished bureaucrats of free lands building houses by day, then rum-sweat and dancing by night. Free people on free land. Naomi had seen the revolutionary societies before they were incorporated into global finance capital.

In his popular history of the Third World, *The Darker Nations*, Vijay Prashad offers a globe-spanning story of decolonial struggles that became new nations. The decolonial struggles had united peasants and workers with landlords and local elites, and the new governments "combined the promise of equality with the maintenance of social hierarchy."[6] By the time Bambara was writing "The Apprentice," cracks had formed in these once-new nations: "Popular demands for land, bread, and peace had been ignored on behalf of the needs of the dominant classes," and "internecine warfare, a failure to control the prices of primary commodities, an inability to overcome the suffocation of finance capital, and more led to a crisis of the budgets of much of the Third World."[7] The era of structural adjustment began. Commercial banks, multilateral and regional development banks, and the Bretton Woods institutions offered short-term loans tied to policies that suffocated what was left of the dream of national liberation.

For each new nation, each liberated former colony, finance capital was waiting. The first crisis, the first recession, the first drought, the first season of failed crops—whatever crisis that couldn't be overcome without foreign direct investment. And then the loan, the conditions on the loan, the debt servicing, the structural adjustments. No matter which way the elections went, the sovereign power of the new state was subservient to the conditions of debt servicing. In "Culture and Finance Capital," Fredric Jameson described financialization as the moment when "capital itself becomes free-floating," as the moment when capital "separates from the concrete context of its productive geography."[8] In important ways, this version of finance capital as "deterritorialized, autonomous, and immaterial" is still how finance is read.[9] We feel its effects, but it is a capitalism separated from the violences that produce value. For Annie McClanahan, the task for contemporary critics is to see how "financial value has as its grounding moment the brutal exploitation of labor, the material violence of the state, and the finitude of natural resources."[10] We must demystify the violence of finance capital.

We face the financialization of our lives. Lives structurally adjusted. Lives of debt servicing. We live these intimate experiences of longer processes of strangling liberation struggle. Like the apprentice, the voice of the story. "Being a revolutionary is something else again. I'm not sure I'm up to it, and that's the truth. I'm too little, too young, and maybe too scarified if you want to know the truth" (33).

Naomi is Bambara's true believer. She believes in what's possible beyond the World Bank, the International Monetary Fund, and imperial America's twentieth-century iterations of the Monroe Doctrine. Liberated people in liberated nations. Collective ownership and collective freedom. And she gets on a roll about it, beating the steering wheel, preaching a new day for a new people. "I can feel the new day Naomi always lecturing about, can feel it pumping through my legs. I want to be there. I'm hoping I live long enough. I'm just about to make some promises to work harder when one of their waitresses rolls up and takes hold of my tray" (39). Somehow the world always comes back. After they eat, Naomi still has gas enough to run back into the kitchen to help clean up:

> I can't see how I'm going to make it back to the car, I'm so beat. No use saying nothing to Naomi, though, bout being tired. I ain't earned the right, to hear her tell it. But hell, it'd been a long, long, long day. (42)

A Walk through a Snowstorm

"The Apprentice" leaves us at the end of a long, long, long day, and "Broken Field Running" thrusts us into the middle of another. The story follows a pair of teachers in a liberated school walking their pupils home through an urban environment in the midst of structural adjustment. The piece grew from Bambara's analysis of the new urban architectures built in response to the urban rebellions of the 1960s. "I'd been observing architectural changes in my community since the street rebellions. Schools, public housing, parks were being designed in such a way as to wreck community sovereignty, to render it impossible for neighbors to maintain surveillance and security of turf. I was enraged. I wrote a blazing essay on the subject, snarling, shooting from both hips."[11] The first draft of the story, according to Bambara, was "baroque in its stridency, bizarre in its tension blend of essay, rally speech, and melodramatic narrative." On the next draft, Bambara made a meteorological change to find the story she meant to tell. "I introduced a snowstorm, originally to lower the temperature of the rhetoric." Bambara's narrator, Lacey, changes with the snowstorm. "There is something irresistibly funny about a self-righteous, angry, propelled/compelled rager trying to move and talk machine-gun fashion while up to her hips in snow and ice."[12]

This way Bambara changed the world of her story recalls Christina Sharpe's formulation of anti-Blackness as the weather, as the "total climate" and "totality of our environments."[13] The snowstorm materializes and metaphorizes the atmospheric violence that has Lacey raging while walking her students home. But Bambara's snowstorm is also clarifying because it does, in fact, operate at a different scale than the violence of urban renewal. There is no stopping a snowstorm. Urban renewal, the spatial and architectural violence of finance capital, can be stopped. Another name for our interregnum might be the experience of state and economic violence as the weather. The cul-de-sac of political possibility feels as natural and unavoidable as a cloudy day.

Bambara plays with this indeterminacy, between the force of weather and the violence of urban renewal. "There's a flurry of snow masking the projects, as though the enemy's ordered a whiteout in our part of town" (44). The snowstorm and the war against Black life, Black collectivity, and Black sovereignty become muddled. When the flurry abates, we see the Lawndale Homes complex in its intended function, "free-flowing terrain designed to leave the issue of territorial control up for grabs" (44). And not only the world of the block has been reconfigured in the name of urban renewal qua urban counterinsurgency, the interior design and infrastructure of the new buildings are weaponized. "We go in the lobby door and a blast of heat gets past the damp and frost to chap my face. Then it goes straight for the eyes. Enemy furnaces to strip the mucous membranes and leave us vulnerable to the viruses cultivated special in the prisons on the rest of our population" (46). These are the structural adjustments of the domestic exterior. Bambara saw a war of position in the new architectures of Black space. These reorganizations of space were one terrain for the reconfigurations of violence called neoliberalism.

Privatization has been the most common name for these reconfigurations of the violences of racial capitalism and state power. The privatization of public space and public goods, the privatization of social services, the privatization of the functions of the state—the welfare state and, just as often, the warfare state. The socialization of risk and the privatization of profit. But there are two limits of this common framing of neoliberalism. First, the politics of anti-Blackness within the prehistory of neoliberalism are rarely acknowledged. Second, in the context of the United States, the framing of privatization obscures the degree to which key functions of the Keynesian state were already privatized.

As teachers in a liberated school, Lacey and Jason represent an alternative response to the era of so-called integration. Recent histories of U.S. public education have shed light on post-*Brown* efforts to demolish Black institutions and to eviscerate the ranks of Black educators.[14] But the summer of 1958 saw the fitful first steps of neoliberalism in the United States. Backed by the force of the federal government, the previous year had seen public schools integrated in communities across the South, and most famously at Little Rock's Central High School. In a number of those communities, the 1958–1959 academic year simply did not begin.

In Little Rock, an attempt was made to rent the facilities of Central High School to a private Christian school. When that was blocked by the courts, the public high schools of Little Rock were shuttered. Without the infrastructure necessary to take education private, the experiment could not sustain itself. After an acrimonious "lost year," it was decided that fighting the specter of social equality, in that way, at least, was not worth the trouble.[15] Little Rock's lost year was an ersatz neoliberalism that anticipated the next several decades: the atavistic, self-destructive, self-preservation of white supremacy.

If public education was, for some, and for some time, a genuine public good in the United States, it might be counterposed by the range of public services that were already effectively private. Historically, and in contrast to other so-called advanced economies, "American workers and their families were uniquely dependent on corporate employers, not just for wages but for the basic social safety net."[16] With both health insurance coverage and retirement pensions tied to employment, the largest parts of the social safety net in the United States were already private endeavors. In important ways, the dynamics most associated with neoliberalism, "increased inequality, decreased mobility, uncertain employment, and an unduly powerful financial class," do not represent the corporatization and privatization of public goods but are outcomes of "the collapse of the corporation and the triumph of a finance-centered ideology."[17] Counterintuitively, it has been the loss of massive public corporations that has hastened the demolition of the social safety net. Many of the most loathsome aspects of our lives as workers are less attributable to corporatization than to the dynamics of shareholder capitalism and the rising power of private equity.

In the same historical moment when Bambara sent Lacey and Jason and their students stumbling through a blizzard, "the owners of capital" faced the question of "what to do with the immense surpluses at their disposal in the face of a dearth of investment opportunities."[18] The rise of the financial sector offered a solution to the contradictions of the postwar Bretton Woods system. Eventually, this new iteration of global finance brought about the present interregnum. Global financial capitalism inaugurated a half century of expanded productivity and stagnated wages—an ongoing crisis of overproduction that presents itself as a sequence of burst bubbles. Fewer people produce more products for which there are fewer potential consumers. Liberalizing access to personal credit was an early approach that remade the domestic space as a new site of insatiable consumption. Responding to the early stages of this shift, Bambara's narrator laments, "Families now are mere cargo cults. Cars, clothes, color TV, eight-track deck, lawn mowers the size of Model T's. And whatcha bring us, boy? How much they offering, girl?" (48). The modalities of structural adjustment touch every part of life. The weather. The city street. The home. The family.

A Boat Ride across the Bay

The titular story in *The Sea Birds Are Still Alive* emerged as Bambara's report to her constituents following her travel to Vietnam in the fall of 1975, after the American withdrawal and the reunification of Vietnam. Bambara went as a member of North American Academic Marxist-Leninist Anti-Imperialist Feminist Women ("it used to take us ten minutes to introduce ourselves") upon the invitation of the Women's Union of North Vietnam.[19] The vignettes, set in a fictionalized Southeast Asian nation aboard a ferry from the provinces to the city, were Bambara's way of telling stories she had seen and heard in Vietnam. It was also a way of bridging discrepant temporalities—from the immediate aftermath of a successful revolutionary struggle to revolutionary movements in the United States struggling to regroup in the new energies of the 1970s.

Bambara's story is told in fragments from the perspectives of the different passengers: peasants, refugees, students, businessmen, and soldiers, a foreign journalist, an American diplomat, a researcher exploring "The Dependency Complex of the Colored Peoples," informants, and militants. The ferry pilot offers a vantage on a regional landlord, returning from his yearly visit to his holdings. His Mercedes Benz below deck is larded with tributes from farmers angling to topple the entire system of property the landlord represents. Bambara offers us his "fat hand" and his "beefy paw," taking and taking from his tenants.

We see the landlord through the hatred of the pilot, himself a member of the resistance: "Soon the people would confront the rich grown fat off the blood and bones of the people. Would accuse them face to face in the people's tribunals.... The landlords, the war lords, the imperialists were no match for the force of the people, the force of justice, once the people moved together" (82). It is through the pilot as well that we see the widow woman from his home district—"a vessel of the old stratagems, a walking manual, having lost a grandfather, a father, six uncles, four sons, two husbands, and a daughter to the French, the Japanese, the Americans" (83). From the perspective of the pilot, Bambara glosses over the necessity of *both* the local elites and the most marginal members of the peasantry for revolutionary decolonial struggle. Closer to home, in the person of old Edward Decker, the head of the Brothers of Canaan Lodge, in "The Apprentice," Bambara grasps the variety and the heterogeneity of class interests that operate together in the making of revolution.

There has been a tendency within U.S. cultural studies to frame neoliberalism within the realm of social relations, where the latter term is treated as analytically distinct from the political economy of racial capitalism and the libidinal economy of anti-Blackness. Neoliberalism is understood as a shift from exclusion to inclusion—as minoritized populations were incorporated into the social, economic, and political machinery of liberal democracies across the latter half of the twentieth century. This framing of neoliberalism is attentive to "the coexistence of diverse forms of power—both repressive and affirmative, necropolitical and biopolitical—at the same time."[20] And because neoliberal power is both repressive and affirmative, because it entwines punishment and care, we "might begin with an understanding that there is no single pure, authentic politics of decolonization or radical antiracism, but rather that all politics emerge out of complex negotiations of care, regulation, and punishment."[21]

In troubling ways, this approach relies on a depoliticized and ahistorical framing of neoliberalism, with stultifying effects on critical cultural studies in the United States. This approach is borne of an unwillingness or inability to distinguish between a critical position (that may be more or less radical) and a class position (in this case, as what Rosa Luxemburg called the "hangers-on of the capitalist class").[22] The tendency within cultural studies to focus on inclusion and formal racial equality has tended to minimize or mystify forms of state violence that seem, at once, to be everywhere but also analytically indistinct. Against this tendency, Paula Chakravarty and Denise Ferreira da Silva point to the ways "the U.S. postracial moment was established with the systematic and effective dismantling of welfare provisions, investments in the carceral system, the growing precarity in labor markets, and the attacks on affirmative action and other race-conscious policies." They add, "This was not because the goals of the civil rights movement had been achieved"; rather, "the few existing mechanisms for redress had been eliminated, and it was time to announce that they were officially obsolete."[23] In crucial and dispiriting ways, cultural studies has been an intellectual accompaniment to the political economic tendencies that created the present interregnum.

Bambara offers an alternative culture of politics. A vision of politics that insists on the work of building a world worth fighting for while, at the same time, "trying to get at how difficult it is to maintain the fervent spirit at a time when the Movement is mute, when only a few enclaves exist."[24]

The throughline of the vignettes on the boat is a young girl and her mother, both militants from the countryside. The girl's mother had survived torture and was living with debilitating explosions of memory, and the girl had learned how to hold her mother through those spells. "'Nothing. I'll tell you nothing.' The girl might manage to get her mother's head up off the floor and into her lap. 'You'll never break our spirits,' soothing her temples. 'We cannot be defeated,' rocking, rocking" (88). The girl herself was recently tortured, and as soon as she was released, her mother took her to the ferry to the city. She was being sent to live with an old woman in the city doing subterranean work for the revolution. The soldier who tortured her left her with a parcel of food. The girl tossed the food to the birds trailing the ferry, amazed when none of them dropped dead into the water. And she thought of him, the soldier, who had tortured her and then let her go with unpoisoned food. Violence. Care. "And pitying him. For what shame would overwhelm him when he reexperienced his natural self and know once more right from wrong. But that, the elders had taught her in the spring, was the wonderful thing about revolution. It gave one a chance to amend past crimes, to change, to be human" (92).

And how many of us meekly acknowledge our complicities with state violence only to avoid imagining revolution as something real, something possible? How many of us sit in the familiar discomfort of our political inertia because we don't want to face what we've done or failed to do? Because we are afraid to change, to be forgiven, to be human.

Hidden in a Bathtub

"The Long Night" is the only of the *Sea Birds* stories not set in Bambara's present. It represents the political horizons of the 1960s. The unnamed narrator is a member of a militant formation, and her apartment building is being raided by police. The careful reader can piece together that the police have murdered a Black man outside the building and are now cleaning up the mess—both initiating a cover-up and engaging in urban pacification, attempting to quash a rebellion before it begins. Our narrator's perspective is limited to her bathtub, with its limited but not insignificant protection from bullets. Even if the police are not looking for her, she understands the state is always consciously or unconsciously looking for her, looking for the information hidden in her apartment.

Bambara dramatizes the social conflict of antiblack state violence through the conflict internal to her narrator. "*They'll find the box. They'll look for me. The blows. The madness. The best of myself splattered bright against the porcelain. No. The best of myself inviolate. Maybe*" (97; italics in original). Maybe. If we tell a story about revolutionary struggle as a genre of certainty, of knowing just what we are for and against, it is always in part an inoculation against indeterminacy. Our revolutionary longing is indeterminacy all the way down. Bambara's narrator experiences her own indeterminacy, the limits of her determination, and the ways she might be overdetermined.

> They'd ask about the others. Cracking her head against the faucet, they'd demand something ungiveable, but settle perhaps for anything snatchable, any anything to sanctify the massacre in the streets below. And would she allow them to tear the best of herself from herself, blast her from the place, that place inviolate, make her heap ratfilth into that place, that place where no corruption touched, where she curled up and got cozy or spread her life leisurely out for inventory. Hurtle her into the yellow-green slime of her own doing, undoing, to crawl on wrecked limbs in that violated place, that place. Could she trust herself. Was she who she'd struggled to become so long. To become in an obscene instant the exact who she'd always despised, condemned to that place, fouled.
>
> She would tell. They would beat her and she would tell more. They would taunt and torture and she would tell all. They'd put a gun in her eye and she would tell even what there wasn't to tell. Chant it. Sing it. Moan it. Shout it. Incriminate her neighbors. Sell her mama. Hawk her daddy. Trade her friends. Turn in everybody. Turn on everything. And never be the same. Dead or alive, never be the same. Blasted from her place. (97–98)

Between "Sea Birds" and "The Long Night," Bambara reckons with torture as one instantiation of state violence. The tendency, across cultural production and cultural studies, to render torture exceptional, has stultified analysis of the violences of both the state and finance capital, as if these forms of violence are detached from the everyday functioning of racial capitalism and state power. They torture. We know they do. They torture in black sites abroad and at black sites here. They will mutilate your life. And for what? For nothing. For nothing. For nothing but the value of a dollar, for floating currencies, for the value of white skin.

They'll kill you for nothing. A counterfeit bill, a loose cigarette, a broken taillight, a TV show. They'll torture you for the nothing that is the base of their power and the value of their currency. And they'll torture you for anything. To write off the loss of an empty housing unit, for the land you happen to be standing on, for just the slightest increase in shareholder value. You're left with whether it matters that you've been killed or some part of you has been killed for no reason or for a bad reason. Life is organized around the potential to face the demand for something ungiveable or anything snatchable. Life is pursued in defiance of that possibility.

This life is both a form of structural adjustment and a form of speculative investment.

These violences and these forms of life, what Bambara articulates with her narrator trapped against the bottom of her bathtub, are the true substance and the remainder of finance capital. Specifically, the iteration of finance capital emerging since the 1970s in the form of the shareholder value movement. The originary intellectual exercise of shareholder capitalism took shape in Michael Jensen and William Meckling's "Theory of the Firm." Jensen and Meckling's argument hinges on two mutually reinforcing ideas: first, that the primary and authentic "owners" of a firm are shareholders and, second, that the only objective measure of a firm's value is its market valuation, the price at which its stock trades. Shareholder capitalism reduced ownership to shareholding and subsumed all other forms of corporate responsibility to a duty to maximize stock prices for shareholders. This is a step beyond the typical exploitation of variable capital, of the wage relation. It extends capitalism's austerity regime to every level of a firm, as all value is redistributed to shareholders, who are, by definition, not obligated to the firm.[25] The subsequent half century—what is called neoliberalism and what we typically think of as a time of privatization and corporatization—was an age of financialization, as money capital was redistributed toward speculative investment; an age when "publicly traded corporations have become less concentrated, less interconnected, shorter-lived, and less prevalent";[26] an age of shareholder capitalism, as all of the functions of a firm were reduced to juicing stock prices, which has had the counterintuitive but predictable effect of destabilizing financial markets; and an age of private equity and asset management, the outcome of the twinned logics of austerity capitalism and the shareholder value movement.

The political provenance of their arguments would later be articulated in hysterical tracts like "Can the Corporation Survive?" in 1978 and *Democracy in Crisis* in 1983. In them, the progenitors of agency theory deplored the demolition of the system of private rights, as politicians and bureaucrats eroded the American free enterprise system. Worse still, they opined that "the courts have in recent years often taken the lead in making new laws that have [consistently] *revoked* previously extant private rights, especially in the so-called 'civil rights' arena."[27] At the outset of shareholder capitalism, it was understood that democracy, to the extent that it might be or become *racial* democracy, was incompatible with capitalism. In the West, the prospect of economic democracy had been forcefully closed off in response to the Russian Revolution, and political democracy, with all of its caveats, began to be phased out as well. At that moment in U.S. capitalism, the prospect of racial democracy had to be stamped out—as a matter of political practice, statecraft, geopolitics, monetary policy, legal philosophy, and domestic and international warfare.

Contemporary cultural studies has focused on an incorporative edge of neoliberalism—as a small number of people from historically excluded groups were granted access to institutions that were otherwise being closed off, consolidated, or disappeared. Largely, we remain inarticulate in the face of the terror that has brought us to the present interregnum, like Bambara's narrator emerging from the long night, our legs weak beneath us, looking down to the street below, wanting to be there. "For the people would be emerging from the dark of their places. Surfacing for the first time in eons into clarity." The clarity of state violence, the clarity we avoid and the clarity that is mystified by the abstract violence of finance. "And she would join the circle gathered round the ancient stains in the street. And someone would whisper, and who are you. And who are you. And who are we" (102).

Sitting on the Healer's Stool

"Are you sure, sweetheart, that you want to be well?"[28]

The critique of neoliberalism has missed something fundamental about the financialization of racial capitalism. Finance capital is the abstraction of very material forms of structural adjustment. Often, this deeply material financialization of living is represented as immaterial, evanescent. The present interregnum is the historical effect of what Malini Ranganathan calls "racial financial capitalism." Ranganathan uses the formulation to attend to both "the inextricability between racialism and the development of capitalism" and, "specifically, the inseparability between racial hierarchy and the financial architectures and mechanisms of capitalism."[29]

Too often, neoliberalism has been reduced to the privatization of social services. It is both the privatization of the former functions of the state, but more directly it has been the evisceration of those social services and the dismantling of social services that were always effectively private. The era of structural adjustment in the new nations emerging from franchise colonialism saw the selling out of the local, regional, and national elites that once made revolution possible. Much of the academic world of critical cultural studies has been caught between the liberal class positions and radical critical positions of its practitioners. In the meantime, we have witnessed the dismantling of the age of corporate capitalism in the name of shareholder value. We have seen the radicalization of austerity capitalism target everyone but the narrowest sector of the ownership class. We're up against the ineffability of racial financial capitalism at a global scale.

When poststructuralism taught us that clarity is a trap, too many of us went searching for some way of touching the world that wasn't a trap. We went looking for nonwounded attachments. We went looking for a radical politics with guarantees. "Folks come in here . . . moaning and carrying on and *say* they want to be well. Don't know what in heaven and hell they want."[30] We went looking like we knew what we wanted, like we knew what it meant to want, like we wanted to be well. The interregnum is both the confluence of crisis and our unwillingness to grasp at the crisis. To be willing to want something different even as we know that what we want won't be the right thing and can't be enough.

If I sound sure, I'm not. It's the certainty of a sentence. A straight line and a period. I walk around the building where I work, craning my neck from side to side. I have tics like my mouth wants away from my face. I shrug invisible hands off my shoulders. I jump when touched. Living in structural adjustment. Living through the financialization of my life and this massive dedemocratization, this dreadful unfreedom, and afraid to want something different. "Take away the miseries and you take away some folks' reason for living. Their conversation piece anyway."[31]

With *The Salt Eaters*, Toni Cade Bambara tried to imagine spirit work against structural adjustment. A way to heal the wasteful split between spirit work and political work. Spirit work can be another name for holding indeterminacy. For inhabiting an indeterminacy against speculation. A world beyond finance capital, a living beyond anti-Blackness.

It asks everything of us. To inhabit a new living. To reckon with the weight of terror. The terror we have lived and the terror of a new living.

"Wholeness is no trifling matter. A lot of weight when you're well."[32]

NOTES

1. Bambara, "What It Is," 153.
2. Bambara, 161.
3. Bambara, 160.
4. Bambara, 165.
5. Bambara, *Sea Birds*, 27. Future references are given parenthetically in the text.
6. Prashad, *Darker Nations*, xvii.
7. Prashad, xviii.
8. Jameson, "Culture and Finance Capital," 251.
9. McClanahan, "Financialization," 241.
10. McClanahan, 242.
11. Bambara, "What It Is," 159.

12. Bambara, "Salvation," 46–47.
13. Sharpe, *In the Wake*, 104.
14. See Fenwick, *Jim Crow's Pink Slip*.
15. On this history, see Gordy, *Finding the Lost Year*.
16. Davis, "After the Corporation," 286.
17. Davis, 293.
18. Foster, "Financialization of Capitalism."
19. Bambara, *Deep Sightings*, 233.
20. Hong, "Neoliberalism," 57.
21. Hong, 62.
22. Luxemburg, *Accumulation of Capital*, 312.
23. Chakravarty and da Silva, "Accumulation, Dispossession, and Debt," 372.
24. Bambara, "What It Is," 159.
25. For a powerful reframing of the history of austerity, see Mattei, *Capital Order*.
26. Davis, "After the Corporation," 284.
27. Jensen and Meckling, "Can the Corporation Survive?," 35; original emphasis.
28. Bambara, *Salt Eaters*, 1.
29. Ranganathan, "Empire's Infrastructures," 493.
30. Bambara, *Salt Eaters*, 8.
31. Bambara, 16.
32. Bambara, 10.

BIBLIOGRAPHY

Bambara, Toni Cade. *Deep Sightings and Rescue Missions: Fiction, Essays, and Conversations*. New York: Vintage, 1996.
———. *The Salt Eaters*. New York: Random House, 1980.
———. "Salvation Is the Issue." In *Black Women Writers (1950–1980): A Critical Evaluation*, edited by Mari Evans, 41–47. Garden City, NY: Anchor Press / Doubleday, 1984.
———. *The Sea Birds Are Still Alive*. New York: Random House, 1977.
———. "What It Is I Think I'm Doing Anyhow." In *The Writer on Her Work: Contemporary Women Reflect on Their Art and Their Situation*, edited by Janet Sternberg, 153–178. New York: W. W. Norton, 1980.
Chakravarty, Paula, and Denise Ferreira da Silva. "Accumulation, Dispossession, and Debt: The Racial Logic of Global Capitalism—an Introduction." *American Quarterly* 64, no. 3 (2012): 361–385.
Davis, Gerald F. "After the Corporation." *Politics and Society* 41, no. 2 (2013): 283–308.
Fenwick, Leslie. *Jim Crow's Pink Slip: The Untold Story of Black Principal and Teacher Leadership*. Cambridge, MA: Harvard Education Press, 2022.
Foster, John Bellamy. "The Financialization of Capitalism." *Monthly Review* 58, no. 11 (2007). https://monthlyreview.org/2007/04/01/the-financialization-of-capitalism/.
Gordy, Sondra. *Finding the Lost Year: What Happened When Little Rock Closed Its Public Schools*. Fayetteville: University of Arkansas Press, 2009.
Hong, Grace Kyungwon. "Neoliberalism." *Critical Ethnic Studies* 1, no. 1 (2015): 56–67.
Jameson, Fredric. "Culture and Finance Capital." *Critical Inquiry* 24, no. 1 (1997): 246–265.
Jensen, Michael C., and William H. Meckling. "Can the Corporation Survive?" *Financial Analyst's Journal* 34, no. 1 (1978): 31–37.

———. "Theory of the Firm: Managerial Behavior, Agency Costs, and Ownership Structure." *Journal of Financial Economics* 3, no. 4 (1976): 305–360.

Luxemburg, Rosa. *The Accumulation of Capital*. London: Routledge, 2003.

Mattei, Clara E. *The Capital Order: How Economists Invented Austerity and Paved the Way to Fascism*. Chicago: University of Chicago Press, 2022.

McClanahan, Annie. "Financialization." In *Transitions in American Literature: 2000–2010*, edited by Rachel Greenwald Smith, 239–254. New York: Cambridge University Press, 2017.

Prashad, Vijay. *The Darker Nations: A People's History of the Third World*. New York: New Press, 2007.

Ranganathan, Malini. "Empire's Infrastructures: Racial Finance Capitalism and Liberal Necropolitics." *Urban Geography* 41, no. 4 (2020): 492–496.

Sharpe, Christina. *In the Wake: On Blackness and Being*. Durham, NC: Duke University Press, 2016.

12

The Interregnum of Care and the Rearticulation of Hegemonic Safe Space

Sean Johnson Andrews

Care is an important emergent framework for thinking about our contemporary hegemonic crisis. In part this is because we have a political economic system in which, as the Care Collective puts it, "for a long time we [have] simply been failing to care for each other, especially the vulnerable, the poor and the weak."[1] But it is important to acknowledge that this inequity of care is a function, not a bug, of the hegemonic system. The distribution of care and safety, vulnerability and trauma, are central to the very functioning of the hegemonic order. One way of conceptualizing the emergent progressive movements is that, like many insurgent communities of the past, they have used the opening provided by new media and communication technologies to forge a set of counterhegemonic values and practices. This is an especially messy process because it is happening in real time, in the open, and largely in a medium—the internet—that never forgets.

For me, this messiness has been very revealing: watching it unfold on multiple fronts, seeing it echoed in media, in conversations with my students, in interactions with my partner, my kids, and our community, paying attention to the feelings it has inspired in my white, cis-hetero-male body. While Judith Butler cautions against posing "racism and homophobia and misogyny as parallel or analogical relations,"[2] from the perspective of a "preferred" or "privileged" subject, these forms of bigotry serve a homologous purpose: they shield people like me from the trauma and vulnerability that they simultaneously empower me to wield. As movements like #MeToo and Black Lives Matter push for a reorganization and redistribution of care, these preferred subjects—subjects like me—will ultimately feel less safe not because we will actually be threatened but because, as preferred subjects, our baseline understanding of safety is relatively elevated. We will suddenly face the possibility that we will be treated like a human in society, forced to account for the consequences of our words, our actions, our mistakes.

If we examine closely the particular norms and concepts these movements have been promoting, it is not merely intended to proselytize a doctrine of "wokeness" or shape the dominant discourse: it is intended to reshape the concrete and continuing reality in which it is safer for some subjects to speak—and to walk, drive, dress, live, breathe—than others. It is a critique of the structural-institutional forces that undergird not the economy but something that has arguably taken on a more essential efficacy. Their aim is to rearticulate hegemonic safe space.

The truth of our hegemonic order is that "safe spaces," "trigger warnings," and "cancel culture" have long existed: they have just been reserved for and wielded by the preferred subjects—and actively secured and maintained by the deference and labors of comfort by those subjects who are not preferred, who are "disinterpellated" into these categories by the threat of the trauma they will face if they trigger white men like me, or trigger the repressive and ideological apparatuses that privilege me even as they interpellate me into this system.

In taking these movements seriously, posing them as central to the hegemonic struggle, to the new that is still waiting to be born, this argument runs counter to some of the dominant strains of the Left. So before I complete the outline of this problematic and the possibilities of its vision, I explore the critiques of some of these movements from both the Left and the Right.

The Old Left Critique Is New Again

In a recent essay, Nancy Fraser gives her account of what is a fairly standard left take on the current interregnum.[3] I generally agree with the existence of what she calls the "hegemonic gap" into which Trump strode back in 2016—with Clinton's progressive neoliberalism on one side and the GOP's reactionary neoliberalism on the other: "Given that neither of the two major blocs spoke for them, there was a gap in the American political universe: an empty, unoccupied zone where anti-neoliberal, pro-working-family politics might have taken root."[4] The political-economic logic of her analyses is sound—the lived reality of race in the United States, for instance, is an effect of the material and institutional inequalities of property and resources, revealing "that the structural bases of racism have as much to do with class and political economy as with status and (mis)recognition."[5]

But I part ways with the emergent (if also long-standing) leftist conclusion that what we might call "the economic" stands as the most logical ground on which to build solidarity and consolidate a new hegemonic bloc. Fraser's comment following the above observation is indicative of a larger tendency:

> Let me be clear. I am not suggesting that a progressive-populist bloc should mute pressing concerns about racism, sexism, homophobia, Islamophobia, and transphobia. On the contrary, fighting these harms must be central to a progressive-populist bloc. But it is counterproductive to address them through moralizing condescension, in the mode of progressive neoliberalism. That approach assumes a shallow and inadequate view of these injustices, grossly exaggerating the extent to which the trouble is inside people's heads and missing the depth of the structural-institutional forces that undergird them.

While some of Fraser's position here can be traced back to her long-standing debate with Judith Butler[6]—which sees concerns around identity as being "merely cultural" or, as Fraser puts it here, "the trouble inside people's heads"— her position here joins critics on the Left (such as in *Jacobin*, the journal edited by her interlocutor in the interview that accompanies her interregnum essay, Bhaskar Sunkara). This position critiques both the episto-ontological basis ("identity" qua "the trouble inside people's heads") and the cultural strategy ("shaming" qua "moralizing condescension") of emergent political movements, but it does so mostly on the assertion that both are offensive to the mythical white working-class majority on whose support the reborn hegemony will rely.

The dominant contemporary tendency on the Left is largely to restructuralize what were once seen as more "cultural" struggles. So Fraser herself has worked alongside Tithi Bhattacharya and Cinzia Arruzza to articulate a "feminism for the 99 percent," which extends from some of the arguments of social reproduction theory.[7] Their arguments reconceptualize feminism and the struggle for gender equity in political economic terms, saying "feminism shouldn't start—or stop—with the drive to have women represented at the top of their profession," a notion they attribute to the elite appropriations of the concept seen in Hilary Clinton's campaign and the "lean in" feminism of the former Facebook COO Sheryl Sandberg.[8] Instead, it positions women's labor—or the labors of care often seen as feminine—as central to the reproduction of capitalism.

This left-oriented position is laudable insofar as it highlights the way that the capitalist class has often found it useful to either split the working class along lines of gender, race, or ethnicity or, when it seems expedient, to adopt and incorporate some version of civil rights, "diversity, equity, and inclusion," or even "Black Lives Matter" to maintain the hegemonic appeal of capitalism. Cedric Johnson's *Panthers Can't Save Us* opens with the now familiar observation that, at the height of the 2020 protests following George Floyd's murder, Amazon was one of many corporate entities that brandished Black Lives Matter banners, despite the very public revelations of the corporations' pandemic-era mistreatment of their largely Black and working-class warehouse workers: "Black Lives Matter to the front office, as long as they don't demand a living wage, personal protective equipment and quality health care."[9] Not only does this "corporate anti-racism" distract from what Fraser calls the "structural-institutional forces" fundamental to the system, but this incorporation is at odds with the long-standing anticapitalist (or at least pro-labor) emphasis of many radical Black movements who frequently sought leftist solidarity with their white working-class counterparts, as Touré Reed elaborates at length in his book *Toward Freedom*.[10]

These leftist critiques of "identity politics" imply that, by working toward the common economic struggle—which will make for a more "universal" hegemonic platform—the most important injuries of marginalization will be assuaged. In building this new hegemonic bloc, then, we can effectively set aside, "grossly exaggerating the extent to which the trouble is inside people's heads," and focus solely on "the structural-institutional forces that undergird them."

I dispute the transparency of these "structural-institutional forces." It is one thing to say that BIPOC people would be better served by an anticapitalist antiracism or that only under socialism will women have true freedom. But it is another thing to say that the economy is the most fundamental force in the struggle of U.S. politics—that people vote with their wallets rather than their ideologies. While I understand (and have regularly defended) this perspective analytically, if the question is how to mobilize a mass of people in support of a hegemonic bloc, it seems ludicrous that we wouldn't begin from the emergent counterhegemonic energies around race and trans/gender politics. Isn't it condescending to say that the constituents of the two largest mass demonstrations in U.S. history so far—the Women's March of 2017 and the Black Lives Matter protests of 2020—should effectively be considered the deluded shills of the capitalist state who don't understand the *true* structural basis of oppression?

Who's/Whose Woke?

Across the political spectrum runs the notion that there is a "woke mob" doling out irrational but disturbingly effective demands for social justice. This is especially true on the political Right, where the term *woke* has been shorn from its origins in Black radical thought and popular culture and turned into a slur and a source of moral panic inspiring not only hyperbolic discourse but political legislation like the state of Florida's Stop WOKE Act.[11] But even purportedly leftist or liberal commentators find much to disdain about the contemporary tone of cultural politics. This ranges from Fraser's tentative warning about the risks of being "condescending" to John McWhorter's assertion that much of the emergent work of antiracist activism is actually "woke racism"—a quasi-religious doctrine that "exploits modern Americans' fear of being thought racist to promulgate not just antiracism, but an obsessive, self-involved, totalitarian, and utterly unnecessary kind of cultural reprogramming."[12]

Ironically, the Stop WOKE Act—where WOKE means "Wrongs to Our Kids and Employees"—takes aim at several of the educational and policy commonplaces that McWhorter says make these "woke mob" tactics unnecessary. In Florida and other states across the country, efforts are underway to make it illegal to teach about forms of structural racism, sexism, homophobia, or transphobia or to use any of these identity markers in hiring or curricular decisions—not to mention the attempt to intervene in the personal medical decisions of parents of transgender kids. In effect, by leaning into the reactionary tide, McWhorter and others like him have made the efforts of the woke mob more necessary than they have been in a generation.

But who is this woke mob? How can it be, simultaneously, an uncontrolled mass of people—a mob whose logic is encapsulated by what Douglas Murray calls "the madness of crowds"[13]—and a quasi-religious group of "elect" elites who can manifest and control a catechism? What kinds of "condescension" are they meting out? Given the manifold categories of identity and subjectivity that are now united under struggles for "wokeness" or "social justice," what (if anything) can be said to be the common threads running through these movements? And how do these movements relate to the hegemonic struggle and the dominant terrain on which it takes place?

Many of these questions lack a clear answer because they are disingenuously framed by both the reactionary and (at least ostensibly) loyal opposition. But on this last point, we can begin by accepting McWhorter's contention that, "ironically, the weapon [the woke mob wields] is so lethal because of the genuine and invaluable change that has occurred in our sociopolitical fabric over the past decades. That change is that to the modern American, being called a racist is all but equivalent to being called a pedophile."[14] To this we could add the accusations of being called a sexist, a homophobe, or a transphobe.

In short, there is general hegemonic agreement that these forms of bigotry are unacceptable. At the root of each is a power differential, where some individuals (because of their categories of subjectivity) feel safer in talking, touching, and taking advantage of others. But how we identify, police, and repair their effects—immediate and historic—remains contentious. Indeed, as the Stop WOKE Act illustrates, it is one of the key fronts in the contemporary hegemonic struggle.

On one front, many institutions have attempted to create structured responses to prevent the effects—mandates on hiring and harassment, training to help inform employees of those mandates, and so on. We cannot say that these structures and processes are in place because of a woke mob except insofar as there has been a long-standing historical struggle against these forms of discrimination and harassment—struggles that have resulted in federal laws and policies, lawsuits, and U.S. Supreme Court precedents that open employers to significant financial liability if it is proven that they have allowed these unacceptable qualities to take root in their workplaces. Employers are thus only "woke" to their bottom line.

One function of the voices of the woke mob is to call out the inadequacy of these institutional efforts. #MeToo and #TimesUp are especially apt examples of this function. Despite all the hand wringing about whether "cancel culture" has gone too far, the original "cancelations" were of men accused of sexual harassment or assault. The accusers were afraid of the power differential that made it unlikely their assailants would be held accountable by the institutions supposedly charged with doing so; often they used the "proper channels" and had been denied remedy. The eventual conviction and imprisonment of Harvey Weinstein—who employed former Mossad spies to protect him and intimidate his accusers—was made possible by these and other very public interventions. The hashtag #BlackLivesMatter emerged from something like the same impulse: the justice system's failure to convict George Zimmerman for the assault and murder of Trayvon Martin.

These interventions may be unruly, but they are hardly unnecessary. It is also hard to see how they can be separated—as McWhorter does—from the longer trajectory of struggles for the rights and protections of women, BIPOC, LGBTQ+, and other marginalized groups. The difference is that social media has upset the role of the commercial press as the sole source of publicizing (and legitimizing) their claims. In introduction to their collection *#HashtagActivism: Networks of Race and Gender Justice*, Sarah Jackson and her coauthors argue that their analysis shows the way "members of these marginalized groups, in the tradition of counterpublics, use Twitter hashtags to build diverse networks of dissent and shape the cultural and political knowledge fundamental to contemporary identity-based social movements."[15] Counterpublics—a concept first introduced by Nancy Fraser—are important not only in the way that they can potentially shape the larger public discourse but the way they serve to develop discursive communities, internal norms, and critical concepts. These communities, norms, and concepts are then transmitted and promoted in the larger public sphere so as to make the values of that "subaltern counterpublic" more widespread.

Rearticulating Hegemonic Safe Space

In this sense, I view these emergent movements, fostered by their online communication and community in accordance with Jackson and her coauthors in *#HashtagActivism*, "as counterpublics [that] use hashtags to make and remake reality in the face of dominant discourses that represent them as undeserving of full inclusion in civil society."[16] This remaking requires a clear-eyed understanding of what came before. Recent work on the everyday trauma of our hegemonic status quo suggests another way of conceptualizing the structural-institutional forces that are at the center of these struggles. I suggest revisiting some key cultural theories to account for the way safety—also known as the insulation from trauma—is central to the constitution of and interpellation into varied forms of subjectivity. A short version of it goes like this.

First, as in Louis Althusser's original problematic, trauma (qua repression) or the threat of trauma is central to the process of interpellation: if we do not answer the police man's call, interpellating ourselves into the role of the subject, we risk not only social ostracization but actual death.[17] Althusser fails to acknowledge some subjects—those who occupy what we can call nonpreferred categories of subjectivity—are at significantly greater risk if they fail to comply.

Second, in his recent book *The Misinterpellated Subject*, James Martel highlights a novel dimension of the process of interpellation: what happens when the subject who answers is not the one called. Martel does not exactly delineate what we might call the hegemonic matrix of possible subjects, possible categories, or possible processes of interpellation, but each of these is illuminated by his concept of misinterpellation. In a series of studies—looking at figures like Franz Fanon, Toussaint Louverture, and the main character of Ralph Ellison's *The Invisible Man*—Martel suggests first that the dominant subjectivity offered by Western, liberal capitalist processes of interpellation is implicitly only meant for a certain unnamed category of subjects: in his study, this delineation is made especially along racial lines, but the gender and sexuality of this preferred subject are easily implied as well.

Third, if there is a preferred subject, the flipside must also be the case: that there are categories of subjects not allowed (or at least not expected) to fill that dominant interpellation (and thus misinterpellated when they show up in that role); and, on the other hand, that there is another role these categories of subject are expected to fill. I term this role "disinterpellation," taking the "dis" from Jose Esteban Munoz's "disidentification."[18] Indeed, we could say that Martel's "misinterpellation" is akin to the "disidentification" of one's "disinterpellation": a refusal to occupy the subservient position designated to one's category of subjectivity. In Martel's words, "This refusal is not purely negative (just as Nietzsche's no saying is also always a yes saying); it has creative and productive aspects wherein these authors (like Fanon) take blackness not as a fate that they cannot escape, but as a subjectivity of their own devising, and in the face of the demand of liberalism that they be [disinterpellated as] the kind of black subject (obedient, downtrodden, etc.) that it calls them to be."[19]

Butler talks about something like disinterpellation when they speak of the "abject," saying the abject "designates here precisely those 'unlivable' and 'uninhabitable' zones of social life which are nevertheless densely populated by those who do not enjoy the status of the subject, but whose living under the sign of the 'unlivable' is required to circumscribe the domain of the subject."[20] Butler's notion of "the domain of the subject" maps onto Martel's concept of interpellation in that there are only some kinds of subjects who are allowed into that zone of "livable"—or safe—life. And I agree with Butler's contention that the zone of the livable is mutually constituted by something like a zone of the "disintepellated."

Finally, following from the recent work on social reproduction theory discussed earlier, I would argue that this zone is not outside of the domain of the subject per se: it is just a domain of subjectivity that is largely meant to serve the preferred subjects, providing them comfort, deference, and care.[21] In effect, they are disinterpellated into a role of maintaining hegemonic safe space for the preferred subjects. And insofar as they work to maintain this comfort, deference, and care, they are rewarded a modicum of safety themselves. But, to return to the repressive apparatus, this arrangement is largely secured by the disproportionate trauma or threat of trauma these abject subjects face if they deviate from their prescribed roles. By addressing trauma here, I call on the emergent set of scholarly, clinical, and activist theories of highlighting marginalized subjects' disproportionate experience of trauma. Resmaa Menekem, Gabor Maté, and Arline Geronimus present clinical evidence of the ways that the stresses and traumas of being a member of a disinterpellated category of subjectivity have measurable effects on the mind and body.[22]

This isn't exactly what theorists of cultural trauma mean by the term, but we can take a page from Christina Sharpe's *In The Wake* and instead talk about our culture itself as the source of the trauma: "Living in the wake means living the history and present of terror, from slavery to the present, as the ground of our everyday Black existence."[23] Elsewhere, Sharpe notes that this terror, this violence, "it is not violence that occurs between subjects at the level of conflict; it is gratuitous violence that occurs at the level of a structure that constitutes the Black as the constitutive outside."[24]

The violence of (dis)interpellation is the structural phenomenon that is ultimately contested in this interregnum. To say that trauma is one of the defining features of these processes is not to say that it is the totality of the life experience of those marginalized populations. Sharpe's metaphor of "the wake" is expansive in this—it is the wake of the ship, the slave ship; the wake following "the afterlives of slavery"; the wake of holding space, of drinking, feasting, and celebration even as we are grieving those lost; and the wake of "being awake," a consciousness that tracks the way the disinterpellated "resist, rupture, and disrupt" the immanence of this trauma.[25] What these have-been and would-be victims are now (and have been) saying is that they will not submit. They will not be deferential to their victimizers. They will not care for their oppressors. Instead, they insist on what we could call an equity of deference, reparations of care.

This is a more accurate elaboration of the definition of identity politics put forth by the Combahee River Collective (CRC).[26] Identity politics for them was bound up with notions of care, love, and communities of struggle. The sites of that struggle lay at the intersection of what I designate here the categories of subjectivity. These categories of subjectivity exist in an implicit—if not explicit—hierarchy. The subjectivity of Blackness in the United States was founded on whiteness as anti-Blackness: both categories continue to be constituted by the lies powerful white people told to bring about their opposition and stratification. Racism—*Racecraft*, as Karen and Barbara Fields call it—constitutes these categories into the racial subjectivities that all must live with, but from which white people automatically benefit, as through

> [sumptuary] rules designed to promote feelings of inferiority and superiority [that] travel in tandem with expectations of deference and with rituals that simultaneously create and express the requisite feelings. In the South just after the Civil War (and, depending on the place, for many years thereafter), a black person was required to step off the sidewalk when a white person approached and, if male, to uncover his head. Obedience usually concealed the intrinsic violence of the rule and kept black people visibly in their place.[27]

If the premises and observations I've laid out are correct, the certainty and comfort of the preferred categories and the structures they mutually constitute rely on the implicit opposition to the safety and security of these disinterpellated categories. To the disinterpellated, these scripts and maps may indeed be useful, but that is only because they are effectively walking through enemy territory and need to know how to watch out for potential triggers and traumas. The framework above highlights the level of abstraction at which some of these struggles take place: #MeToo and Black Lives Matter primarily concern the meaning and hierarchy of the categories of subjectivity. But they intersect with many trans and queer activists as well, whose struggles are the most provocative because they attack the structure at the level of what Susan Stryker calls bodily being, arguing especially against the binary morphological distinctions of sex.[28]

As Rogers Brubaker observes, we are living in a trans moment, where identity categories of all kinds have come to seem fragile and unsettled.[29] In some ways this explains the reason behind the greatly outsized moral panic that the reactionary Right has raised about gender affirming care and trans rights. It strikes at the most fundamental level of this hegemonic structure determining who is allowed to feel safe in their most basic, bodily being.

In this light, the interregnum we are living through is not adequately described as a struggle over economic structure. It is a more fundamental shift in the structures of safety and subjectivity. While this is a disturbing moment for these erstwhile defenders of the status quo ante, it poses an exciting opportunity to effectively throw out all these rules about the relationships between bodily being, categories of subjectivity, and the performance of identity.

But coupled with this, it is also a moment that demands a lot of what Hil Malatino calls "aftercare," after the care that is needed following surgical transition. This is especially the case for those disinterpellated subjects who have never enjoyed a truly safe space. As Malatino puts it, "Care is necessary in the wake of profound recalibrations of subjectivity and dependency. We need care in order to heal from transformative physical and emotional experiences. We need it when the milieu we inhabit becomes radically reorganized."[30]

In this sense, the trans experience serves as a bellwether for our general level of progress—as Shon Faye puts it, riffing off the CRC, "The liberation of trans people would improve the lives of everyone in our society"—and the rearticulation of safe space will inevitably create "a profound recalibration of subjectivity" for us all. As this old order is dying, and a new order is born, we must all be especially supportive of an order that provides care to those closest to the current traumas of the disinterpellated and works to eliminate the structures mutually constituted by the processes and protocols of disinterpellation.

NOTES

1. Care Collective, *Care Manifesto*, loc. 40.
2. Butler, *Bodies that Matter*, 38.
3. Fraser, *Old Is Dying*.
4. Fraser, loc. 287.
5. Fraser, loc. 287.

6. Fraser, "Heterosexism, Misrecognition, and Capitalism"; Butler, "Merely Cultural."
7. Bhattacharya, *Feminism for the 99%*; Bhattacharya, *Social Reproduction Theory*.
8. Sandberg, *Lean In*.
9. Johnson, *Panthers*, loc. 102.
10. Reed, *Toward Freedom*.
11. Romano, "Woke"; Migdon, "Stop WOKE Act."
12. McWhorter, *Woke Racism*, 25.
13. Murray, *Madness*.
14. McWhorter, *Woke Racism*, 23.
15. Jackson et al., *#HashtagActivism*, 23.
16. Jackson et al., 23.
17. Althusser, "Ideology," 141–177, esp. 174.
18. Munoz, *Disidentifications*.
19. Martel, *Misinterpellated Subject*.
20. Butler, *Bodies that Matter*, xiii.
21. Bhattacharya, *Social Reproduction Theory*.
22. Kolk, *Body*; Menakem, *Grandmother's Hands*; Maté, *Myth of Normal*; Geronimus, *Weathering*.
23. Sharpe, *In the Wake*, 28.
24. Sharpe, 44.
25. Sharpe, 34–36.
26. Taylor, *How We Get Free*, loc. 279.
27. Fields and Fields, *Racecraft*, 35.
28. Stryker, "Caitlyn Jenner."
29. Brubaker, *Trans*.
30. Malatino, *Trans Care*, loc. 112.

BIBLIOGRAPHY

Althusser, Louis. "Ideology and Ideological State Apparatuses." In *Lenin and Philosophy and Other Essays*, translated by Ben Brewster, 121–176. Monthly Review Press, 1971.

Bhattacharya, Tithi. *Feminism for the 99%: A Manifesto*. Verso, 2019.

———, ed. *Social Reproduction Theory: Remapping Class, Recentering Oppression*. 1st ed. Pluto, 2017.

Brubaker, Rogers. *Trans: Gender and Race in an Age of Unsettled Identities*. Princeton University Press, 2016.

Butler, Judith. *Bodies That Matter: On the Discursive Limits of Sex*. 1st ed. Routledge, 2011.

———. "Merely Cultural." *New Left Review* I/227 (January/February 1998): 33–44.

The Care Collective, Andreas Chatzidakis, Jamie Hakim, Jo Litter, and Catherine Rottenberg. *The Care Manifesto: The Politics of Interdependence*. London: Verso, 2020.

Fields, Karen E., and Barbara J. Fields. *Racecraft: The Soul of Inequality in American Life*. London: Verso, 2014. Kindle.

Fraser, Nancy. "Heterosexism, Misrecognition and Capitalism: A Response to Judith Butler." *New Left Review* I/228 (March/April 1998): 140–149.

———. *The Old Is Dying and the New Cannot Be Born: From Progressive Neoliberalism to Trump and Beyond*. Verso, 2019.

Geronimus, Arline T. *Weathering: The Extraordinary Stress of Ordinary Life in an Unjust Society*. Little, Brown Spark, 2023.

Gill-Peterson, Jules. *Histories of the Transgender Child*. 3rd ed. University of Minnesota Press, 2018.
Haider, Asad. *Mistaken Identity: Race and Class in the Age of Trump*. Verso, 2018.
Jackson, Sarah J., Moya Bailey, Brooke Foucault Welles, and Genie Lauren. *#HashtagActivism: Networks of Race and Gender Justice*. Illustrated ed. Cambridge, MA: MIT Press, 2020.
Johnson, Cedric. *The Panthers Can't Save Us Now: Debating Left Politics and Black Lives Matter*. London: Verso, 2022.
Kolk, Bessel van der. *The Body Keeps the Score: Brain, Mind, and Body in the Healing of Trauma*. 1st ed. Penguin Books, 2014.
Malatino, Hil. *Trans Care*. University of Minnesota Press, 2020.
Martel, James R. *The Misinterpellated Subject*. Duke University Press Books, 2017.
Maté, Gabor. *The Myth of Normal: Trauma, Illness, and Healing in a Toxic Culture*. Avery, 2022.
McWhorter, John. "The Dehumanizing Condescension of 'White Fragility.'" *The Atlantic*, July 15, 2020. https://www.theatlantic.com/ideas/archive/2020/07/dehumanizing-condescension-white-fragility/614146/.
———. *Woke Racism: How a New Religion Has Betrayed Black America*. Portfolio, 2021.
Menakem, Resmaa. *My Grandmother's Hands: Racialized Trauma and the Pathway to Mending Our Hearts and Bodies*. Central Recovery, 2017.
Migdon, Brooke. "What Is DeSantis's 'Stop WOKE Act'?" *The Hill* (blog), August 19, 2022. https://thehill.com/changing-america/respect/diversity-inclusion/3608241-what-is-desantiss-stop-woke-act/.
Muñoz, José Esteban. *Disidentifications: Queers of Color and the Performance of Politics*. University of Minnesota Press, 2013. Kindle.
Murray, Douglas. *The Madness of Crowds: Gender, Race, and Identity*. 1st ed. Bloomsbury Continuum, 2019.
Reed, Touré. *Toward Freedom: The Case against Race Reductionism*. London: Verso, 2020.
Romano, Aja. "How Being 'Woke' Lost Its Meaning." Vox, October 9, 2020. https://www.vox.com/culture/21437879/stay-woke-wokeness-history-origin-evolution-controversy.
Sandberg, Sheryl. *Lean In: Women, Work, and the Will to Lead*. 1st ed. Knopf, 2013.
Sharpe, Christina. *In the Wake: On Blackness and Being*. Illustrated ed. Duke University Press Books, 2016.
Stryker, Susan. "Caitlyn Jenner and Rachel Dolezal: Identification, Embodiment, and Bodily Transformation." *AHA Today* (blog), July 13, 2015. https://www.historians.org/publications-and-directories/perspectives-on-history/summer-2015/caitlyn-jenner-and-rachel-dolezal-identification-embodiment-and-bodily-transformation.
Taylor, Keeanga-Yamahtta, ed. *How We Get Free: Black Feminism and the Combahee River Collective*. Haymarket Books, 2017. Kindle.

13

Co-opting Liberation Technology

John R. Decker

How It Started, How It's Going

In a 2010 article titled "Liberation Technology," Larry Diamond hailed cell networks, politically active online forums, Facebook, Twitter (now X), and other technologies for their promise of facilitating self-expression, aiding self-organization, championing social and governmental transparency, making politicians and businesses more accountable to the people, and their ability to circumvent the power of authoritarian rulers.[1] In short, Diamond considered the internet and social media to be the means for empowering people to stand against tyranny and build ideal democracies. Diamond's analysis came in the wake of the Arab Spring (2010), in which the internet and social media played a major role. In the years that have passed since the publication of the article, however, a great deal has changed—from the rise of mass-scale harvesting and monetization of personal data, to the engineering of methods to capture user attention, to the creation of "post-truth" mediascapes, to the ubiquitous tracking of personal devices and habits, and to the upswing of technically savvy authoritarian movements that use these technologies to recruit members to their cause, to name only a few.[2]

In this chapter, I discuss these changes in terms of interregnal thinking. As the editors note in their introduction, an interregnum can be thought of as an in-between place in which the future is formed in the present. In particular, I situate the changes I discuss in the context of what I see as an apocalyptic moment of democratic unwinding that has taken place in the United

States and Europe since 2010. The term *apokalypsis*, which means "revelation," "unveiling," "laying bare," or "a disclosure of truth," is particularly apt here. The word describes a moment in which patterns of being—seen and unseen, comprehensible and incomprehensible—become apparent and, for the period of unveiling, accessible and knowable. In a prophetic sense, an *apokalypsis* is a moment in which a potential future is unveiled by laying bare the lived realities of present existence. Unlike the Judeo-Christian use of the term in which the revealed prophecy is a foretaste of an inevitable reality, however, I employ it in a more contingent form—as a prediction of things that may come, rather than a fixed certainty. Understanding that the outcome is not guaranteed is important because this interregnal moment is a contest to decide the future. It is a fight between diametrically opposed views of what a "good," "fair," and "desirable" world looks like and is being forged in the space between democratic ideals and authoritarian fantasies.

I must admit that I am pessimistic about the possibility of a liberation technology largely because the concept itself—a technological means of building and sustaining democratic norms—presumes a univalent use of technology that does not reflect reality. As I discuss further in this chapter, the technologies that played a crucial role in the Arab Spring have already been co-opted by various governmental power structures. Zeynep Tufekci, for example, has noted that the governments who were caught off guard during the Arab Spring were unfamiliar with what was a fairly new technology.[3] In the period since 2010, social media, smartphones, and other electronic communications media have become ubiquitous, and those in power have learned how to use them effectively to sway opinion and police people. Moreover, the technologies in question were never designed for liberation but were brought to market to meet business needs and purposes. As such, it is unrealistic to pin any hopes of creating lasting change for the better on them or on the capitalist logics that underlie them.

As a result, I argue that we must realign how we think of liberation technologies. Rather than thinking of these tools in terms of liberation, understood in relation to liberal democratic norms, we should think of them in terms of resistance. As a lens, resistance allows us to appreciate the potential benefits encapsulated in the term *liberation technology* while at the same time acknowledging that the agency of groups and individuals can complicate matters. Resistance cuts both ways—resistance to tyranny as well as resistance to liberal democracy; resistance to racism and hate as well as resistance to multiculturalism and inclusivity; resistance to surveillance and a loss of privacy as well as resistance to behavior that is perceived as "secretive," "unacceptable," or "unpatriotic." The tension between extremes here is important because the moral valence of a tool depends on how and by whom it is used.

A hammer, after all, may be used to build shelter for those in need or to tear down a shelter to spite them.

Revisiting "Liberation Technology"

As Diamond's article is the starting place for my thoughts on the issue, it will be useful to briefly rehearse his major points. To begin, he defines liberation technology as "any form of information and communication technology (ICT) that can expand political, social, and economic freedom."[4] This includes but is not limited to cell phones, computers, and social media platforms. For the author, the great promise of liberation technology is that it "enables citizens to report news, expose wrongdoing, express opinions, mobilize protest, monitor elections, scrutinize government, deepen participation, and expand the horizons of freedom."[5] It also "provides efficient and powerful tools for transparency and monitoring."[6] As support for his thesis, Diamond offers examples from Malaysia, China, the Philippines, Ukraine, and Iran to demonstrate how the use of liberation technologies helped to champion the cause of participatory governance. In each of these cases, technologies like cellular communication and social media platforms amplified the voices of the people thanks to their speed, scale, accessibility, and reach. These factors, as well as the often ad hoc means by which people used technology to organize, allowed dissidents and ordinary citizens to defy the power of authoritarian governments. These are not the only use cases he cites, but they are illustrative of his main arguments.

Diamond tempers his techno-optimism, however, by noting that in some cases initially successful protests did not translate to lasting, positive change. This reality leads Diamond to acknowledge that authoritarian regimes can use the same or similar strategies to spread propaganda, mobilize loyalists, and exert state control against protesters and dissidents. He notes that some companies operating in democratic countries facilitate the subversion of liberation technologies by being willing to provide surveillance tools to authoritarian states. In addition to state-level actions, he cautions that the technologies used to bring people together also have the potential to fragment them by breaking them into groups of like-minded individuals, which could harm the cause of democracy. Finally, Diamond notes that the secure means of communication that liberation technologies require can enable illegal and exploitative behaviors that could damage the social fabric. These notes of caution, however, are largely overshadowed by the more positive potential he sees liberation technologies offering. Unfortunately, these caveats have proven to be more prescient than Diamond could ever have imagined—a set of circumstances he has written about in the intervening years since penning "Liberation Technology."[7] Further, the very actions that the author ascribed to authoritarian countries—the subversion of liberation technologies to antidemocratic ends—have become standard operating procedures even for democratic regimes.

The Rise of Tech and Social Media Companies as Corporate Giants

One of the most significant changes since 2010 has been the meteoric rise of internet technology companies. Corporate valuations for Google, Facebook, and X, the key platforms used during the Arab Spring, as well as Apple, whose smartphones helped fuel global social media use, have increased dramatically. As of 2022, each of these corporations controlled nation-level wealth and had global brand recognition. The rise of these companies and their competitors was due in part to the ubiquity of the internet for communication and commerce. As of 2022, for example, roughly 63 percent of the world's population used the internet and social media platforms.[8] A nearly equal amount used smartphones worldwide.[9] In highly technological countries, connectivity has become or rapidly is becoming the "fourth utility," behind power, water, and gas.[10] Access to the internet, or lack thereof, can drastically affect a person's social, economic, and educational prospects. As the 2019 COVID pandemic demonstrated, persistent digital divides have very real effects for poor and vulnerable populations even in heavily wired countries like the United States.[11]

The demand for connectivity has driven an explosion in the manufacture of devices as well as the software to run them. The vast array of connectivity technologies (from physical devices to search engines) provides the companies who make and supply them with troves of information about individual users. The mass-scale collection and analysis of personal data obtained through various devices and services is the source of the wealth of these tech companies and their peers.[12]

Big Data and Behavioral Engineering

When a user carries out a search on a platform like Google, the results they see are "personalized" in various ways depending on a number of factors, including search history, location, type of computer or device, and language.[13] For personalization to work, companies must track and monitor a user's behavior. By 2020, internet firms had an estimated 59 zettabytes of data at their disposal, and projections anticipate this will almost triple by 2024.[14] The information contained in these data not only allows companies to make adjustments to their proprietary software; it also is a commodity that they sell to other companies and governments. Shoshana Zuboff has dubbed this business model "surveillance capitalism" and argues that it has the power to make companies more powerful—and less accountable—than governments.[15]

Data collection by corporations has become pervasive despite widespread discomfort with it. A 2019 U.S. study, for example, indicated that 84 percent of respondents did not feel that they were in control of their own data, and that 62 percent did not believe that it was possible to avoid data collection efforts.[16] The question arises: Why collect all these data if it makes people uncomfortable? In large part, the answer to this is that large datasets provide those who collect them with the raw materials for understanding and shaping behavior on both individual and societal levels. At its most benign, the data collected from billions of individuals can make it possible to analyze trends that may be hard to see without those observations. Such analyses have the potential to lead to breakthroughs in health, make society more functional and humane, or simply make it easier to maneuver traffic. Less altruistic applications include the ability to target advertising to individuals or groups and use the patterns evident in their online behavior to induce them to stay engaged and buy more products.

In short, corporations have engineered social media and ICTs to meet their underlying commercial goals. Repurposing these tools to organize people, form communities, spread political and social messages, and support ideologies does not remove their primary business focus. While the technology in question has affordances that allow non-business-oriented communication and social organization, these features still trade on the underlying objective of increasing engagement with the platform. Platform dependency, in turn, ensures that organizations and individuals seeking to organize for personal or political reasons do so within the constraints established by companies who have vested interests in converting engagement to profit.

Echo Chambers, Filter Bubbles, Disinformation

Engagement with a site or platform not only increases corporate profits; it also facilitates the creation of social and intellectual echo chambers. While the political landscape in the United States arguably has seen increased levels of partisanship on cultural issues since at least the Reagan era, divisions between citizens—down even to the level of political demographics—appear to have quickened their pace since 2010.[17] These divisions are being solidified by an increased self-segregation into like-minded enclaves.[18] This behavior is problematic on its own, but its effects are amplified by personalized search results and social media feeds giving rise to closed informational loops, or "filter bubbles."[19] These self-sustaining thought-worlds reinforce systems of belief and can potentially lead people to adopt extreme points of view. This is not to say, however, that the information found on the internet or through social media acts like a mental contagion. Very often, people are consuming extremist narratives because it accords with their preexisting beliefs.[20] This, in turn, increases demand for similar content, which media-savvy authoritarians are able to monetize through platforms like YouTube.

Antidemocratic groups seeking to recruit new members are able to game the engagement strategies employed by various platforms by offering "hot button" topics and other clickbait targeted at those receptive to their message. These efforts leverage the invisible and automatic adjustment of information that is a routine part of search and social media activity. This is troubling especially as social media users in the United States report that they have difficulty discerning whether or not the information encountered on social media is true or false. According to a 2019 Pew Research poll on trust in society, almost half (48 percent) of the respondents stated that they had trouble with this issue.[21] Difficulty in discerning truth from falsity on social media is a larger problem than it might first appear. A 2019 U.S. poll on social media and the news shows that a majority of people (55 percent) sometimes or often get their news from social media, and 28 percent often use social media to stay up-to-date.[22] Those who primarily relied on social media for news, however, were less able to correctly answer questions regarding fundamental political knowledge and current events than those who got their news from a mixture of sources.[23] Indeed, those who consumed news primarily through social media were more likely to be exposed to unproven claims and fringe theories and were more likely to believe them.[24] The consequences of this for political discourse are all too evident in the QAnon conspiracy that began in 2017 and in the "Stop the Steal" narrative that sprang up after the 2020 U.S. election.

Government, Intelligence, and Police Use of Similar Technologies

Corporations are not the only entities with access to the massive amounts of information generated by internet technologies. Governments have shown that they also are able to obtain data about individuals through a variety of means. In the United States, for example, the Immigration and Customs Enforcement Agency (ICE) has been using fake Facebook accounts to carry out sting operations against undocumented workers since at least 2015.[25] They also use information from such databases as Thompson Reuter's CLEAR to track down and detain undocumented people.[26] Further, ICE was able to purchase cell phone location data from data aggregators like Venntel to help them track potential targets.[27] The government's use of private data does not end with tracking and detaining undocumented people. These techniques are also being used to track and profile citizens.

In the wake of the U.S. Supreme Court's 2022 decision to overturn *Roe v. Wade*, the landmark case that granted abortion rights, multiple states criminalized the termination of unwanted pregnancies.[28] In response, police agencies in states that have limited or completely outlawed abortion have turned to various means to enable them to track and triangulate the movements of suspects.[29] The Electronic Frontier Foundation (EFF) has raised concerns that police investigating suspected abortions will increasingly make use of data aggregation services to monitor suspects' movements.[30] One service in particular, Fog Reveal, which is used by at least eighteen state and local law enforcement agencies, boasts access to billions of geolocation signals from cell phones and allows both "area searches" and "device searches," which can be used to construct so-called pattern-of-life information.[31] According to an EFF analyst, "all [police] need to do is know where [the abortions are] happening, then click and drag a box on a map and then follow all of the cellphones in the city to wherever they go next."[32] The police agencies that use this service, and presumably others, have actively worked to keep the use of the tool secret from the public and the court.[33]

The examples thus far have been drawn from the United States, but patterns of digital surveillance of smartphone data and social media activity are available across the globe. China, for example, requires that users of social media and internet accounts use their real names and provide biometric information so that each person's digital data are directly linkable to them.[34] Russian authorities are able to "collect, analyze, and conduct sentiment analysis on social media content relating to President Vladimir Putin and other topics of interest to the government." Nigerian officials used social media posts regarding corruption to sentence a journalist to prison.[35] European democracies are also engaging in such efforts. In the United Kingdom, for example, the police "monitored nearly 9,000 activists from across the political spectrum . . . using geolocation tracking and sentiment analysis on data scraped from Facebook, Twitter, and other platforms."[36] Governments worldwide—even democratic nations—are using social media platforms, as well as other technologies and the power of the state, to track people. This capability blunts the ability of antiauthoritarian groups to use technologies to organize themselves free of government oversight. Moreover, the tactics employed in state surveillance weaponize these technologies against vulnerable groups and individuals (e.g., undocumented workers, ethnic minorities, dissidents).

A Resurgence of the Extreme Right

Authoritarian movements, white nationalists, neo-Nazi groups, and extreme antigovernment libertarians like the Boogaloo Bois, Proud Boys, and the Oath Keepers use various social media platforms to spread their messages. Paradoxically, many of these groups claim that they are standing against authoritarianism and see their uses of ICTs as being in the name of liberty and liberation. They use memes and wordplay to avoid filtering algorithms and often employ coded language and group-specific slang as a means of identifying themselves to others. Their mildly clever and colorful façades aside, members of these groups have proven to be violent.

The Boogaloos, for example, are one of the newest in a long line of antifederalist militias in the United States who have armed themselves in anticipation of a coming civil war.[37] Like many online groups, the Boogaloos are loosely organized, with a great deal of regional variation. One of the few commonalities that binds members, however, is "a willingness, if not an outright desire, to bring about the collapse of American society."[38] This willingness was on full display during the attempted insurrection of January 6, 2021.

Militia groups including the Boogaloos, the Proud Boys, the Oath Keepers, the Three Percent Militia, and a large contingent of QAnon adherents—with a good deal of overlap between militia membership and belief in QAnon narratives—stormed the U.S. Capitol building in an attempt to prevent the certification of the 2020 election.[39] Plans for the attack, including the stockpiling of caches of weapons in nearby hotels, were worked out via various social media platforms and channels.[40] Despite the failure of the attempt, militias and the extreme Right continue to prosecute their beliefs in a stolen election via social media, including Truth Social and Parler, as well as encrypted communication platforms like Signal and WeChat. Movements like QAnon, Stop the Steal, and various militias make clear that ideas of liberty, liberation, and freedom are not stable and can be claimed by multiple groups with wildly different ideologies. Internet technologies are just as capable of spreading conspiracy theories, toxic libertarian dogma, and hate speech as they are of lifting up the voices of the powerless and oppressed.

Liberation Technologies—Ambivalence and Complexity

Developments since 2010 have largely upended the liberation abilities of the technologies that played a role in the Arab Spring. Diamond's caveats regarding the likelihood of governments using similar strategies to their own ends, the willingness of technology companies to help regimes track citizens, the fragmentation of people into echo chambers, and the use of secure communications for illegal and exploitative behavior have proven to be true. In large part, this seems to be a result of the fact that the technologies in question were not primarily meant as tools of liberation but as tools of commerce. Social media products were designed to create connections between people and brands as a means of driving engagement and putting eyes on ads. The use of these technologies for self-organization (democratic or otherwise) is a secondary feature. This is important because it is immaterial to the business models of the companies that brought these technologies to market if the groups creating and engaging with content are pro- or antidemocratic. The more engaging the subject matter and the more passionate those who follow it, the more time that is spent on ad-bearing pages and, hence, the more potential for revenue. In other words, social media companies not only have financial incentives to accommodate the ambivalence of how their tech is used; their businesses thrive on it.

Similarly, governments are too easily tempted to use the vast amounts of information generated by information technologies to prosecute their own interests. While less profit-driven than the businesses who gather and control the information, governmental actions are just as ambivalent and prone to abuse. Arguably, tracking the habits of a suspected pedophile constitutes a social good. Alternatively, using personal information to find and deport migrants or prosecute people seeking abortions is not a social good—or, at the very least, is only a social good as far as extreme conservative (and ostensibly authoritarian) factions in society are concerned.

In social media spaces, controlling narratives and capturing attention allow individuals or groups to amplify their messages. Political and social movements can leverage this feature to build support.[41] The amplification dynamic of social media has no built-in guardrails against being used for antidemocratic purposes, however. People can use online tools to fight for their rights, and at the same time, extremist factions have embraced and co-opted liberation technologies to disseminate their messages, recruit members, and mobilize people to take aggressive, even violent, actions. Further, many of the actors driving and consuming antidemocratic ideas and narratives consider themselves to be "patriots" who are fighting for their way of life, which they consider to be the only legitimate approach, and who are defending their perceptions of freedom.[42]

Can liberation technologies still liberate? Perhaps, but like any double-edged tool, they require great care when using them. The same social media mechanisms activated to mobilize people to support anti-racist protests all over the United States, for example, are the same ones used to call insurrectionists to Washington, DC, on January 6, 2021. Resistance takes many forms; not all of them are aligned with the ideals of liberal democracy. The corporations who peddle these technologies fly the banner of self-expression and free speech to the benefit of their brands in the marketplace. They are also the same companies, though, that control nation-level wealth and power, monetize their customer's habits and information, and make their product available to governments, authoritarians, and bigots as equally as to everyone else.

NOTES

1. Diamond, "Liberation Technology."
2. Noble, *Algorithms of Oppression*; Webb, *Coding Democracy*; *Age of Surveillance Capitalism*; McIntyre, *Post-Truth*; Wu, *Attention Merchants*.
3. Tufekci, *Twitter and Tear Gas*.
4. Diamond, "Liberation Technology."
5. Diamond.
6. Diamond.
7. Diamond, "Road to Digital Unfreedom"; Diamond, "Democracy's Arc."
8. "Internet and Social Media Users in the World 2022."
9. "Smartphone Users in the World 2025."
10. Hughes, "Internet Connectivity."
11. Patrick, "How the COVID-19 Pandemic."
12. Noble, *Algorithms of Oppression*; Zuboff, *Age of Surveillance Capitalism*.
13. Bar-Ilan, "Manipulating"; Feiner, "Google Exercises"; Noble; Statt, "Google Personalizes."
14. Statista, "Total Data Volume Worldwide 2010–2024."
15. Zuboff, *Age of Surveillance Capitalism*.
16. Auxier et al., "2. Americans."
17. Chinni, "Parties."
18. Bishop, *Big Sort*.
19. Pariser, *Filter Bubble*.
20. Munger and Phillips, "Right-Wing YouTube."
21. Auxier et al., "2. Americans."
22. Shearer and Grieco, "Americans."
23. Mitchell et al., "Americans."
24. Mitchell et al.
25. Holmes, "ICE"; Rivlin-Nadler, "How ICE."
26. Currier, "Legal Scholars"; Funk, "How ICE"; Rivlin-Nadler.
27. Molla, "Forget Warrants."
28. Totenberg and McCammon, "Supreme Court"; Diamondstein, "Abortion."
29. Belanger, "Sneaky Ways."
30. Cyphers, "Inside Fog Data."
31. Cyphers.
32. Quoted in Belanger, "Sneaky Ways."
33. Belanger; Cyphers, "Inside Fog Data"; "Maryland State Police_Magnet Forensics Discussion of Fog."
34. McDonnell, "China Social Media."
35. Shahbaz and Funk, "Social Media Surveillance."
36. Shahbaz and Funk.
37. Sottile, "Inside the Boogaloo."
38. Sottile.
39. Diaz and Treisman, "Members."
40. Wamsley, "On Far-Right Websites."
41. Tufekci, *Twitter and Tear Gas*. Tufekci points out that the ability to amplify a message and control a narrative is a vital aspect of gaining traction as a movement.
42. Hochschild, *Strangers*.

BIBLIOGRAPHY

"Alphabet Net Worth 2010–2022 | GOOGL." MacroTrends, 2022. https://www.macrotrends.net/stocks/charts/GOOGL/alphabet/net-worth.

Amarasingam, Amarnath, and Marc-Andre Argentino. "The QAnon Conspiracy Theory: A Security Threat in the Making?" Combating Terrorism Center at West Point, July 31, 2020. https://ctc.usma.edu/the-qanon-conspiracy-theory-a-security-threat-in-the-making/.

Anti-Defamation League. "Online Hate and Harassment Report: The American Experience 2020." Anti-Defamation League, June 9, 2020. https://www.adl.org/online-hate-2020.

"Apple Net Worth 2010–2022 | AAPL." MacroTrends, 2022. https://www.macrotrends.net/stocks/charts/AAPL/apple/net-worth.

Auxier, Brook, Lee Rainie, Monica Anderson, Andrew Perrin, Madhu Kumar, and Erica Turner. "2. Americans Concerned, Feel Lack of Control over Personal Data Collected by Both Companies and the Government." Pew Research Center, November 15, 2019. https://www.pewresearch.org/internet/2019/11/15/americans-concerned-feel-lack-of-control-over-personal-data-collected-by-both-companies-and-the-government/.

Bar-Ilan, Judit. "Manipulating Search Engine Algorithms: The Case of Google." *Journal of Information, Communication and Ethics in Society* 5, no. 2/3 (January 1, 2007): 155–66. https://doi.org/10.1108/14779960710837623.

Belanger, Ashley. "Sneaky Ways Cops Could Access Data to Widely Prosecute Abortions in the US." *Ars Technica*, November 23, 2022. https://arstechnica.com/tech-policy/2022/11/sneaky-ways-cops-could-access-data-to-widely-prosecute-abortions-in-the-us/.

Bishop, Bill, and Robert G. Cushing. *The Big Sort: Why the Clustering of Like-Minded America Is Tearing Us Apart*. Houghton Mifflin Harcourt, 2008.

Chinni, Dante. "Parties See Massive Demographic Changes despite Overall Static Split." NBC News, January 19, 2020. https://www.nbcnews.com/politics/meet-the-press/parties-see-big-demographic-changes-despite-overall-static-split-n1118521.

"Countries by GDP 2022." PopulationU, 2022. https://www.populationu.com/gen/countries-by-gdp.

Cox, Kate. "Former Facebook Manager: 'We Took a Page from Big Tobacco's Playbook.'" *Ars Technica*, September 24, 2020. https://arstechnica.com/tech-policy/2020/09/former-facebook-manager-we-took-a-page-from-big-tobaccos-playbook/.

Currier, Cora. "Legal Scholars to LexisNexis, Thompson Reuters: Stop Helping ICE." *The Intercept*, November 14, 2019. https://theintercept.com/2019/11/14/ice-lexisnexis-thomson-reuters-database/.

Cyphers, Bennett. "Inside Fog Data Science, the Secretive Company Selling Mass Surveillance to Local Police." Electronic Frontier Foundation, August 31, 2022. https://www.eff.org/deeplinks/2022/08/inside-fog-data-science-secretive-company-selling-mass-surveillance-local-police.

Diamond, Larry. "Democracy's Arc: From Resurgent to Imperiled." *Journal of Democracy* 33, no. 1 (January 2022): 163–179. https://www.journalofdemocracy.org/articles/democracys-arc-from-resurgent-to-imperiled/.

———. "Liberation Technology." *Journal of Democracy* 21, no. 3 (July 2010): 69–83. https://www.journalofdemocracy.org/articles/liberation-technology/.

———. "The Road to Digital Unfreedom: The Threat of Postmodern Totalitarianism." *Journal of Democracy* 30, no. 1 (January 2019): 20–24. https://www.journalofdemoc

racy.org/articles/the-road-to-digital-unfreedom-the-threat-of-postmodern-totalitarianism/.

Diamondstein, Megan. "Abortion Is Now Illegal in 11 U.S. States." Center for Reproductive Rights, August 30, 2022. https://reproductiverights.org/abortion-illegal-11-states/.

Diaz, Jaclyn, and Rachel Treisman. "Members of Right-Wing Militias, Extremist Groups Are Latest Charged in Capitol Siege." NPR, January 19, 2021. https://www.npr.org/sections/insurrection-at-the-capitol/2021/01/19/958240531/members-of-right-wing-militias-extremist-groups-are-latest-charged-in-capitol-si.

Duffy, Clare. "Twitter Relaunches Option to Pay for Blue Check Marks." CNN Business, December 12, 2022. https://www.cnn.com/2022/12/12/tech/twitter-verification-relaunch/index.html.

Duggan, Maeve. "Online Harassment 2017." Pew Research Center, July 11, 2017. https://www.pewresearch.org/internet/2017/07/11/online-harassment-2017/.

Ellis, Emma Grey. "4Chan Is Turning 15—and Remains the Internet's Teenager." *Wired*, June 1, 2018. https://www.wired.com/story/4chan-soul-of-the-internet/.

"Facebook Net Worth 2009–2020 | FB." MacroTrends, 2020. https://www.macrotrends.net/stocks/charts/FB/facebook/net-worth.

Feiner, Lauren. "Google Exercises More Direct Control over Search Results than It Has Admitted, Report Claims." CNBC, November 15, 2019. https://www.cnbc.com/2019/11/15/google-tweaks-its-algorithm-to-change-search-results-wsj.html.

Fowler, Geoffrey. "Twitter's $8 'Verification' Makes Blue Check Marks Mostly Meaningless." *Washington Post*, November 11, 2022. https://www.washingtonpost.com/technology/2022/11/11/twitter-blue-checkmark/.

Funk, McKenzie. "How ICE Picks Its Targets in the Surveillance Age (Published 2019)." *New York Times*, October 2, 2019. https://www.nytimes.com/2019/10/02/magazine/ice-surveillance-deportation.html.

Goldman, David, and Stacy Cowley. "Apple's Value Soars to $600 Billion." CNNMoney, April 10, 2012. https://money.cnn.com/2012/04/10/technology/apple_market_cap/index.htm.

Hochschild, Arlie Russell. *Strangers in Their Own Land: Anger and Mourning on the American Right*. New York: New Press, 2016.

Holmes, Aaron. "ICE Is Using Fake Facebook Accounts to Carry out Raids, Report Says." *Business Insider*, October 3, 2019. https://www.businessinsider.com/ice-used-fake-facebook-accounts-for-raids-report-2019-10.

Hughes, Steve. "Internet Connectivity, the Fourth Utility." Medium, September 26, 2019. https://medium.com/@_SteveHughes_/is-internet-connectivity-the-fourth-utility-df1c00b13e0b.

"Internet and Social Media Users in the World 2022." Statista, accessed December 27, 2022. https://www.statista.com/statistics/617136/digital-population-worldwide/.

Kramer, Adam D. I., Jamie E. Guillory, and Jeffrey T. Hancock. "Experimental Evidence of Massive-Scale Emotional Contagion through Social Networks." *Proceedings of the National Academy of Sciences* 111, no. 24 (June 17, 2014): 8788–8790. https://doi.org/10.1073/pnas.1320040111.

LaFrance, Adrienne. "QAnon Is More Important than You Think." *The Atlantic*, June 2020. https://www.theatlantic.com/magazine/archive/2020/06/qanon-nothing-can-stop-what-is-coming/610567/.

Manovich, Lev. "The Algorithms of Our Lives." *Chronicle of Higher Education*, December 16, 2013. https://www.chronicle.com/article/the-algorithms-of-our-lives/.

"Maryland State Police_Magnet Forensics Discussion of Fog." Accessed December 29, 2022. https://www.documentcloud.org/documents/22189131-maryland-state-police_magnet-forensics-discussion-of-fog.

McDonell, Stephen. "China Social Media: WeChat and the Surveillance State." BBC News, June 7, 2019. https://www.bbc.com/news/blogs-china-blog-48552907.

McIntyre, Lee C. *Post-Truth*. MIT Press Essential Knowledge Series. Cambridge, MA: MIT Press, 2018.

"Meta Platforms Net Worth 2010–2022 | META." MacroTrends, 2022. https://www.macrotrends.net/stocks/charts/META/meta-platforms/net-worth.

Mitchell, Amy, Mark Jurkowitz, J. Baxter Oliphant, and Elisa Shearer. "Americans Who Mainly Get Their News on Social Media Are Less Engaged, Less Knowledgeable." *Pew Research Center's Journalism Project* (blog), July 30, 2020. https://www.journalism.org/2020/07/30/americans-who-mainly-get-their-news-on-social-media-are-less-engaged-less-knowledgeable/.

Molla, Rani. "Forget Warrants, ICE Has Been Using Cellphone Marketing Data to Track People at the Border." *Vox*, February 7, 2020. https://www.vox.com/recode/2020/2/7/21127911/ice-border-cellphone-data-tracking-department-homeland-security-immigration.

Montag, Christian, Bernd Lachmann, Marc Herrlich, and Katharina Zweig. "Addictive Features of Social Media/Messenger Platforms and Freemium Games against the Background of Psychological and Economic Theories." *International Journal of Environmental Research and Public Health* 16, no. 14 (July 2019). https://doi.org/10.3390/ijerph16142612.

Munger, K., and J. Phillips. "Right-Wing YouTube: A Supply and Demand Perspective." *International Journal of Press/Politics* 27, no. 1 (2022): 186–219. https://doi.org/10.1177/1940161220964767

Noble, Safiya Umoja. *Algorithms of Oppression: How Search Engines Reinforce Racism*. New York: New York University Press, 2018.

Ortutay, Barbara. "Twitter's Blue Check: Vital Verification or Status Symbol?" AP News, November 3, 2022. https://apnews.com/article/kanye-west-twitter-inc-technology-business-19d0726ed7f819b0649cec6eaefd56bb.

Pariser, Eli. *The Filter Bubble: What the Internet Is Hiding from You*. New York: Penguin, 2011.

Patrick, Anna. "How the COVID-19 Pandemic Shed Light on the Digital Divide." Government Technology, June 10, 2020. https://www.govtech.com/network/How-the-COVID-19-Pandemic-Shed-Light-on-the-Digital-Divide.html.

Prokop, Andrew. "Cambridge Analytica Shutting Down: The Firm's Many Scandals, Explained." *Vox*, March 21, 2018. https://www.vox.com/policy-and-politics/2018/3/21/17141428/cambridge-analytica-trump-russia-mueller.

Rivlin-Nadler, Max. "How ICE Uses Social Media to Surveil and Arrest Immigrants." *The Intercept*, December 22, 2019. https://theintercept.com/2019/12/22/ice-social-media-surveillance/.

Roose, Kevin. "What Is QAnon, the Viral Pro-Trump Conspiracy Theory?" *New York Times*, September 3, 2021. https://www.nytimes.com/article/what-is-qanon.html.

Selinger, Evan, and Woodrow Hartzog. "Facebook's Emotional Contagion Study and the Ethical Problem of Co-opted Identity in Mediated Environments Where Users Lack Control." *Research Ethics* 12, no. 1 (January 1, 2016): 35–43. https://doi.org/10.1177/1747016115579531.

Sen, Ari, and Brandyu Zadrozny. "QAnon Groups Have Millions of Members on Facebook, Documents Show." NBC News, August 10, 2020. https://www.nbcnews.com/tech/tech-news/qanon-groups-have-millions-members-facebook-documents-show-n1236317.

Shahbaz, Adrian, and Allie Funk. "Social Media Surveillance." Freedom House, accessed October 23, 2024. https://freedomhouse.org/report/freedom-on-the-net/2019/the-crisis-of-social-media/social-media-surveillance.

Shearer, Elisa, and Elizabeth Grieco. "Americans Are Wary of the Role Social Media Sites Play in Delivering the News." *Pew Research Center's Journalism Project* (blog), October 2, 2019. https://www.journalism.org/2019/10/02/americans-are-wary-of-the-role-social-media-sites-play-in-delivering-the-news/.

"Smartphone Users in the World 2025." Statista, accessed December 27, 2022. https://www.statista.com/forecasts/1143723/smartphone-users-in-the-world.

Sottile, Leah. "Inside the Boogaloo: America's Extremely Online Extremists." *New York Times*, August 19, 2020. https://www.nytimes.com/interactive/2020/08/19/magazine/boogaloo.html.

Statista. "Google: Net Income 2001–2015." Statista, 2020. https://www.statista.com/statistics/266472/googles-net-income/.

———. "Total Data Volume Worldwide 2010–2024." Statista, 2020. https://www.statista.com/statistics/871513/worldwide-data-created/.

Statt, Nick. "Google Personalizes Search Results Even When You're Logged Out, New Study Claims." *The Verge*, December 4, 2018. https://www.theverge.com/2018/12/4/18124718/google-search-results-personalized-unique-duckduckgo-filter-bubble.

Stone, Biz. "Not Playing Ball." X (blog), June 6, 2009. https://blog.twitter.com/en_us/a/2009/not-playing-ball.

Totenberg, Nina, and Sarah McCammon. "Supreme Court Overturns *Roe v. Wade*, Ending Right to Abortion Upheld for Decades." NPR, June 24, 2022. https://www.npr.org/2022/06/24/1102305878/supreme-court-abortion-roe-v-wade-decision-overturn.

Tufekci, Zeynep. *Twitter and Tear Gas: The Power and Fragility of Networked Protest*. New Haven, CT: Yale University Press, 2017.

"Twitter (TWTR)—Market Capitalization." Companies Market Cap, accessed December 27, 2022. https://companiesmarketcap.com/twitter/marketcap/.

Wamsley, Laurel. "On Far-Right Websites, Plans to Storm Capitol Were Made in Plain Sight." NPR, January 7, 2021. https://www.npr.org/sections/insurrection-at-the-capitol/2021/01/07/954671745/on-far-right-websites-plans-to-storm-capitol-were-made-in-plain-sight.

Webb, Maureen. *Coding Democracy: How Hackers Are Disrupting Power, Surveillance, and Authoritarianism*. Cambridge, MA: MIT Press, 2020.

Wu, Tim. *The Attention Merchants: The Epic Scramble to Get inside Our Heads*. New York: Vintage Books, 2017.

Zuboff, Shoshana. *The Age of Surveillance Capitalism: The Fight for a Human Future at the New Frontier of Power*. New York: PublicAffairs, 2019.

Tactics for the Interregnum

14

Afro-Asian Solidarity in the Interregnum

Revisiting Cold War Politics in Da 5 Bloods *and* Lovecraft Country

Evyn Lê Espiritu Gandhi and Rachel Haejin Lim

In the summer of 2020, the film *Da 5 Bloods* and the television series *Lovecraft Country*—both of which juxtapose the ongoing afterlives of anti-Black slavery and U.S. militarism in Asia—premiered on Netflix and HBO, respectively.[1] Both popular cultural productions were regarded as "timely" or "prescient," capturing the zeitgeist of the moment of their release.[2] Indeed, summer 2020 was the apex of the resurgent Movement for Black Lives, which responded to the state-sanctioned murders of Ahmaud Arbery, Breonna Taylor, David Prude, George Floyd, and many others. At the same time, as the ongoing COVID-19 pandemic exacerbated existing health and economic inequalities among minoritized and racialized populations, the rise of anti-Asian xenophobia and violence coincided with increasingly hateful rhetoric toward China, activating older stereotypes of Asian Americans as vectors of disease and foreign pollutants to the nation. In response to these accumulated crises, Asian American activists and artists reignited urgent conversations on anti-Blackness in Asian immigrant communities and sought to recover Black-Asian histories of shared struggle, while Black movement organizations affirmed their solidarity with Asian Americans in ways that highlighted the divisive role of white supremacy.[3] In a raucous public conversation that crosscut digital platforms, public writing, and community spaces, the responsibility to move past "indifference" and toward antiracist and coalitional solidarity emerged as a key framing for a better and more just form of multiracial politics.[4]

Since the first Black Lives Matter protests in 2013, there has been a wave of films, such as *Selma* (2013), *Hidden Figures* (2016), and *One Night in Miami* (2021), that situate the Movement for Black Lives within the United States' much longer history of anti-Black racism, with a particular focus on the Cold War period. But *Da 5 Bloods* and *Lovecraft Country* uniquely reflected the political moment of their emergence in three ways. First, they center the role that U.S. imperialism—signified by U.S. wars in Korea and Vietnam—had on shaping Black subjectivity and Black politics, both during the Cold War period and today. Second, both move beyond the Black-white binary to center the fraught relationships between Black and Asian communities. Finally, both texts conscientiously rework the contradictions of their inherited genres—the Vietnam War film in the case of *Da 5 Bloods* and Lovecraftian horror in the case of *Lovecraft Country*—to imagine more capacious pasts and futures. As such, *Da 5 Bloods* and *Lovecraft Country* mark the inflection point in the protracted interregnum between multiple geopolitical and racial regimes that defined 2020: the American Century and the Pacific Century, the increased visibility of police violence and the rise of the Movement for Black Lives, the myth of the model minority and the uptick in anti-Asian violence during the pandemic, and the rearticulation of white supremacy under Trump and seeming "return to 'business as usual'" under Biden.[5]

In this chapter, we interrogate *Da 5 Bloods* and *Lovecraft Country* for what they might teach us about the current interregnum and, more importantly, the kinds of political responses this time between world orders might require. By turning to film and television, we echo Stuart Hall's essential insights about popular culture as a site of struggle, where political uses and abuses both cohere and disappear.[6] While recognizing that selling multiculturalist and antiracist cultural productions was popular and indeed profitable in 2020, we nevertheless contend that it is important to take seriously the antiracist and anti-imperialist politics that these cultural texts offer to diagnose the contemporary conjuncture and help us envision a more radical future. In fact, we argue that both *Da 5 Bloods* and *Lovecraft Country* represent two attempts to, in Hall's words, "analyse ruthlessly" the embedded histories of accumulated crisis crystallized in the structures of anti-Black racism in the United States and U.S. imperialism in Asia.[7] By returning to an earlier period of Afro-Asian relations, these cultural productions reckon with Black American involvement in Cold War military conflicts—what Erica R. Edwards theorizes as "Black intimacy with state-sanctioned terror"—and provide new mappings for Afro-Asian coalition building in a moment in which Asia is increasingly figured as a threat to U.S. global hegemony.[8]

Still, while *Da 5 Bloods* and *Lovecraft Country* narrate the connections between histories of anti-Black racism, anti-Asian violence, and U.S. imperialism, both texts ultimately subsume the potentiality of radical internationalism to a history of U.S. civil rights. In *Da 5 Bloods* and *Lovecraft Country*, messy histories of imperial relationalities and transpacific entanglements become domesticated and ultimately resolved through the multicultural family frame. Probing the limits of solidarity based on models of heteronormative kinship, this chapter draws from a Black feminist tradition that sidesteps a patriarchal reproductive order to work through the current interregnum. Instead of accepting a return to a neoliberal status quo or awaiting the deferred possibility of future generations, this model of critique demands, in Alexander Weheliye's words, "the imagination of liberation in the future anterior tense of the NOW."[9] Wrestling with the contradictions of the "NOW" necessitates the mapping of "novel assemblages of relation" that move beyond "the grammar of comparison."[10]

Our reading of *Da 5 Bloods* and *Lovecraft Country* thereby brings intersectional and anti-imperialist analyses into the same frame—a critical move that positions Afro-Asian solidarity not as a question of multicultural alliance but as intimacies across transnational matrixes of race, empire, gender, and sexuality. Understanding the interregnum as a "space of looseness and possibility, not yet overcoded and fixed in meaning, signification, or representative economy," to quote the trans studies scholar Hil Malatino, we ultimately contend that genuine Afro-Asian solidarity must be grounded in queer, feminist, and anti-imperialist politics, which provide new horizons for coalition building.[11]

Historical Antecedents: The Cold War and Its Afterlives

The Cold War was a defining period of Black subject formation. On the domestic front, African Americans fought for civil rights: the right to eat at desegregated lunch counters, vote free of intimidation, live in multiracial neighborhoods, and work at well-paying jobs—in sum, the right to aspire toward the American Dream. This was the era of *Brown v. Board of Education*, the Montgomery Bus Boycott, and the March on Washington. On the international front, Black men played a key role in America's imperial ventures, marking the "troubling reality of Black responsibility for the state-sponsored terror that keeps Black people in danger but also unleashes itself without predictable fealty to modern racial formations."[12] The Korean War marked the first time that the U.S. army was desegregated. The Vietnam War, which followed soon after, highlighted the bitter ironies of integrating the military while domestic neighborhoods remained violently segregated. As Martin Luther King Jr. powerfully noted in his famous "Beyond Vietnam" speech, delivered on April 4, 1967: "[We watch] Negro and white boys on TV screens as they kill and die together for a nation that has been unable to seat them together in the same schools. So we watch them in brutal solidarity burning the huts of a poor village, but we realize that they would hardly live on the same block in Chicago."[13]

During the Cold War period, Black leaders and activists debated the best way to guarantee Black freedom. The civil rights movement emphasized the domestic context, privileging nonviolent forms of protest to fight for equal rights and inclusion. These activists ultimately believed that the United States could overcome its fraught history of slavery and racial capitalism to guarantee freedom and liberty for all, regardless of race. The Black radical tradition, epitomized by the Black Panther Party and Black Maoists, took a more internationalist approach, understanding Black America as an internal colony of the United States that should build solidarities with other colonized subjects across the Third World, such as China, Korea, and Palestine.[14] The Black Panthers in particular promoted a politics of intercommunalism, which sought to transcend nation-state borders in order to articulate solidarities between different colonized communities suffering from the violence of U.S. imperialism.[15]

At the same time, Black feminists such as Angela Davis, June Jordan, and the Combahee River Collective emphasized a need for an analysis through and across race, gender, and sexuality, to critique the heteronormativity and hypermasculinity pervasive in the majority of Black activist spaces as well as the white supremacist cultures they sought to counteract. In the words of the Combahee River Collective, "The liberation of all oppressed peoples necessitates the destruction of the political-economic systems of capitalism and imperialism as well as patriarchy."[16] Such lessons, which underscore the importance of an intersectional politics for calling forth Afro-Asian solidarity, remain integral for confronting the contemporary interregnum. The political limitations of failing to do so—that is, of sacrificing a critique of imperialism, capitalism, and patriarchy in favor of a one-dimensional analysis of domestic racism—are acutely represented in two cultural productions from the conjunctural moment of the summer of 2020: *Da 5 Bloods* and *Lovecraft Country*.

Afro-Asian Intimacy and the Heteronormative Family Frame: *Da 5 Bloods* (2020)

Spike Lee's film *Da 5 Bloods* follows the journey of a band of four African American Vietnam War veterans—the eponymous "Bloods"—who return to Vietnam in the contemporary moment to find the remains of their fallen squad leader as well as the gold fortune he helped them to hide. The film juxtaposes activism from the contemporary Movement for Black Lives with visual and audio clips of Black activism during the Vietnam War, including quotes and images of Malcom X, Martin Luther King Jr., and Muhammad Ali, marking the historical antecedents of the current interregnum. In its treatment of Black veterans and their war experiences, the film is an important corrective to Vietnam War films such as *Green Berets* (1968), *Apocalypse Now* (1979), and *Full Metal Jacket* (1987) that centered the white GI perspective. At the same time, *Da 5 Bloods* reproduces the visual and narrative tropes of this filmic tradition that overwrite and, in effect, erase Vietnamese subjects: communists and anticommunists, soldiers and civilians, the ethnic Kinh majority and native ethnic minority groups. As Viet Thanh Nguyen writes in his *New York Times* review of the film: "In putting Black subjectivity at the center, Lee also continues to put American subjectivity at the center. If one can't disentangle Black subjectivity from dominant American (white) subjectivity, it's impossible to apply a genuine anti-imperialist critique."[17]

In other words, by narrowing the scope of Black activism to the domestic field of white-Black relations, *Da 5 Bloods* misses the opportunity to tap into the anti-imperialist politics of the Black radical tradition. Furthermore, by centering the Black male GI experience, *Da 5 Bloods* also overlooks Black feminist politics, which offers an astute critique of the toxic masculinity underwriting American imperial war making, both during the Cold War and today. Indeed, there is a missed opportunity in the film's treatment of Tien, a former Vietnamese lover of one of the Bloods, Otis, and their mixed-race daughter Michon. Although the film does feature the Black-Vietnamese model and actress Sandy Huong Pham, herself the daughter of a South Vietnamese mother and an African American GI father, as Michon, for the most part this celebration of representational politics is eclipsed by the film's failure of the promise of Afro-Asian solidarity, insofar as *Da 5 Bloods* reproduces common stereotypes about Asian women. Tien, whom the Bloods need in order to smuggle out the gold, recalls older iterations of the "dragon lady," a mysterious figure who uses deceit and cunning to get her way.[18] In the film, other Vietnamese reject Tien and call Michon racial slurs, reminding viewers of the trope of the "tragic mulatta"—a beautiful, mixed-race woman who fails to find belonging in either Vietnamese or Black communities.[19]

In one of the film's final scenes, Otis is finally introduced to his daughter Michon. They embrace warmly. Michon says, "I miss you. And I love you so," and Otis responds, "And I love you." This scene of familial reconciliation is particularly notable because, more often than not, *Da 5 Bloods* focuses on the incommensurabilities between the Black veterans and the people of Vietnam. In fact, the film portrays a litany of hostile encounters with Vietnamese *men*: gangsters, merchants, and hired mercenaries. Additionally, the very reason the Bloods were in Vietnam in the first place was to retrieve buried gold, which had been intended as a payment to Indigenous Lahu soldiers allied with the U.S. military—a claim that is framed as "reparations." According to the Bloods' fallen leader Norman (played by Chadwick Boseman), "We repossessed this gold for every single Black boot who never made it home, every brother and sister stolen from Mother Africa." In this framework, which understands racial violence solely within the U.S. racial frame, "reparations" is presented as a zero-sum game that occurs at the expense of an already marginalized group in Southeast Asia.

Michon's immediate acceptance of her father, who had been unaware of her existence, is presented as a reparative act that heals the wounds of the broken Afro-Asian family, born of the violence of imperialism, and allows Michon to reconnect with her Black identity. The final shot of Michon and Otis presents them shoulder to shoulder, grinning straight into the camera in a manner reminiscent of a family portrait. But Michon's mother, Tien, is not included; instead, her spectral image appears unfocused and blurry in the background, like a forgotten spirit. That is, the film suggests that the restoration of Michon's connection to her Black father cannot coexist on equal terms with her relationship with her Vietnamese mother. This representation of Afro-Asian familial intimacy depends on a patriarchal definition of family in terms of biological reproduction rather than an ongoing feminist ethics of care. By using the family snapshot to exclude Tien, *Da 5 Bloods* ultimately concludes by literally centering Black men against the backdrop of Vietnamese women.

In so doing, *Da 5 Bloods* reflects the contradictions of the interregnum of the summer of 2020, in which the potential of Afro-Asian solidarity, emerging from the contemporaneous accumulated crises of anti-Black police vio-

Figure 14.1 Michon and Otis in Spike Lee's *Da 5 Bloods* (2020).

lence and anti-Asian pandemic-fueled hate, harkened back to an earlier moment of Afro-Asian relations during the Cold War for political inspiration. By setting the film in Vietnam, Spike Lee posits that U.S. race relations—both anti-Black racism and Black (masculinist) heroism—were/are negotiated not only on the home front but in spaces of U.S. empire, such as Cold War Asia. *Da 5 Bloods* tantalizingly gestures toward the promise of a radical internationalist framing of solidarity; this promise, however, is ultimately foreclosed, sacrificing a more capacious feminist, anti-imperialist Afro-Asian politics for a domesticated, heteronormative family frame.

Queering Afro-Asian Solidarity: *Lovecraft Country* (2020)

Lovecraft Country (2020), set in the 1950s, directs our attention to earlier moments of Black politics and subject formation: the space-time of the slave plantation, indexing the gendered violence suffered by Black female slaves raped by white slave masters, as well as the Tulsa Massacre, marking a defining moment of white terrorism.[20] Like *Da 5 Bloods*, *Lovecraft Country* grapples with Black subjectivity during the Cold War's "hot wars" in Asia, though this time the Vietnam War is replaced by the Korean War, which preceded the former by a decade and a half. Like *Da 5 Bloods*, *Lovecraft Country* centers a Black male veteran protagonist, Atticus "Tic" Black (played by Jonathan Majors). Unlike in *Da 5 Bloods*, however, Tic's story is eclipsed by an ensemble of Black queer and/or female characters that surround him: his queer father Montrose, his aunt Hippolyta, his cousin Diana, his lover Leti, and her queer sister Ruby. Indeed, in contrast to *Da 5 Bloods*, *Lovecraft Country* was written and directed by Black women, Misha Green and Victoria Mahoney, whose outlook profoundly shaped the show's representation of not only Black subjectivity but also Afro-Asian relations as routed through Black queer feminist interventions.

Throughout the first half of the show, Tic is haunted by memories of the Korean War, which manifest as the guilt and fear he shows whenever he thinks about his relationship with Ji-ah (played by Jamie Chung) while in Korea. In episode 6, "Meet Me in Daegu," *Lovecraft Country* shifts from the U.S. home front to the space of Korea to explain Ji-ah's backstory: she is a *kumiho*, the nine-tailed fox of East Asian lore who shapeshifts into a woman to seduce male victims and consume their flesh. *Lovecraft Country* gives its own twist to this East Asian legend, making the kumiho a spirit that possesses Ji-ah until she feeds on the souls of one hundred men. While Ji-ah spends her days tending to men's wounds as a nurse, at night she preys on their desires, exemplifying what Suiyi Tang calls a "monstrous" "yellow woman."[21] Embodying

Figure 14.2 Ji-ah and Tic in HBO's *Lovecraft Country* (2020).

both the "nurse" and "femme fatale" archetypes of Korean women common to media productions about the Korean War, she lures them to a candle-ringed room where she seduces them and, with Cthulhu-like tentacles, absorbs their memories and explodes them into a shower of blood.

Ji-ah first crosses paths with Tic when the U.S. military suspects that there is a communist spy among the Korean nurses. Tic is one of the soldiers who brutally participates in the murder of two innocent nurses and the torture of Young-ja, a communist agent and Ji-ah's best friend, underscoring the complicity of Black soldiers with U.S. Cold War violence. When Ji-ah encounters Tic again, wounded in the hospital, she is filled with a desire for revenge and decides that he will be her one hundredth and final victim. However, Ji-ah and Tic then fall in love, bonding over a mutual appreciation of Hollywood films and Western literature in a somewhat predictable pattern. But when Ji-ah loses control of her kumiho powers with Tic, foreseeing his impending death and revealing her supernatural abilities, Tic becomes terrified and flees.

Korea in *Lovecraft Country*, like Vietnam in *Da 5 Bloods*, risks becoming a mere backdrop on which to write the Black male protagonists' stories. And "Meet Me in Daegu" teeters dangerously on this line. Reflecting the contradictions of the current interregnum, the show is at its weakest when it centers Tic's guilt for the violence he committed against innocent Korean civilians and uses Ji-ah's love and forgiveness to absolve him of what are in fact heinous war crimes. Indeed, nearly 2 million civilians were killed during the Korean War—including targeted massacres—constituting about 10 percent of Korea's prewar population. For Korean American viewers, the familiarity of the English-inflected Korean accents of *Lovecraft Country*'s Korean

American cast presented a continuous reminder that in the show, Korea was primarily positioned as a stage upon which a set of questions about U.S. race relations were negotiated.

However, in its final two episodes, *Lovecraft Country* circumvents this foreclosure of Afro-Asian solidarity via the surprising narrative arc of Ji-ah, in turn pointing a way forward through the present interregnum. In the show's penultimate episode, Ji-ah shows up at Leti's house in Chicago in search of Tic, the last remaining human that she had loved as a kumiho. Tic—arguably scared and emasculated by his last sexual encounter with Ji-ah, as well as worried that Ji-ah might disrupt his new romantic relationship with Leti—initially misreads Ji-ah's desire to reconnect as a plea for heterosexual love and forcefully drives her out of the house. Later, he reaches out to Ji-ah and apologizes, affirming that the love that he kindled with Ji-ah in Korea was real and that it persists, albeit now within the valence of familial, platonic love. Ji-ah, unburdened by human distinctions between romantic, familial, and platonic love, accepts Tic's apology and tentatively inserts herself into Tic's extended family, which includes not only his blood relatives but also Leti, pregnant with Tic's son, and her queer sister Ruby.

In the final climactic scene of episode 10, Ji-ah sacrifices herself to help Tic—a sacrifice that, for those familiar with American orientalist narratives of the abandoned Asian lover, from *Madame Butterfly* (1932) to *Miss Saigon* (1989), is altogether expected. What is *unexpected*, though, is that Ji-ah *does not die*. Instead, in a stunning reversal, it is the American male protagonist, Tic, rather than the scorned Asian lover, Ji-ah, who ultimately sacrifices his life for the "greater good"—understood in *Lovecraft Country* as the cessation of white Americans' monopoly over magic rather than the preservation of white Americans' nuclear family structure, as other cultural texts of this genre depict. By demonstrating her *willingness* to sacrifice her body to the darkness out of love for Tic and his family, even though she does not die, Ji-ah exemplifies a queer Afro-Asian love that is irreducible to heterosexual desire. And it is precisely this queer Afro-Asian love that exceeds and ultimately defeats the white supremacist patriarchal order of the Sons of Adam (which, in typical white feminist fashion, Christina Braithwhite, played by Abbey Lee, had sought to circumvent by literally sacrificing a Black male subject to gain access into, rather than tear down, the white male patriarchal order that had excluded her). Such a queer Afro-Asian love posits Black struggles against racism and Asians struggles against militarism as intimately entangled.

Ji-ah, like the rest of Tic's family, is pained by Tic's death but not consumed by it. In other words, the show ends with an opening—a gesture toward a queer, feminist Afro-Asian futurity, a new horizon beyond our current interregnum. As Ji-ah walks somberly with the rest of Tic's family with the fallen Tic in their arms, the show suggests that she will stay with Leti to help raise their baby, creating a queer, Afro-Asian family formation. This reading of the show's ending and possible epilogue is supported, perhaps even foreshadowed, by two previous scenes of queer family formation. In a heartwarming scene from earlier in episode 10, Ji-ah joins Tic, Montrose, Hippolyta, Dee, Leti, and Ruby in singing the Chords' version of "Sh-Boom" as they drive together to Ardham, cementing her role as part of the family despite her non-Black Korean status. In an earlier scene, Tic's mother, Dora, explains to Tic why and how she loved both his father Montrose and his uncle / possible biological father George, and why her refusal to choose between the two brothers made Tic stronger, since he could then inherit the qualities of all three adults. In making the case for queer family formations that exceed the heteronormative nuclear family, Dora sets a precedent for Ji-ah's future role in parenting Tic's child: a queer transnational kinship relation that could undermine American tendencies—including Black American tendencies—to read "Asia" as forever foreign and suspect.

At the same time, however, Ji-ah's assimilation into the American family—and, by extension, the U.S. body politic—reminds viewers that *Lovecraft Country* is ultimately an American story, in which the decolonial struggles of the Korean people are ultimately collapsed back into the framework of U.S. race relations. Bereft of her closest familial and friendship ties in Korea, Ji-ah's migration across the Pacific echoes a long history in which post–Korean War marriage migrants, adoptees, and mixed-race children gained legibility as American subjects via their uneasy incorporation into families across the United States.[22] That is to say, the show's gesture toward the emancipatory potential of Afro-Asian kinship relations is still limited by the elisions of more anti-imperialist political futures represented by characters such as Young-ja, whose untimely murder forecloses the possibility of representing Asian women as political agents in their own right.

Nonetheless, the narrative interventions embodied by Ji-ah's character evoke new forms of queer, feminist Afro-Asian intimacy that are rarely represented in mainstream American media. Why, though, is the character of Ji-ah able to forge such intimacy with *Lovecraft Country*'s Black American characters, in a way that was otherwise foreclosed in *Da 5 Bloods*? Is there something particular about the Korean War and Black subjects' relation to it—an earlier moment of inchoate possibility, a different interregnal moment of conjuncture—that became foreclosed by the time of the Vietnam War (which, it should be noted, South Korea joined on behalf of the United States)?[23] Were political divisions between the civil rights movement and the internationalist Black radical tradition too entrenched by the Vietnam War era, collapsing the possibility of a more dialogical approach to Black politics?

In some ways, Ji-Ah reproduces Cold War stereotypes of the Korean friendly, since she aspires for incorporation into the American life represented in Hollywood films.[24] In other ways, however, she exceeds Cold War politics: although located in South Korea, she is not invested in anticommunist politics per se and even locates her most fulfilling friendship in Young-ja, the communist secret agent. Considering the fact that the Korean War is often called the "forgotten war," it is notable that one of her kumiho powers is an ability to absorb the experiences of her Korean and American victims, making her a living archive of multiplicitous—albeit exclusively male—memories. While Ji-Ah arguably does not forward a clear anti-imperialist critique—understood as a decentering of U.S. empire in favor of a recentering of the Korean decolonial struggle—her mutual love for Tic and his family exceeds a dichotomous and ultimately limiting Cold War framework, pointing toward a more queer and feminist form of Afro-Asian intimacy in the wake of the Korean War.

Lessons for the Present Interregnum

The summer of 2020 brought into stark visibility the contradictions of the contemporary interregnum. The moment marked the culmination of decades of accumulated crises: the trenchant anti-Blackness that marks Black subjects as targets of "premature death" and the persistent nativism that depicts Asian subjects as threats to the U.S. body politic, both at home and abroad.[25] The year 2020 also marked the revival of Cold War tensions, exemplified by the antagonism of communist North Korea and China as political and economic threats to a declining U.S. hegemony. It is in this sociopolitical moment that *Da 5 Bloods* and *Lovecraft Country* emerged, offering us glimpses of Afro-Asian solidarity rooted in an earlier Cold War moment and yet bearing profound lessons for our current moment of conjuncture. For we are indeed writing at an inflection point: the 2020 election of President Joe Biden and Vice President Kamala Harris—heralded as a victory for Black-Asian representational politics—in many ways indexed a return to neoliberal multiculturalist "politics as usual." Then the U.S.-backed Israeli genocide in Palestine followed by the election of former President Trump over Vice President Harris in 2024 underscored the reality of protracted crisis. It is in this moment that we turn to cultural productions for glimpses of a more radical politics of Black internationalism routed through queer Black feminism, which would refuse the collapsing of Black-Asian race relations into the domestic, heteronormative family frame. Representational politics, of course, will not save us. But cultural representations *can* point us toward queer, feminist, and anti-imperialist Afro-Asian possibilities and futurities. We draw inspiration from the images and narratives depicted in *Da 5 Bloods* and *Lovecraft Country*, which present cultural blueprints for relating otherwise.[26]

NOTES

1. A previous version of this chapter was published online by Heung | 흥 Coalition on November 17, 2020, under the title "Toward a New Afro-Asian Solidarity: Revisiting Cold War Politics in DA 5 BLOODS, WATCHMEN, and LOVECRAFT COUNTRY" (https://www.heungcoalition.com/writings/toward-a-new-afro-asian-solidarity). The authors thank Heung | 흥 Coalition for permission to revise and republish the piece.
2. Debruge, "'Da 5 Bloods'"; Jones, "Lovecraft Country Review."
3. Movement for Black Lives, "M4BL Statement."
4. Yellow Horse et al., "Asian Americans' Indifference"; Kuo, "Racial Justice Activist Hashtags."
5. Hall and Massey, "Interpreting the Crisis."
6. Hall, "Notes."
7. Hall and Massey, "Interpreting the Crisis," 58.
8. Edwards, *Other Side of Terror*, 13.
9. Weheliye, *Habeas Viscus*, 39.
10. Weheliye, 13.
11. Malatino, "Future Fatigue."
12. Edwards, *Other Side of Terror*, 13.
13. King, "Beyond Vietnam."
14. Kelley and Esch, "Black Like Mao"; Young, "*Juche* in the United States"; Lubin, *Geographies of Liberation*.
15. Rodriquez, "Long Live Third World Unity!"
16. Combahee River Collective, "Combahee River Collective Statement [1978]."
17. Nguyen, "Vietnamese Lives."
18. Clark, "Disturbing Stereotypes."
19. Raimon, *"Tragic Mulatta" Revisited*.
20. Spillers, "Mama's Baby, Papa's Maybe."
21. Tang, "Of Monsters and Ornaments."
22. Cho, *Haunting the Korean Diaspora*; Woo, *Framed by War*.
23. Lee, "Surrogate Military."
24. Park, *Cold War Friendships*.
25. Gilmore, *Golden Gulag*, 28.
26. Gilmore, *Golden Gulag*, 28.

BIBLIOGRAPHY

Cho, Grace M. *Haunting the Korean Diaspora: Shame, Secrecy, and the Forgotten War*. Minneapolis: University of Minnesota Press, 2008.

Clark, Audrey Wu. "Disturbing Stereotypes: Fu Man/Chan and Dragon Lady Blossoms." *Asian American Literature: Discourses and Pedagogie*s 3 (2012): 99–118.

Combahee River Collective. "Combahee River Collective Statement [1978]." Accessed October 24, 2024. http://circuitous.org/scraps/combahee.html.

Debruge, Peter. "'Da 5 Bloods' on Netflix: Film Review." *Variety*, June 10, 2020. https://variety.com/2020/film/reviews/da-5-bloods-review-spike-lee-chadwick-boseman-1234629971/.

Edwards, Erica R. *The Other Side of Terror: Black Women and the Culture of US Empire*. New York: New York University Press, 2021.

Gilmore, Ruth Wilson. *Golden Gulag: Prisons, Surplus, Crisis, and Opposition in Globalizing California*. Berkeley: University of California Press, 2007.

Hall, Stuart. "Notes on Deconstructing 'the Popular' (1981)." In *Cultural Theory: An Anthology*, edited by Imre Szeman and Timothy Kaposy, 72–80. New York: John Wiley & Sons, 2010.

Hall, Stuart, and Doreen Massey. "Interpreting the Crisis." *Soundings* 44 (2010): 57–71.

Jones, Ellen E. "Lovecraft Country Review—Are People Scarier than Monsters?" *The Guardian*, Aug 17, 2020. https://www.theguardian.com/tv-and-radio/2020/aug/17/lovecraft-country-review-are-people-scarier-than-monsters.

Kelley, Robin D. G., and Betsy Esch. "Black Like Mao: Red China and Black Revolution." *Critical Journal of Black Politics and Culture* 1, no. 4 (1999): 6–41.

King, Martin Luther, Jr. "Beyond Vietnam." Riverside Church, New York, April 4, 1967. http://kingencyclopedia.stanford.edu/encyclopedia/documentsentry/doc_beyond_vietnam/.

Kuo, Rachel. "Racial Justice Activist Hashtags: Counterpublics and Discourse Circulation." *New Media and Society* 20, no. 2 (2018): 495–514.

Lee, Jin-kyung. "Surrogate Military, Subimperialism, and Masculinity: South Korea in the Vietnam War, 1965–73." *Positions: East Asia Cultures Critique* 17, no. 3 (2009): 655–682.

Lubin, Alex. *Geographies of Liberation: The Making of an Afro-Arab Political Imaginary*. Chapel Hill: University of North Carolina Press, 2014.

Malatino, Hil. "Future Fatigue: Trans Intimacies and Trans Presents (or How to Survive the Interregnum)." *Trans Studies Quarterly* 6, no. 4 (2019): 635–658.

Movement for Black Lives. "M4BL Statement on Anti-Asian Violence." Accessed January 21, 2023. https://m4bl.org/statements/anti-asian-violence/.

Nguyen, Viet Thanh. "Vietnamese Lives, American Imperialist Views, Even in 'Da 5 Bloods.'" *New York Times*, June 24, 2020. https://www.nytimes.com/2020/06/24/movies/da-5-bloods-vietnam.html.

Park, Josephine Nock-Hee. *Cold War Friendships: Korea, Vietnam, and Asian American Literature*. Oxford: Oxford University Press, 2016.

Raimon, Eve Allegra. *The "Tragic Mulatta" Revisited: Race and Nationalism in Nineteenth-Century Antislavery Fiction*. New Brunswick, NJ: Rutgers University Press, 2004.

Rodriquez, Besenia. "'Long Live Third World Unity! Long Live Internationalism': Huey P. Newton's Revolutionary Intercommunalism." *Souls* 8, no. 3 (2006): 119–141.

Spillers, Hortense J. "Mama's Baby, Papa's Maybe: An American Grammar Book." *Diacritics* 17, no. 2 (1987): 64–81.

Tang, Suiyi. "Of Monsters and Ornaments: Yellow Femininity, Afrofuturism, Form." Paper presented at the ACLA 2022 conference, National Taiwan Normal University, Taipei, Taiwan, June 15–18, 2022.

Weheliye, Alexander G. *Habeas Viscus: Racializing Assemblages, Biopolitics, and Black Feminist Theories of the Human*. Durham, NC: Duke University Press, 2014.

Woo, Susie. *Framed by War: Korean Children and Women at the Crossroads of US Empire*. New York: New York University Press, 2019.

Yellow Horse, Aggie J., Karen Kuo, Eleanor K. Seaton, and Edward D. Vargas. "Asian Americans' Indifference to Black Lives Matter: The Role of Nativity, Belonging and Acknowledgment of Anti-Black Racism." *Social Sciences* 10, no. 5 (2021): 1–19.

Young, Benjamin R. "*Juche* in the United States: The Black Panther Party's Relations with North Korea, 1969–1971." *Asia-Pacific Journal* 13, no. 12 (2015). https://apjjf.org/2015/13/12/benjamin-young/4303.

15

NdN Popular Culture

Musings on Cultural Appropriation

Kyle Mays

Before beginning, I want to offer my positionality: I am Afro-Indigenous, African American, and Saginaw Chippewa. I am speaking specifically to an Indigenous studies audience, though I'm sure that other marginalized groups will certainly get something from the larger points I am attempting to make. As an Afro-Indigenous person, I see this particular moment of colliding Afro-Indigenous futures, an interregnum, consisting of uncertainty but with grand possibilities for our collective futures rooted in kinship and solidarity. I also want to mention that this is not written in the style of your typical academic essay. I write from the perspective of someone who believes that one way of challenging academic discourses is using Black language and challenging the language of wider (whiter?) communication, or what some inappropriately refer to as "standard English." I have written like this elsewhere but have been deeply influenced by the work of the linguists Geneva Smitherman and H. Samy Alim.

We are at a point of contention within Indigenous popular culture (hereafter, NdN popular culture) and representation.[1] NdN popular culture consists of the symbols, signs, and meanings produced by Indigenous people to tell stories about their lives. Produced within the context of a settler colonial, capitalist space, it offers the possibility to create fugitive, anticolonial art, ripe with possibilities for Indigenous futures. The modes of NdN popular culture include but are not limited to aesthetics and visual cultures, fashion, literary production, the utilization of social media, music, dance, and film. It seems we are in a positive stage in NdN cultural production for mainstream audiences. We have two seasons of two highly successful shows, including *Reservation Dogs* (Hulu) and *Rutherford Falls* (Peacock). And there are several other shows with Indigenous characters and themes focused on Indigenous issues, including *Missing* and *Murdered Indigenous Women*. And yet there remains a limitation on cultural appropriation. For example, during the first season of *Reservation Dogs*, I received numerous messages from a variety of Indigenous folks asking my opinion on the appropriation of Black culture on the show. I wanted to wait and see the entire season before I rushed to judgment. A major critique levied by some of the show was hip-hop's representation, including the performance of Mvskoke Creek rapper Sten Joddi's "Greasy Frybread." After watching the entire show and the music video, I did not see the level of appropriation that everyone else claimed. This is not the only incident.

Thus, there seems to be two things in tension: an uncritical discussion of cultural appropriation and the desire for more representation. How do we come to exploring these tensions?

It makes sense why some have hope for Indigenous representation in the current political moment. We live in a settler colonial society that is dedicated to erasing and distorting Indigenous identities and cultures for the purposes of land accumulation. To be fair, there is currently the first Indigenous secretary of the interior leading the charge on Indigenous issues. Secretary Deb Haaland is helping return land to Indigenous nations. She is also helping restore discussions around the boarding schools that occurred in the United States, which focused on destroying Indigenous cultures and identities. While she is doing this work to further entrench tribal sovereignty, there is a potentially devastating case before the U.S. Supreme Court relating to the Indian Child Welfare Act (ICWA), with the possibility of destroying one of the cornerstones of modern Indigenous sovereignty. So the tension centers on a question: What does more representation mean if tribal sovereignty is at stake? In our efforts to do something positive, are we also reifying the settler colonial nation-state? I think this is the context in which discussions of cultural appropriation exist. In other words, we are in a moment of crisis and the facade of possibilities. For example, the interregnum within NdN popular culture is shifting, stuck in place, and teetering on moving to the future simultaneously. It is stuck between a hyperfocus on non-Indigenous people stealing and exploiting Indigenous cultures and the ability to produce relevant expressive culture not set to the limits of the settler colonial gaze. I offer a few examples below.

In Sten Joddi's "Greasy Frybread" video from season 1 of *Reservation Dogs*, he is wearing a tank top in one scene and then an Oklahoma City Thunder jersey in the other. He is wearing Native bling, a combination of powwow beads and gold chains.[2] He also has a grill on the top row of his teeth, a popular Black southern aesthetic that has been popularized within hip-hop and Black culture for decades. The video is a parody. It is funny; he has aunties and uncles and elders dancing in the background. The video is filmed primarily in Okmulgee, the original capital of the Mvskoke Cree Nation, and not far from Tulsa, Oklahoma. When it first aired, I had Afro-Indigenous and Indigenous peers texting me and DMing me, and I saw tweets about the inappropriate nature of the video; they said Joddi was making a mockery of Black aesthetics and culture. I watched the video and saw a parody that was not meant to make fun of Black culture at all—it was making fun of Indigenous cultures and a humorous approach to hip-hop. And to be fair, Indigenous peoples wear grills, too.

The other component of season 1 of the show is that there was a lack of Black and Afro-Indigenous characters. I understand that folks want to see more of themselves on television. But the first question is why? There are hardly any representations of Indigenous peoples or Afro-Indigenous peoples across the board, and while the show is not perfect and perhaps could do more, it does not take away from its brilliance. I would enjoy seeing an Afro-Indigenous, primarily urban show that would add to NdN popular culture, but I suppose I will have to wait to see that. Not every show has to check every box, and lazily levying critiques of a show with cultural appropriation is not helpful in expanding our range of possibilities in our current times.

I remain unsatisfied with the discussion of cultural appropriation, though. There is a juncture where we are fixated on cultural appropriation to the detriment of Indigenous cultural development that is not solely consumed with the white gaze. I think that the discourse of cultural appropriation from Indigenous studies is, well, not all that critical. It is so reactionary that whenever I see another story about some white person or famous person "playing Indian," I almost roll my eyes—at the perpetrator *and* the people who are writing about it. I'm not the only one. As the Anishinaabe intellectual Leanne Betasamosake Simpson wrote in the aftermath of the Idle No More movement, cultural appropriation has become a central source of our reactionary political movements. I quote her at length:

> There has been a significant lack of discussion and action about land issues. While it has become the practice for segments of Canadian society, particularly the more liberal and well-meaning segments, to condemn racist stereotypes, this same group is immobilized with regard to land issues. As a result, it is possible to get, for instance, music festivals to ban hipsters from wearing Native headdresses, or sports teams to change their name from the Nepean Redskins, or even the word *squaw* to be removed from maps. These efforts have my respect but also my worry. Changing stereotypes are easy wins right now. They

are easy because they are acceptable to the oppressor, and they only give the illusion of real change. It is not acceptable to wear a headdress to a dance party, but it is acceptable to dance on stolen land and to build pipelines over stolen land.[3]

Though writing about Canada, I think it is important to think about Simpson's point as a way to think deeper about culture. She is not saying that we should not challenge racist stereotypes—she just sees that as a limited way of thinking about things. Yes, of course, we should challenge racist stereotypes and cultural appropriation. But is that really a form of radical resurgence?

Radical resurgence is the idea that Indigenous cultures and lifeways will not return to traditional ways but rather, in this moment of crisis, will build on the resilience of their ancestors and create futures known and unknown, outside of the white supremacist, settler colonial gaze. Is it engaging in liberal forms of dissent? Simpson is referring to the relationship between culture and decolonization in the Fanonian sense. Frantz Fanon writes in the chapter "On National Culture" in *Wretched of the Earth*, "What is the relationship between the struggle, the political or armed conflict, and culture? During the conflict is culture put on hold? Is the national struggle a cultural manifestation? . . . In other words, is the liberation struggle a cultural phenomenon?"[4] Fanon's questions stem from his attempt to think critically about the importance of culture to decolonial efforts and to consider how systematically settlers attempt to destroy Indigenous cultures. But, for Fanon, decolonization is not simply producing culture in response to colonialism but about a specific focus on returning land and ending settler colonialism once and for all. Expressive culture, or more precisely representation, has its place in anticolonial movements, but it cannot be the only thing. I think some believe that getting more positive representation will lead in some way to decolonization. Without the return of land and the creation of representations and expressive cultures outside the colonial gaze, we will never be free.

After settlers stop using mascots, then what? Will they return land and restore better relations or engage in radical resurgence? I think history tells us that it is a no! The current land-back movement has allowed for us to keep the main thing central: the unequivocal return of Indigenous land.

So, in this essay, I ask this: Is cultural appropriation it? We must reject the colonial politics of recognition within the realm of NdN popular culture. At this moment, right now, we need to think differently about cultural appropriation, we need a new language, and we need new interventions. The interregnum of NdN popular culture might require a new language that is not only focused on appropriation but is instead focused on the actual production of Indigenous expressive cultures.

Cultural appropriation is the idea that a dominant group takes, at will, cultural markers from a powerless group and appropriates them for capital gain. They seek to assign themselves as the "Indigenous" creators of a cultural element, and because of their origin story, they seek to profit from it. In other words, the appropriation of culture is not far removed from the appropriation of land because they both require erasure and a justification for that erasure for the purpose of capital. The interesting thing today is that cultural appropriation is basically what Philip Deloria called "playing Indian" back in 1998. Many folks are rehashing arguments from playing Indian. Deloria writes, "Playing Indian is a persistent tradition in American culture, stretching from the very instant of the national big bang into an ever-expanding present and future. It is, however, a tradition with limitations. Not surprisingly, these cling tightly to the contours of power."[5] Playing Indian is as American as cherry pie and green bean casserole. It is a tradition like eating turkey and stuffing. So why has the discourse not changed? To be clear, I am not saying we should not criticize non-Indigenous people for playing Indian, but we need a new way of talking and to be proactive versus reactionary. Let me further break down my reasons below.

Problem Number One: Where Is Class in Cultural Appropriation?

I am not trying to sound like a Marxist-dude-bro who reduces everything to class. Race, indigeneity, gender, and other social, economic, and political identities matter just as much as class status. However, mainstream Indigenous responses to popular culture are basically reduced to identity politics.[6] That is, "white-settlers can't do X because they are white and profiting off of Indigenous 'cultures.'" OK: If we follow that logic, then can an Indigenous person do X because they are Indigenous and should therefore be able to profit? What happened to a critique of racial capitalism? This is a bad version of identity politics, one that ignores or avoids any intersectional analysis. As Stuart Hall argues, there is little distinction today between political economy and the media or, more precisely, cultural production.[7] There is no *one* form of Indigenous cultural expression; it is diverse. And who gets to determine who is and is not able to profit from Indigenous cultural expressions?

To break this down, let me turn to the Black feminist understanding of identity politics, coming from the Combahee River Collective Statement. According to Keeanga-Yamahtta Taylor, the "CRC statement identified 'class oppression' as central to the experience of Black women, as in doing so they helped to distinguish radical Black feminist politics from a developing middle-class orientation in Black politics that was on the ascent in the 1970s."[8] Furthermore, as Patricia Hill Collins and Sirma Bilge argue, "the explicit focus on institutional transformation of key figures who introduced intersectionality to the academy suggest that, when it comes to questions of identity, intersectionality has long emphasized a combination of structural and cultural analyses."[9] We can understand the authors use of structural analysis to include social inequality, a class analysis.

I include class here because the cultural appropriation vanguard lacks a basic critique of capitalism that critiques whites for engaging in capitalist gain while not also doing the same of Indigenous peoples. I would assume that if they were serious about decolonization, then that would include a direct assault on the foundations of both dispossession and enslavement: capitalism. Again, just because you are Indigenous, that does not mean you should also make profit from Indigenous cultures.

Problem Number Two: Essential Authenticity

The problem with cultural appropriation, in its present form, is that its logic is based on some "authentic" understanding of Indigenous culture(s) without respecting the diversity of Indigenous North America. When an incident of white colonial fuckery—I mean cultural appropriation—occurs (almost always someone wearing a headdress), the responses logically work like this: (1) "There are over 560 tribal nations, many state recognized, blah blah." (2) "Most white Americans don't know the history of oppression that Native Americans have experienced in this country." (3) "And, as a Native person, I'm deeply offended because these stereotype us as timeless beings."

Yes, we know. This same scenario is used, over and over, like the story your auntie or uncle tells you every Christmas, like clockwork. But aren't the headdresses and the majority of stereotypes about Indigenous peoples connected with the Plains First Nations? I don't, for the most part, see white people appropriating Anishinaabe anything, besides the time I was in a bar in Michigan and this woman told me she was the descendant of an "Ojibwe princess," but that is pretty rare.

And yet, non-Plains First Nations talk specifically about things appropriated from Lakota and Dakota peoples' history as if it's their own, as if they have a right to it. I have a solution: if white people want to wear headdresses that are associated with the Plains First Nations, why don't we let the Plains First Nations handle that in the arena over the cultural appropriation wars? If we are so diverse, that's their problem. I'm not saying don't speak up, but if there is a public conversation and you are asked, pass the mic. Unless Dakotas or Lakotas ask you directly to be a spokesperson, keep quiet and pass the mic. If there are no other Indigenous people around when something happens, you should speak up on principle. But if you're asked to go on television or radio or whatever—tell them to contact someone from that tribal nation.

Or, more recently, former president Donald Trump kept using the name Pocahontas in relation to Senator Elizabeth Warren. If you recall, she claimed to be Cherokee, but the Cherokee Nation dismissed those claims. But why do people who are not from the tribal nation of Pocahontas always got something to say about Pocahontas? Let Pocahontas's peoples handle that. In addition, a major component of cultural appropriation talk is rooted in this idea of victimization—I don't mean it in a conservative sense (more on that later).

Are we going to spend most, if not all of our energy, using the language and ideology of victimhood and reacting to what settlers do and think? I'm not saying Indigenous people aren't targets to the ongoing settler project—I think the Dakota Access Pipeline and the water crises that are happening in Flint and Detroit (lest we forget—Indigenous people live there, too!) demonstrate that. But as Scott Richard Lyons reminds us: "It is always entirely possible to promote a resistance identity that rejects the dominant culture and the political status quo without falling prey to the temptation of defining ourselves as Other and/or always defined by a history of victimization. It is important (and more historically accurate) to assert an identity and culture that consists of more than grievances or stories about abuses suffered at the hands of the white man."[10] I completely understand, and as my comrade Amber Starks writes, "I fundamentally believe our arrival at Black Liberation and Indigenous Sovereignty will certainly require us to remember who we are outside of our oppressors' institutions, ideologies, and imaginations."[11] Seeing ourselves outside of these limited positions is important for our futures in the aftermath of settler colonialism and white supremacy. I think this could take many forms. For example, the Cree hip-hop artist Eekwol did a video "For Women, by Women," which is a wonderful example of the interregnum of NdN popular culture in motion. The video is multigenerational and includes children, young adults, and elders. The chant "for women, by women" is a call to respect Indigenous women, that they are our past, present, and future. Perhaps most importantly, they have the ability to do things for themselves, without the patriarchy that exists within Indigenous communities.

Seeing ourselves outside of the colonial gaze does not mean appealing to whiteness. Further, why should we expect different from those invested in whiteness? Haven't centuries of colonization taught us anything about whiteness? The discourse goes from noble savage (we should be like the Indians, the people of the land) to the binary of savagery and civilization (premodern and modern). Indigenous cultures have been bought and sold and reimagined for the benefit of settlers.[12] As my auntie once told me, "White folks gone be white folks." She did not mean to say all white people are racist, but she offered me the same thought that W. E. B. Du Bois articulates in *Black Reconstruction*: that whites have historically chosen their whiteness over their economic interest and various possibilities of solidarity.[13] Again, I'm not suggesting we should not confront cultural appropriation, but we need to focus on creating a better language and ways of talking about it. But there is an important part to this: Indigenous people appropriating non-Indigenous cultures. This forces us to ask the question: Are any cultures pure? What do we risk when we play the game of cultural essentialism and authenticity? I would argue that the stage of NdN popular culture requires less talk of appropriation and more analyses on the art itself. A focus on essentialism and authenticity not only limits the possibilities of Indigenous expressive culture but disallows for the necessary critique to continue producing creative, abstract, and meaningful art for Indigenous and non-Indigenous audiences alike.

We know from Philip Deloria that it is about white Americans' sense of entitlement and the construction of self.[14] So why do we keep rehashing the same argument? I propose this: How about we focus more on our artistic practices and invention and less so on what white people are doing or, more precisely, how they engage in cultural appropriation? I know, the next retort is going to be that until we get rid of mascots, until white people see us as human beings, then we won't be able to get anything else going. I disagree with that on two levels. First, our Indigenous relatives in Canada and in Mexico, while still having to deal with the white imagination and anti-Indigenous policies, continue to produce interesting and conceptual art. And second, focusing so much on white people reproduces the power of whiteness—especially the idea of their superiority. Let me be clear, I am not saying we ignore white power and white terrorism as if they don't have real consequences; we should fight that wherever it exists. But our language on cultural appropriation, our collective discourse, is limited.

A consequence of focusing on more positive mainstream representation is that it reinscribes the idea that white standards of cultural validation are the norm and the standard, and it suggests that if settlers see Indigenous peoples as three-dimensional human beings, it might in some way lead to decolonization. It won't. Settler capitalists aren't going to willingly return land, which should be the goal of decolonization. We need to focus on our artistic development and critiques of that art.

If we go back in history, do people remember the Apollo Theater back in the 1960s? You would get booed off the stage if the crowd wasn't feeling you. Where is the metaphorical Indigenous Apollo Theater? Just because settlers view Indigenous people as invisible, that doesn't mean they can't be critiqued for the expressive culture they produce. Just because you're Indigenous, it does not mean your work is above critique; cultural criticism is a necessary part of producing expressive culture, and it isn't always hating. Not everything an Indigenous person does is "good art"—whatever that may mean in a given moment. I don't believe everything I write is good, and I'm certainly OK with it being criticized. They should be booed off the stage, with love.

If you write, you deserve (constructive) criticism. I'm not talking about those who want to talk shit, criticize, and say nothing—I don't believe in being mean-spirited, but there needs to be another level to our collective artistic practices. For instance, we both want to be respected as Indigenous people and yet continue to appeal to the white imagination with art.

I believe that there is a lot of possibility in exploring NdN popular cultures that are not invested in the colonial politics of representation. The interregnum of NdN popular culture is a moment of opportunity for Indigenous creatives. We have a duty not only to our current generation but the future one, to critique, dismantle, and create NdN futures that are not bound to the colonial imaginary. I appreciate the work of the Cree rapper Supaman, whose video "Alright" blends the past and the future. He goes back into time to tell his ancestors about the future generations. In a car similar to the one featured in *Back to the Future*, he ends his video by going back into time and putting in the year 1491, suggesting that he is going to warn Indigenous folks on the changing world ahead of them with the onset of colonization, or perhaps he wants to completely shift history by directly challenging Christopher Columbus. It is hard to know, but this is the type of work that I think is on the cutting edge of NdN cultural futures. This work exists, and I look forward to more, for our collective futures.

NOTES

1. Mays, *Afro-Indigenous History*. See chapter 7 on Black and Indigenous popular culture.
2. Mays, *Hip Hop Beats*, 55.
3. Simpson, *As We Have*, 113.
4. Fanon, *Wretched of the Earth*, 171.
5. Deloria, *Playing Indian*, 7.
6. Reed, *Stirrings in the Jug*, 15.
7. Hall, "Centrality of Culture," 317.
8. Taylor, *How We Get Free*, 9.
9. Collins and Bilge, *Intersectionality (Key Concepts)*, 124.
10. Lyons, *X-Marks*, 98.
11. Starks, "Envisioning Black Liberation."
12. Meyer and Royer, "Selling the Indian," xii.
13. Du Bois, *Black Reconstruction in America*, 700.
14. Deloria, *Playing Indian*, 4.

BIBLIOGRAPHY

Collins, Patricia Hill, and Sirma Bilge. *Intersectionality (Key Concepts)*. Cambridge: Polity, 2016.

Deloria, Philip, *Playing Indian*. New Haven, CT: Yale University Press, 1998.
Du Bois, W. E. B. *Black Reconstruction in America: 1860–1880*. New York: Free Press, 1998.
Fanon, Frantz. *The Wretched of the Earth*. New York: Grove, 2004.
Hall, Stuart. "The Centrality of Culture: Notes on the Cultural Revolutions of Our Time." In *Selected Writings on Marxism*, 316–334. Durham, NC: Duke University Press, 2021.
Lyons, Scott Richard. *X-Marks: Native Signatures of Assent*. Minneapolis: University of Minnesota Press, 2010.
Mays, Kyle T. *An Afro-Indigenous History of the United States*. Boston: Beacon, 2021.
———. *Hip Hop Beats, Indigenous Rhymes: Modernity and Hip Hop in Indigenous North America*. Albany: SUNY Press, 2018.
Meyer, Carter Jones, and Diana Royer. "Selling the Indian: Commercializing and Appropriating American Indian Cultures." In *Selling the Indian: Commercializing and Appropriating American Indian Cultures*. Tucson: University of Arizona Press, 2001.
Reed, Adolph, Jr. *Stirrings in the Jug: Black Politics in the Post-Segregation Era*. 1st ed. Minneapolis: University of Minnesota Press, 1999.
Simpson, Leanne. *As We Have Always Done: Indigenous Freedom through Radical Resurgence*. Minneapolis: University of Minnesota Press, 2017.
Starks, Amber. "Envisioning Black Liberation and Indigenous Sovereignty." U.S. Department of Arts and Culture, September 22, 2021. https://usdac.us/news/2021/9/21/envisioning-black-liberation-and-indigenous-sovereignty.
Taylor, Keeanga-Yamahtta. *How We Get Free: Black Feminism and the Combahee River Collective*. Chicago: Haymarket Books, 2017.

16

Kanaka Maoli Radical Resurgence

Walking the ʻĀina, Past, Present, and Future

Mary Tuti Baker, Candace Fujikane, and C. M. Kaliko Baker

The introduction to this volume provides in broad strokes a vision of the interregnum as an era of potentiality and revolution. As the editors note, "Gramsci illustrates that an interregnum is not merely a conjunctural point of no return or a crisis without a clear resolution. Rather, it is a breakdown in and a possibility for change in the order of meaning making itself."

We see Kanaka Maoli resurgence as such a historical moment where ancestral social formations are reemerging to bring back ecologies of life that have existed for millennia. As planetary crises are exacerbated by state structures that support the accumulation of wealth at the expense of these ecologies of life, a critical mass of Kanaka Maoli are working toward living in relationship to their places despite this onslaught, persisting in the face of exploitation and death brought on by settler colonial capital. In this conversation, we reflect on this existential threat and discuss the ways that Kanaka Maoli knowledge keepers and settler allies work against toxic settler colonial and capitalist relations in Hawaiʻi.[1]

This chapter features three activist scholars who were born to the islands: C. M. Kaliko Baker (Kanaka Maoli), whose work centers on the revitalization of ʻōlelo Hawaiʻi (Hawaiian language); Mary Tuti Baker (Kanaka Maoli), Kaliko's aunty, who studies the intersection of Indigenous and anarchist political theory; and Candace Fujikane, a fourth-generation Japanese settler and author of *Mapping Abundance for a Planetary Future: Kanaka Maoli and Critical Settler Cartographies in Hawaiʻi*.

We began our conversation with a question: How are Kanaka Maoli and settlers forging reciprocal relationships that move beyond the domination paradigms upon which the colonial conquest and capitalist expropriation of resources is built? More importantly, how do we move forward in Hawai'i to open creative spaces for social, political, and economic transformation? We found that our inquiry into solidarity and transformation repeatedly circled back to *aloha 'āina*, the deep love that Kanaka Maoli have for lands, waters, and skies, who are *kūpuna* (ancestors) as expressed in genealogical chants.[2] Aloha 'āina is born out of the ways that Kanaka walk the land, particularly on the island of Kaho'olawe: an island that was used by the U.S. military as a bombing target from 1941 to 1990, an island where Native Hawaiians took a stand against U.S. occupation, and an island that is now a beacon of aloha 'āina, Kanaka Maoli resurgence, and ecological stewardship, led by the Protect Kaho'olawe 'Ohana (PKO, also referred to here as 'Ohana).

The Conversation

We gathered on Kaliko's *lānai* (outdoor gathering area) under the *malu* (shelter) of the Ko'olau Mountains towering above us. The three of us spent the day sharing stories about work and family and *'ono* grinds (delicious food) prepared by Haili'ōpua Baker, Kaliko's partner. We begin this excerpt of the day's conversation with Tuti's question to Candace.

TUTI: So, Candace, your book maps Kanaka Maoli practices of abundance in such profound ways, articulating alternatives to capitalist economies of scarcity with Kanaka Maoli economies of abundance and a careful attention to stories of kūpuna. I was intrigued—but maybe not surprised—to see that you worked so closely with an 'ōlelo Hawai'i editor. What was that process like?

CANDACE: That's a great question, Tuti! In *Mapping Abundance*, I draw from *mo'olelo* [stories/histories] that were printed in nineteenth-century Hawaiian-language newspapers. Kaliko was my *kumu* [teacher] at the time, and when I thought about Kanaka Maoli economies of abundance, I thought about the kind of translation work that you [*turning to Kaliko*] do in the classroom. You have a deep knowledge of the mo'olelo and the most beautiful translations into 'ōlelo Hawai'i. I knew you would be an amazing editor because you really love the mo'olelo. You are also very demanding and very precise. I learned so much about the nuances of 'ōlelo Hawai'i working on the translation with you. So we would have breakfast at IHOP [International House of Pancakes], and you would look at passages that I had translated, and you would say, "Yeah, this is good," or you would say, "No, no, no, it's more like this—" One time, I remember us having a conversation about Kāneikawaiola,

Kāne of the Living Waters, and I asked you, is there such a thing as water that isn't alive?

KALIKO: Yeah, that was a good question. No, there is no water that is dead that I can think of offhand. But then again, I don't pray people to death. So maybe there were or are waters that bring death. The *-ola* here means that the water brings *ola*, or "life." Even Kanaloa's references as the god of the ocean and the hot depths are that which gives life.

CANDACE: Yes! Even stagnant, still water like the *hauna* [smelly] part of a fishpond is rich and fertile. In the *mele* [song, incantation, poetic expression], Kanaloa takes the *kino lau* [bodily form] of Kanaloa Heʻe Haunawela. Kanaloa is the *akua* [god and/or elemental form] of the hot, slimy waters of creation.[3]

TUTI: Really! Missionaries saw Kanaloa as the devil. I guess it makes sense that the invaders demonize the akua that unifies all of Moana Nui. Traveling the Pacific, we encounter Kanaloa in so many forms. I remember in Rarotonga in the Cook Islands many years ago attending a Catholic service packed with islanders from across the Pacific. At the peak of the homily, the Cook Island Maori priest opened his arms to the congregation and declared, "And who unites us all here in Te Moana Nui?" And whispers of "Tangaroa" rolled through the crowded pews. I thought, "Of course, it is Kanaloa that unites us." [Tangaroa is the South Pacific variant of Kanaloa.]

KALIKO: Yeah!

CANDACE: And when I think about this kind of ʻōlelo Hawaiʻi work, I think about you, Kaliko, saying that Hawaiian language has to provide the foundation, the common ground, for regrowing the lāhui Hawaiʻi [Hawaiian collective or nation]. And when we think about ʻōlelo Hawaiʻi, we also remember that Kanaloa is the older place-name that the Protect Kahoʻolawe ʻOhana (PKO) recovered for the island of Kahoʻolawe: Kanaloa Kahoʻolawe. Your work at bringing back Kanaloa Kahoʻolawe has been so much about ʻōlelo Hawaiʻi. You do the important research to find the original names for places as well as to *haku* [compose] new names for places that have changed over time.

KALIKO: We were fortunate that when the movement to protect Kahoʻolawe started in the seventies, we still had some kūpuna who knew names—like Uncle Harry Mitchell and others from Molokaʻi. They knew a lot about the place-names. There was a map, and they wrote on it where they thought all the place-names were. So we had that. And, you know, the ʻOhana didn't have much knowledge of ʻōlelo Hawaiʻi, like most Hawaiians in the 1970s, so we didn't know what the place-names meant. People like Uncle Harry, Aunty Clara Kū, I believe, and others from Molokaʻi were part of the last generations of native speakers of ʻōlelo Hawaiʻi outside of Niʻihau—they knew what the place-names meant. But there was also so much going on with the PKO. How you gonna stop and take time to break down the names, root word by root word, you know? And so there's a lot left to be interpreted.

We have this one ʻOhana member now, CJ Elizares, and he has genealogical connections to the ranchers at Honuaʻula. He lives on Maui, and he's motivated, not only as a Kanaka but as somebody whose kūpuna lived there. He's got to be a thirty-something, a younger guy, but his knowledge of *wahi pana* [storied places] on Kahoʻolawe—it just blows my mind!

TUTI: And does that come from listening to the kūpuna?

KALIKO: Yeah, we all are listening, reading, and walking the land. CJ has, along with other people like Syd Kawahakui, Attwood Makanani, and others. They have walked the entire island. They've walked through different districts. That's their research process—methodology, I guess—that they use to acquire their knowledge.

CANDACE: Yeah, I talked with CJ, and he studied botany and hydrology, so he has that academic background, but he applies that to what he sees on the ground as a KUA [a longtime PKO restoration crew member], a planter, and a fisherman. Every day, he's out on the water observing wind and cloud patterns and thinking about what they mean for planting on Kahoʻolawe.

TUTI: He's combining haole [foreign] science with kūpuna knowledge as he walks the land.

CANDACE: Yes, I think of the ways that all three of us have had the experience of walking the land at Kahoʻolawe, which has such a long history. I grew up on Maui, and I used to hear about the PKO as a kid. I remember a five-hundred pound bomb floated from the island to lands on Maui leased by Elmer Carvalho, who was mayor at the time. I used to think about how Hawaiians were fighting for the island when no other groups were, that they had a special connection to this land that those of us who aren't Hawaiian don't. Since then I've read so much about the 1976 landings, especially of the Kahoʻolawe Nine [Walter Ritte, Emmett Aluli, Ellen Miles, Karla Villalba, Steve Morse, Kimo Aluli, George Helm, Gail Kawaipuna Prejean, and Ian Lind] when the U.S. military was still bombing the island.

TUTI: I was living in the Pacific Northwest back then, and the news spread through the continental coconut wireless[4] about those crazy Hawaiians.

CANDACE: Yes, and I'm thinking about the fourth landing, when Walter Ritte and Richard Sawyer hid on the island for 35 days while the navy dropped bombs around them. They were constantly moving to seek cover, as Walter wrote in his journal at the time. They were later arrested and served six months in prison.[5] The 'Ohana never stopped standing for the protection of the island, and they are a large part of the reason why President George Bush stopped the bombing, not because it was the right thing to do but because the Republicans knew that the island meant a lot to Hawaiians, and they wanted to garner votes for the Republican congressional candidate Pat Saiki.[6]

TUTI: I have fond memories of helping my sister, Leilani Wilson, lay out the edition of the PKO newsletter announcing the stopping of the bombing. We celebrated even though we knew that the battle to save the island was not over.

Kahoʻolawe was the *kāhea* [calling] for me to return home. In the seventies, living on the continent, I experienced the uprising centered on Kahoʻolawe unfolding through the eyes of friends, especially my sister. And then in 1990, she got sick, and I came home to be with her. She'd been involved with the PKO for a few years. She went to Kahoʻolawe with a *hula hālau* [school of hula] and, like so many Hawaiians, was compelled by her cultural awakening to join PKO. She was a talented photographer and journalist, so she helped with the PKO newsletter. I shared in her passion and excitement for the movement, and when she was too sick, I would help her with the newsletter and take her to KUA meetings. And eventually I went on an access trip to Kahoʻolawe.[7] Walking that *ʻāina* really brought me back home.

In the 1990s I went on access about half a dozen times. Every access was accompanied by a navy EOD [explosive ordnance disposal] technician who gave us the obligatory lecture on live ordnance, which I took seriously, sort of. It was hard, though, to keep the very real possibility of setting off a bomb with an errant stumble in the front of my mind when on the island. I wanted to—needed to—walk the island. I remember walking the dusty, uninviting hardpan up to Moaʻulaiki and seeing the lone wiliwili tree along the way—

CANDACE: Yes! I saw that wiliwili tree! She's still there! We chanted, "E ulu ē," and made offerings to honor her. We also laid our hands on her.

KALIKO: She had seeds in November. She's gotta be two, three hundred years old, if not more.

Figure 16.1 Wiliwili tree on Kahoʻolawe, November 2022. Photo by Momi Wheeler.

Figure 16.2 A seed on the wiliwili tree, November 2022. Photo by Momi Wheeler.

TUTI: That is such good news! Back then, after the bombing stopped, that was the hope. The person leading the hike told us that there used to be a wiliwili forest at the top of the island. They were full of hope. "Someday," they told us, "she will give seeds." And look now—get seeds!

Back then most of us on access didn't know any chants or blessings. In the PKO, cultural practice was still *mohala aʻela* [unfolding like a flower].

KALIKO: Learning cultural practices on Kahoʻolawe is a lifelong project, right, a multigenerational project. I think that one of the most important things that George Helm and Emmet Aluli understood in the early days is that they had shortcomings in Hawaiian knowledge. They acknowledged that and embraced that, and until today, people like them, including Davianna McGregor, Craig Neff, and others, they all go back to check sources, and it's so important to *ʻimi naʻauao* [seek knowledge], *ʻimi noiʻi* [investigate], the endeavors that we have to go through just to be better stewards of the land. They consulted with Emma Defries, Sam Lono, Harry Mitchell, Parley Kanakaole, just to name a few.[8]

In 1993, Pua Kanakaʻole Kanahele and the Edith Kanakaʻole Foundation authored a report called *E Mau Ana ʻo Kanaloa*.[9] Later, in 2009, the foundation published *Kūkulu ke Ea o Kanaloa*, the cultural plan for the restoration of the island.[10] So research is at the *kahua* [foundation] of all that we do.

There's always this drive for us to understand our place, so much so that now ʻōlelo Hawaiʻi and fluency in traditional narratives and practices is required for Moʻo Lono [Lono priests] training. We are renewing our relationship with traditional knowledge.[11]

CANDACE: Yes, I'm thinking of the document *Kīhoʻihoʻi Kānāwai*, or the "laws of regeneration," as they have been described by Pualani Kanakaʻole Kanahele and her team of researchers at the Edith Kanakaʻole Foundation. They have been key to the restoration of places all over Hawaiʻi. The law of regeneration is all about renewing our relationships with the akua, the elements.

What is so important to me is the way that people like CJ Elizares have an intimate knowledge of the winds that they share with others. I learned so much from CJ on a huakaʻi to Kahoʻolawe with Kekuhi Kealiikanakaoleohaililani's land stewardship class, Hālau ʻŌhiʻa. As we were hiking up to Moaʻulanui and Moaʻulaiki, CJ asked us, "How do you know the path of the wind? You look at where the plants grow because the wind carries the seeds. On Kahoʻolawe, we are planting the ʻaʻaliʻi because of that ʻōlelo noʻeau: 'He ʻaʻaliʻi kū makani; ʻaʻohe makani nāna e kūlaʻi' [I am a wind-resisting ʻaʻaliʻi, no gale can push me over]."[12] This was an epithet for the people of Kaʻū, but it's also the epithet that the ʻOhana has taken for the people of Kanaloa

Kahoʻolawe and for the island itself, where the people must *kanu* [plant] those plants who stand strong in the face of powerful winds blowing away topsoil and, even worse, the bombing over the years. The ʻaʻaliʻi can survive the strongest of winds, the severest of drought, the bombing. So CJ shows us that the ʻaʻaliʻi seeds have papery wings, so when the winds blow, the seeds disperse.

CJ tells us, "Follow the ʻaʻaliʻi to know where the wind blows and the rain falls. And that's how you plant Native plants like naio above ground on a windblown island like Kahoʻolawe. We all know about the Nāulu wind and rain that come from Haleakalā that creates a cloud bridge to Kahoʻolawe, but Uncle Harry Mitchell reminds us that there are many, many, many different winds, 300 winds that hit Hālona Point, and you cannot just rely on the thinking that there is one dominant wind. He taught us that the winds will shift, and you have to be prepared for that."[13] On an island where you cannot dig into the ground to plant because 91 percent of the island hasn't been cleared of subsurface unexploded ordnance, you have to plant above ground, and so what happens to a lot of these seeds is they get caught in the crevices of the island, and that's where they take root. So the ʻOhana lays the irrigation lines where they see the ʻaʻaliʻi, and that was just so amazing to me because we are learning chants about birthing clouds, and the winds are critical to that birthing.

And how do you know what CJ knows unless you have an intimate knowledge of the island? Through CJ, I came to know and love the winds of Kahoʻolawe. And you see that hardpan [packed dirt]. And you realize, yeah, it's hard to grow things in that hardpan when the water just rolls off the surface of the earth. How do you green an island that has been so devastated?

KALIKO: To green the island, ceremony is so important because we need to ask the akua to come to the island. George Helm in all his wisdom and his connection to Lonoikamakahiki, sought counsel with our revered elders. Aunty Edith Kanakaʻole was adamant about bringing Makahiki back because what the island needed was Lono and what the lāhui needed was also Lono. The reason that the island needed Lono was for Lono's earthly body forms, *kino lau*, which include rain clouds and moisture, and those elemental phenomena that are necessary to regreening the ʻāina. To keep it simple, Lono is the god of Makahiki. All offerings made during Makahiki are offerings to Lono, and our offerings on Kahoʻolawe are intended to regreen the island.

The PKO consulted with Aunty Edith's daughter Kumu Hula [hula master] Nālani Kanakaʻole of Hālau o Kekuhi, and in 1982, the PKO conducted the first Makahiki ceremonies on the island. Nālani Kanakaʻole did the research and trained the first set of Moʻo Lono. She chose nine men as *kahu*, or "caretakers," of the Lono ceremonies, thus creating a genealogy of Lono practitioners.

TUTI: Kaliko, you are a part of that genealogy of Moʻo Lono. How long have you been at the helm of the Moʻo Lono on Kahoʻolawe?

KALIKO: Since 2003. Started training in 1993. ʻŪniki [graduation rites] was around 2000.

We are responsible for gathering the appropriate hoʻokupu [offerings], carrying out the ceremonies and properly reciting the incantations while maintaining the kapu, the sanctity and sacredness of our ceremonies.[14]

Regreening the island is dependent on water, and therefore, we continue to do Makahiki and will continue ā mau ā mau [forever and ever].

CANDACE: As Moʻo Lono, how do you call out to Lono?

KALIKO: During Makahiki, we feed Lono, and he brings his kino lau to regreen Kanaloa Moku. Our Makahiki on Kahoʻolawe is based on traditional accounts of Makahiki that Aunty Nālani adapted for our current needs. So we have nine prescribed hoʻokupu. The number nine is symbolic of the first nine who landed in Kūheia, Kahoʻolawe. Those offerings are the major kino lau of Lono. We erect an akua loa [a long god] to symbolize Lono's presence in our ceremonies. Lono, thus, presides over all that we do during Makahiki. It's our intention to appease Lono through our offerings and the akua loa is the conduit through which our mana [divine energy and power] flows to Lono.

TUTI: Isn't it the other way around, that Lono's mana flows to the people? You know manna from heaven...

KALIKO: Well... No, I don't, sorry. Mana, as we say, is minimally a concept that predates Christian contact.

Mana is reciprocal. I'm building off of the Hawaiian concept of religion: hoʻomana. The Christian ideology is that divine energy and power comes from God, but that's not what we believe. What we believe is that mana flows through all of us, and we must give mana, hoʻomana, to get mana. So our hope is that Lono reciprocates our mana-filled offerings to keep his kino lau on Kahoʻolawe so that Kahoʻolawe is once again greened. That's how we fulfill our kuleana [responsibility, privilege, purview]. Makahiki is a collective effort.

The island named Kanaloa is the island that brings Lono back to us and is itself a conduit of our connection to one another. Because we've had our religious practices stripped away from us through colonization and are reawakening our current practices based on traditional ways and customs, we are free to adapt for present ceremonial needs. It's important that the connection is made now, because we are a living people.

Only extinct people don't evolve.

As much as we try to hold on to tradition, precolonization ancestors adapted ceremonies for their needs, thus so should we, modern Kānaka Maoli, face the needs of today.

TUTI: I remember in all those legal proceedings where so many archaeologists testified that the PKO was just making things up when asked about religion and Kahoʻolawe.

CANDACE: Yes, the archaeologists reduced Kanaka Maoli practices of adaptation and survival to what they called, in academic terms, "the invention of culture," which the courts took up as something imaginary and opportunistic. According to Western courts, only precontact practices are "real," which doesn't allow for the vitality and thriving of living cultural practices.

KALIKO: Ultimately, that's racist. Simply stated, the American court attempted to deny the humanity of Kānaka Maoli by recruiting and hearing testimony that we, Kānaka Maoli, have no rights to evolve with the times. Thus, we are extinct.

TUTI: Kaliko, doesn't this have something to do with the -hoʻolawe part of the island's name.

KALIKO: Yes, that's the dual path of the word *hoʻolawe*. It doesn't have to only mean to subtract. It can also mean simply "to cause to bring, take, or transport." So Kahoʻolawe is a *kīpuka* [oasis] through which Kānaka Maoli reconnect to ʻāina and thus to akua, which requires ceremony because that's how we connect akua, ʻāina, and kānaka. Now we find ourselves in this reciprocating religious pattern where every year we walk the ʻāina in ceremony calling our akua, Lonoikamakahiki, to be present with us and bless the land with his kino lau: his rains, mists, dew, and so on.

TUTI: That's so beautiful.

CANDACE: Amazing and beautiful description of ceremony!

KALIKO: *Mahalo nui i nā kūpuna* [Thanks to the elders]! They bless us with what we know today.

TUTI: So what's the relationship between this reciprocating religious pattern and the ecological restoration practices that go on for the rest of the year?

KALIKO: We have to make good on what Lono provides. Therefore, we have water catchment systems on island. The Kahoʻolawe Island Reserve Commission (KIRC) donated two 2,500-gallon water tanks to the PKO.[15] These water catchment systems provide the water we need in Hakioawa, the PKO's base camp. There are other catchment systems on Kahoʻolawe that provide irrigation to other planting areas. Since 2021, the PKO has been planting in Hakioawa and using the reservoir water to nourish the plants, and we've seen a dramatic turnaround in the landscape of Hakioawa.

And the important thing is, it wasn't just Kānaka Maoli who were thinking about this. It's non-Kanaka too. It's the allies. Good allies come in with this technology, this filtration system. The filtered water in Hakioawa is far more *ʻono* [delicious] than the Maʻalaea hose water that we take over. Far more ʻono. You have to have a good filtration system because you can get real sick from water catchments, and you have to take care of them really well. It's those sorts of efforts in forging forward and creating abundance that make good on what Lono provides.

Right now, we have *ʻuala* [sweet potatoes] growing *ma uka* [in the upland]. Paul Higashino of the KIRC staff and longtime PKO member puts stones in the ruts—erosion furrows—creating *kīpuka* where dust gathers resulting in a fertile environment for growth. ʻUala have grown in these kīpuka to the size of my hand. Those ruts up mauka are fertile.

CANDACE: How do the ʻuala get water?

KALIKO: It's amazing! In the ruts, there aren't any irrigation lines. The moisture is simply caught in the wind. It's the moisture in the wind that feeds the ʻuala. Once in a while there is rain, but for the most part, the ʻuala are fed by the moisture in the wind.

Someday we will harvest the other hoʻokupu from Kahoʻolawe to feed Lono.

CANDACE: We have seen the abolition of the military on Kahoʻolawe, the *hoʻāla* [reawakening] of the island in ceremony, and the EAducation that gives the people hope in seeing the rising of the ʻāina and the kānaka.[16] So what decolonial futurity do you envision for Kahoʻolawe and for the lāhui?

KALIKO: Being able to feed the people on Kahoʻolawe with food grown on Kahoʻolawe and being able to make offerings to Lono from Kahoʻolawe with kino lau grown on Kahoʻolawe would be ideal goals to strive toward. That would be a good *hōʻailona* [sign] that the ʻāina is responding to the reciprocal relationship reestablished through ceremony.

This regreening is and will be symbolic of the reawakening of our lāhui, engaging our identity through practice, through self-awareness, through our humanity.

TUTI: A decolonial futurity is rooted in the work of our kūpuna that we carry forward. Kaliko, seeing you carry on, on Kahoʻolawe, I think about my *kaikuaʻana* [older sister of a female], your aunty Leilani. She really carried me to Kahoʻolawe. She was one of the many women who worked behind the scenes.

CANDACE: Yes, this reminds me, too, of Noelani Goodyear-Kaʻōpua's interviews with the women of the PKO in *Nā Wāhine Koa*, Loretta Ritte, Moanikeʻala Akaka, Maxine Kahaulelio, and Terrilee Kekoʻolani-Raymond, as well as the women like Davianna McGregor who write about Kahoʻolawe.[17]

TUTI: On one visit to Kahoʻolawe, I got to hang out with an unsung *wahine koa*. I even think her name was Wahine. We were having early morning coffee in the kitchen at Hakioawa, when some kids came running into camp shouting that there were guys taking ʻopihi down at the shore. We follow the kids to the cliffs above the bay, and there they are scraping ʻopihi off the rocks below. Wahine yelled at them that the ʻopihi were kapu [protected]. One of the guys yelled back, "It's for our baby lūʻau!" and she yells back, "OK, you can take one small bag for your baby lūʻau, and everything else you have to let go." She had so much authority that the guys did just that. Of course, now there is a pile of ʻopihi on the rocks. She told the kids, "Let's see how much ʻopihi we can put back—how many can survive." And I thought that is Kahoʻolawe justice. It's having compassion and not making those ʻopihi pickers into criminals. And it was a great lesson for the *keiki* [children], too, rescuing those ʻopihi.

KALIKO: Lessons are abundant on Kahoʻolawe. Whether coming from caregivers, elders, or peers, there are always lessons to be learned. Your *moʻopuna* [grandchild], Aunty Tuti, gets his name from our ceremonies on Kahoʻolawe. Kaipulaumakaniolono is a reference to the wind gourd of Lono. Those winds are the winds that carry the moisture in the air that feed many of the plants on island. Kaipulaumakaniolono's name came to me while in procession for Makahiki ceremony when my *wahine* [wife] was pregnant with him. Kaipu, as we call him, is now a young adult and is a Moʻo Lono and loves to compose and perform traditional chants.

On the day of Kūpau of Makaliʻi, November 30, 2022, we lost Noa Emmett ʻAuwae ʻĀluli, one of the first nine to land on Kahoʻolawe at Kūheia on January 4, 1976, the one who brought suit against the navy, which resulted in the consent decree, which guaranteed access to Kahoʻolawe for the PKO, one of the first nine Moʻo Lono to be trained in this modern era for Kahoʻolawe, the elder statesman of the PKO who guided the PKO and the KIRC to what it is today. Kaipu and I mourn how we know how to, through composition of *kūmākena* [laments]. I was present while Emmett's *kupapaʻu* [body] was prepared to be viewed at his *hoʻolewa* [funeral]. I did my *kūmākena* then, just Emmett and I. Kaipu came in later, and we, with a few others, kept watch over the kupapaʻu as people visited Emmett for the last time. Emmett loved Kaipu. He saw so much hope in him, as he did in many of the people he mentored through the PKO and his medical profession. As Emmett's cousins sang their last song and people sang along, we who were attending the kupapaʻu approached Emmett knowing that those were our final minutes with him. Kaipu was obviously emotional and began his kūmākena quietly. As the family's song ended and they realized that Kaipu was lamenting, a silence came over two hundred plus mourners gathered that day. Kaipu's voice got louder. He must have lamented for about ten minutes. Poetry, mele composed with purpose to honor his kupuna who was always there for him and all of us. The *kahu* [officiant] of the hoʻolewa, Luana Busby-Neff, came near as Kaipu was lamenting with tears in her eyes, and as Kaipu's kūmākena ended, she said, "Now the ceremony is *pau* [done]." We sang "Hawaiʻi Aloha," one final mele together to lighten and uplift our spirits.

Emmett knows that the efforts of the PKO and other endeavors of reindigenization, that is reclaiming our knowledge to reaffirm our Kanaka Maoli identity through practice, is being realized and will endure and persevere.

We are *kanaloa* [securely established, unconquerable].

NOTES

1. Kanaka Maoli is a common phrase for Native Hawaiian. Kānaka Maoli with the macron is the plural form. Kupuna and kūpuna used here function similarly in that kupuna (elder, ancestor) is singular and kūpuna is the plural form. Not all words function the same way.

2. For example, the Kumulipo is a *koʻihonua*, or "genealogical chant," chronicling the birth rite of Kalaninuiʻīamamao as chief and, in doing so, uses Kanaka epistemologies to illustrate the cosmology of Kānaka Maoli.

3. Pualani Kanakaʻole Kanahele defines *akua* as both "deity" and "elemental form" or "energetic" in Kanahele, *Ka Honua Ola*, 5.

4. By this we mean the informal communication networks in the diaspora.

5. Ritte and Sawyer, *Nā Manaʻo Aloha o Kahoʻolawe*.

6. Miller, "Bush Halts Kahoolawe Bombing."

7. Access to the island is restricted. In 1990 the PKO was the only organization allowed to bring people to the island, and access was granted by the navy. In 2003, control of access was passed to the state of Hawaiʻi.

8. For detailed discussion of cultural developments on Kahoʻolawe, see Kanahele, "Ke Au Lono i Kahoʻolawe"; McGregor, *Nā Kuaʻāina*, 249–285.

9. Edith Kanakaole Foundation, *E Mau Ana ʻo Kanaloa*.

10. Kanahele et al., *Kūkuku Ke Ea a Kanaloa*.

11. According to Kelou Kamakau in Fornander's Puke IV, there were eight major *kāhuna* (priest) types. They were ranked in order. Moʻo Kū, or those dedicated to the order of Kū, were first. The second were the Moʻo Lono. Fornander, *Account of the Polynesian Race*.

12. ʻŌlelo Noʻeau #507, in Pukui, *ʻŌlelo Noʻeau*, 60.

13. Christopher John Elizares interview, Puakalani, October 31, 2022.

14. Edith Kanakaole Foundation, *E Mau Ana o Kanaloa*, 50. See also Protect Kahoʻolawe ʻOhana; and McGregor, *Nā Kuaʻāina*, 249–285.

15. KIRC is a governmental organization that manages the Kahoʻolawe Island Reserve. Kaliko served as a commissioner from 2011 to 2018 (https://www.kahoolawe.hawaii.gov/home.php).

16. Leilani Basham and Noelani Goodyear-Kaʻōpua have discussed the term *ea* as meaning "life," "breath," and "a rising," the rising of the people for political independence. Kahoʻokahi Kanuha came up with the term *EAducation* to describe a new kind of education in political independence for children, young people—for all people in Hawaiʻi. For a discussion of EAducation, see Kanuha, quoted in Fujikane, *Mapping Abundance*, 135–136.

17. Goodyear-Kaʻōpua, *Nā Wāhine Koa*; McGregor, *Nā Kuaʻāina*.

BIBLIOGRAPHY

Edith Kanakaʻole Foundation. *E Mau Ana o Kanaloa, Hoʻi Hou: "The Perseverance of Kanaloa, Return!" The Cultural Practices and Values Established at Kanaloa/Kahoʻolawe Past and Present*. Kahoʻolawe Island Conveyance Commission consultant report no. 12. Accessed December 26, 2022. http://www.kahoolawe.hawaii.gov/KICC/12%20E%20MAu%20Ana%20O%20Kanaloa%20Ho%27i%20Hou.pdf.

Elizares, Christopher John. Interview. Pukalani, October 31, 2022.

Fornander, Abraham. *An Account of the Polynesian Race; Its Origins and Migrations, and the Ancient History of the Hawaiian People to the Times of Kamehameha I*. Rutland, VT: C. E. Tuttle, 1969.

Fujikane, Candace. *Mapping Abundance for a Planetary Future: Kanaka Maoli and Critical Settler Cartographies in Hawaiʻi*. Durham, NC: Duke University Press, 2021.

Goodyear-Kaʻōpua, Noelani, ed. *Nā Wāhine Koa: Hawaiian Women for Sovereignty and Demilitarization*. Honolulu: University of Hawaiʻi Press, 2018.

Kanahele, Pualani Kanakaʻole. *Ka Honua Ola: ʻEliʻeli Kau Mai / The Living Earth: Descend, Deepen the Revelation*. Kamehameha, 2011.

———. "Ke Au Lono i Kahoʻolawe (The Era of Lono at Kahoʻolawe, Returned)." *Mānoa* 7, no. 1 (Summer 1995): 152–167.

Kanahele, Pualani Kanakaʻole, Huihui Kanahele Mossman, Ann Kalei Nuʻuhiwa, and Kaumakaiwapo ʻohalahiʻipaka Kealiʻikanakaʻole. *Kūkuku Ke Ea a Kanaloa: The Culture Plan for Kanaloa Kahoʻolawe*. Edith Kanakaʻole Foundation, 2009.

McGregor, Davianna. *Nā Kuaʻāina: Living Hawaiian Culture*. Honolulu: University of Hawaiʻi Press, 2007.

Miller, Ken. "Bush Halts Kahoolawe Bombing." *Honolulu Star Bulletin*, October 22, 1990.

Protect Kahoʻolawe ʻOhana. "Home." Accessed October 28, 2024. http://www.protectkahoolaweohana.org/.

Pukui, Mary Kawena. *ʻŌlelo Noʻeau: Hawaiian Proverbs and Poetical Sayings*. Bernice P. Bishop Museum special publication no. 71. Honolulu, Hawaii: Bishop Museum, 1983.

Ritte, Walter, and Richard Sawyer. *Nā Manaʻo Aloha o Kahoʻolawe: Hawaiʻi Warriors Love for Land and Culture*. 2nd ed. Aloha ʻĀina o Nā Kūpuna, 2022.

Contributors

Sean Johnson Andrews is Associate Professor in the School of Communication and Culture at Columbia College, Chicago, and is author of *The Cultural Production of Intellectual Property Rights* (Temple University Press, 2019).

C. M. Kaliko Baker is assistant professor at the Kawaihuelani Center for Hawaiian Language at the University of Hawai'i at Mānoa.

Mary Tuti Baker is assistant professor in comparative Indigenous studies at Western Washington University.

James Bliss is visiting assistant professor of communication at Tulane University.

Robert F. Carley is associate professor of international affairs at Texas A&M University, College Station, and author of *The Cultural Production of Social Movements*, *Cultural Studies Methodology and Political Strategy*, and *Culture and Tactics*.

Jorge E. Cuéllar is assistant professor of Latin American, Latino, and Caribbean Studies at Dartmouth College.

John R. Decker is associate professor at the School of Information at Pratt Institute.

Brian Dolber is associate professor of communication and media studies at California State University, San Marcos, and co-author of *The Gig Economy: Workers and Media in the Age of Convergence*.

Anne Donlon is an independent scholar.

CONTRIBUTORS

Evyn Lê Espiritu Gandhi is associate professor of Asian American studies at the University of California, Los Angeles, and is author of *Archipelago of Resettlement: Vietnamese Refugee Settlers and Decolonization across Guam and Israel-Palestine*.

Candace Fujikane is professor of English at the University of Hawai'i at Mānoa and is author of *Mapping Abundance for a Planetary Future: Kanaka Maoli and Critical Settler Cartographies in Hawai'i*.

Alexis Pauline Gumbs is a 2023 Windham-Campbell Prize winner in Poetry and 2022 Whiting Award winner and is author of *Survival Is a Promise: The Eternal Life of Audre Lorde*.

Chris Hall is assistant professor of English at the University of the Ozarks and author of a book project in progress on race, gender, species, and the biopolitics of global modernism.

Beenash Jafri is assistant professor of gender, sexuality, and women's studies at the University of California, Davis, and author of *Settler Attachments and Asian Diasporic Film*.

Anna Karthika is a candidate of the Interdisciplinary PhD Programme in Social Studies at the Makerere Institute of Social Research.

Manu Karuka is associate professor of American studies at Barnard College and author of *Empire's Tracks: Indigenous Nations, Chinese Workers, and the Transcontinental Railroad*.

Laura J. Kwak is associate professor of socio-legal studies at York University.

Eero Laine is associate professor and chair of the Theatre and Dance Department at the University at Buffalo, State University of New York, and coauthor of *Mourning the Ends: Collaborative Writing and Performance*.

Rachel Haejin Lim is assistant professor of Asian American studies in the Department of Ethnic Studies at California State University, Sacramento.

Najwa Mayer is Society of Fellows postdoctoral scholar at Boston University.

Kyle Mays is professor of African American studies, American Indian studies, and history at UCLA and is author of *City of Dispossessions: Indigenous Peoples, African Americans, and the Creation of Modern Detroit*.

Andrew Ó Baoill is lecturer in the School of English, Media and Creative Arts at University of Galway.

Yumi Pak is associate professor of Black studies at Occidental College.

Therí A. Pickens is the Charles A. Dana Professor of English and Africana at Bates College and author of *New Body Politics* (Routledge 2014) and *Black Madness :: Mad Blackness* (Duke 2019). Her debut poetry collection is *What Had Happened Was* (Duke 2025).

SAJ is an independent scholar and associate editor at Punctum Books.

Sami Schalk is associate professor in the Department of Gender and Women's Studies at University of Wisconsin–Madison and author of *Bodyminds Reimagined: (Dis)ability, Race, and Gender in Black Women's Speculative Fiction*.

Leanne Betasamosake Simpson is an independent academic, writers and musician, She is the author of eight books including *As We Have Always Done: Indigenous Freedom through Radical Resistance*. Leanne is a member of Alderville First Nation.

Chris Alen Sula is associate provost for academic affairs and associate professor at Pratt Institute.

Tia Trafford is reader in philosophy and design at University for the Creative Arts (London) and author of *Everything is Police* and *The Empire at Home: Internal Colonies and the End of Britain*.

Index

Abolition, 9–10; of gender, 23, 26; of matriliny, 97–99, 102 (*see also* Matriliny); of police and military, 144, 233 (*see also* Police violence)

Access Living, 89

African American activist groups: Black Maoists, 202; Black Panther Party for Self-Defense, 64, 202. *See also* Black Lives Matter (BLM); Movement for Black Lives

African American Motion Picture, 200; *Da 5 Bloods*, 199–205, 209; *Lovecraft Country*, 199–201, 205–209

Afro-Asian: futurity, 207–208; media, 199–200, 203–207, 209; solidarity, 199–209; relations during Cold War, 200–209

Afro-Indigenous, 32, 212, 214. *See also* Cultural appropriation

Agamben, Giorgio, 22, 25–26; *Work: Where Are We Now?*, 22

Ahmad, Aijaz, 49–53

Aloha ʻĀina, 223, 226, 230, 232–233

Aluli, Emmett, Kahoʻolawe Nine, 226, 228, 234–235. *See also* Kahoʻolawe Nine

Amazon, 120, 125, 174

American Century, 200

American dream, 201

Anishinaabe Nation, practices, 33, 36, 39

Anti-Asian. *See* Asian: xenophobia and violence

Anti-Black: ideology, origins of, 72, 142, 179, 200; policing, 70–71; politics, 160, 163; violence, 26, 69–71, 74, 76–77 (*see also* Police violence)

Anticolonial, 51; feminism, 100; nationalism, 50; social movements, 137, 212, 215. *See also* Decolonization

Anti-Fascist, struggle, 50, 53. *See also* Fascism

Anti-imperial: futurity, 200; nationalism, 51; neoliberalism, 51; politics, 201, 203, 205

Anti-Indigenous, 219. *See also* Indigenous: violence

Anti-racism, 174, 191; activism, 175, 199–200; education, 82; politics, 163, 174

Anti-trans. *See* Transgender: anti-trans violence

Apocalypse, 82, 87, 183–184

Arab Spring, 123–124; liberation technology, 183–186, 190

Arbery, Ahmaud, murder of, 199

Asian: American identity, 199, 209; class struggle, 50; media, 207; women, 203, 208; xenophobia and violence, 199–200, 205. *See also* Afro-Asian

Assimilation, of immigrants, 44, 208
Authoritarian populism, 51, 116

Babri Masjid, demolition of, 48, 50
Bambara, Toni Cade: writing, 156–158, 160, 162, 167; Works: *The Sea Birds Are Still Alive*, 157–159, 162–164; *The Salt Eaters*, 164–165, 168
Banana Republic, 107–108; Capitol Riot, 107–108, 111, 115; racialized contexts, 107–109, 113–117; term, origin of, 109; U.S. political culture, 107–113, 115. *See also* Big Lie; Capitol Riot
Banana Wars, 108
Bartleby the Scrivener (Melville), 59–60, 66
Biden, Joe, Capitol Riot response, 111, 140; 2020 presidential election, 140, 200, 209
Big Lie, 108
Big Tech, 124. *See also* Amazon, Social media; Surveillance; Technology
Biopolitics, 22–24, 26–28, 163
Biopower, 22–23, 26
Black America, 200–202
Black and queer, 59, 82–83, 85, 205; literature, 57, 59–60, 65; family formation, 207–208; feminism, 206, 207–209; media representation, 205, 207–209
Black disability: ableism, 84; activism, 81, 83–85, 89–90; pandemic, 88
Black Disability Politics (Sami), 84
Black Feminism, 40; perspectives from, 156–157, 203, 209, 216; political resistance/liberation, 201–202
Black freedom: historic efforts for, 202; politics, 84; struggle, 122
Black Lives Matter (BLM): critique of, 171–172, 174, 180; 2020 pandemic protests, 127–128, 143, 174
Black Madness . : : Mad Blackness (Pickens), 84
Black Maoists, 202
Blackness: biopower as and beyond, 23–24; and colonial modernity, 75; historical studies on, 72, 74, 75; and transness, 24
Black Panther Party for Self-Defense, 64, 202
Black protest, 122; Brixton Uprising, 71. *See also* Black Lives Matter (BLM): 2020 protests
Black Trans Feminism, 26

Blind Man with a Pistol (Himes), 58, 60
Bolshevik Revolution. *See* World War I
Bourgeoisie: rise of, 47; conservatism, 49, 52
Brixton Uprising, 71. *See also* Police: reform; 1999 Macpherson Report
Broadcasting, threat to middle class, 121, 128
Burney-Scott, Omisade, 38
Bush, George W., Jr., 110, 114
Bush, George W., Sr., 226
Butler, Judith, 171, 178
Butler, Octavia E., 82, 86–87. Work: *Parable of the Sower, Parable of the Talents*, 82

Capitalism, 166; crisis of, 20, 22, 45, 141; exploitation from, 25; global, 22, 162; governance, 22, 25, 108, 167; monopoly, 47, 121; and imperialism, 149; racial, 157, 160, 163, 167–168, 202
Capitol Riot, 115–116, 140; global response, 109, 112–113; motivations of, 146; planning of, 189–191; U.S. political response, 140. *See also* Extremism; United States Elections: 2020 Presidential
Care networks. *See* Crip doula-ing
Chakrabarty, Dipesh: writing, 48–49, 95–96. Work: *Postcoloniality and the Artifice of History*, 48
Chauvin, Derek, 76, 120. *See also* Floyd, George: murder of
Chronopolitics, 70, 74
Class mobility, 124
Class struggle, 43, 46, 52–53; interpretations of, 46–47; South Asian, 50
Climate crisis, 32, 34, 36–39, 82, 222
Cold War, 43, 46, 108; Asia, 204–205; Black American involvement in, 200–202; representation in media, 205–206, 209
Collectivism, 40, 160; rejection of, 45 (*see also* Individualism)
Colonialism: function of, 35, 215; imperial, 113; justification for, 72. *See also* Decolonization; Settler colonialism
Colonial modernity. *See* Colonialism; Racial Temporality
Combahee River Collective, 179, 202, 216
Communism, defeat of, 44, 51
Cosmopolitanism, 49, 73
Counterextremism, 138, 145; approach to, 146–147; and Capitol Rioters, 146, 148; Department of Homeland Security, 145; racial, religious targeting, 139, 145. *See*

also September 11 terror attacks; Surveillance: anti-Muslim
Counterterrorism, 138, 145; policy, 143; racial, religious targeting, 139, 145. *See also* September 11 terror attacks; Surveillance: anti-Muslim
COVID-19 pandemic, catastrophe of, 20, 23; governance, 120; health, 88–89, 199; labor and economy, 124–126, 199; social tensions, 121, 128
Crip doula-ing, 88–89; as care network, 90
Crisis of legitimacy, 109
Crusades, modern extremist inspiration from, 141, 146
Cultural appropriation, 214–219; Playing Indian, 214, 216

Da 5 Bloods (Lee), 199–205, 209
Darker Nations, The (Prashad), 158
Davis, Angela, 8–9, 202
Decolonization, 7–8, 96, 215, 219; culture after, 163, 215, 219; of gender, 97, 102–103; and futurity, 233; radicalism after, 50–51
Dehistoricizing: gendered bodies, 96, 100; and depoliticizing, 147
Derrida, Jacques, 26–28
Disability, 83–91; communities, 89–90; justice, 86; literature, 84
Disability doula-ing, 88–89; as care network, 90
Disinformation, 187–188

Ecotone, as ecology, 33, 36
Eco-Tones (art project), 34
Edith Kanaka'ole Foundation, 228–229
Elders, role of, 38; intergenerational sharing and, 36–40; Indigenous, 42
Ellison, Ralph, *The Invisible Man*, 177
End of History, The (Fukuyama), 47–48
Episto-ontological, identity, 173
Ethnonationalism, 149; ideals of, 110; United States, culture of, 111 (*see also* Capitol Riot); and religious supremacy, 51, 141, 148 (*see also* under Indian). *See also* Extremism
Eurocentric: enlightenment, 49; history, modernity, 96, 102–103; ideals, 48–49, 100; universalism, 95–97, 100–101
Extremism, 148; Far Right groups, 138, 189; media treatment of, 140; and systemic racism, 151n59; susceptibility to, 188, 191

Family structure, 207, 209; Black, 71; colonial influence on, 100, 205; and kinship, 97–98, 201; multicultural, 201
Fanon, Frantz: insights of, 73–75, 177, 215; literary references to, 177–178. Work: *Wretched of the Earth*, 215
Fascism, rise of, 51; and class struggle, 51, 141; as nationalism, 50, 141–142, 149; Hindu, 51; Italian, 46, 50
Fatalism, through progress, 76–77. *See also* Racialized temporality
Federal Housing Authority, early actions of, 122
Floyd, George, murder of, 76; global response and protest to, 120, 127, 143, 174, 199. *See also* Black Lives Matter (BLM): 2020 protests
Fraser, Nancy: counterpublics, 176–177; progressive neoliberalism, 124, 172–173; writing, 25, 124, 174
French Revolution, conservatism and class, 49
Friedman, Milton, 45–46. Works: *Free to Choose*, 45; *Why Government Is the Problem*, 45
Fukuyama, Francis: arguments of, 43–44, 46; critique and related literature, 46–48. Work: *The End of History*, 47–48
Futurity: modernity and, 70, 72; decolonial, 233

Gallagher, Mike, 110
Gathara, Patrick, use of political cartoons, 112
Global North, 70
Global South, 96, 102, 115. *See also* Third World
Gopinath, Gayatri, 99
Gramsci, Antonio: argument/insights, 12, 20, 43–44, 46–50, 58, 109–110; influence of, 25, 47–49, 51–52; writing, 27–28, 44, 144
Great Compression, 121
G7, 44
Gunboat Diplomacy, 108

Haaland, Deb, 213
Hall, Stuart, 13, 48, 200, 216
Harlem Detective Series (Himes), 58, 60
Harriet Tubman Collective, 89
Health care system: access to, 88, 174; collapse of, 88, 90; critiques of, 120, 125

Hegel, G. F. W., 72–75
Helm, George, Kahoʻolawe Nine, 226, 228, 230
Heteronormative: gender formation, 96–97, 99, 102, 104n43; marriage and family structure, 97, 100, 201–202, 205, 208–209
High Brahminism, 49
Himes, Chester: life, 64, 66; unfinished and posthumous work, 60–63; writing, 58–64. Works: *Blind Man with a Pistol*, 58, 60; *Harlem Detective Series*, 58, 60; *If He Hollers Let Him Go*, 58; *My Life of Absurdity*, 57–58; *Negro Martyrs are Needed*, 63–64; *Plan B*, 58, 60–64, 66; *The Quality of Hurt*, 57–58; *Tang*, 60, 64–66
Hindutva, 48–50; concerns of, extremism, 51, 141, 148
Historicism, 95
Historico-politics, 115
Housing, government interventions, 122, 159

Idle No More movement, 214
If He Hollers Let Him Go (Himes), 58
Imperialism: conquest, 72, 113; liberal, 50, 99; triumphalism, 44, 51, 74; United States, 108, 115, 117, 148, 200; Western, knowledge production, 96, 102, 147. *See also* Universalism: European
Indian: class struggle, 50; colonization, 97, 99–102 (*see also* Matriliny: abolition of); ethnonationalism, 49–51, 54n34; social class, 51, 99–101, 103n9
Indian Child Welfare Act (ICWA), 213
Indigenous: history, 39, 218, 223; popular culture and media, 213–217; sovereignty, 218; violence, 143, 149, 223
Indigenous peoples: Alderville First Nation, 33; Saponi Nation, 34; Shinnecock Nation, 34. *See also* Anishinaabe; Kanaka Maoli
Individualism, 122; care networks, 89; and consumption, 123; Western culture of, 45, 122
Infinite postponement, 75–77
Intercommunalism, 202
Interim, 59
Intersectional: analysis, 201–201; failed attempts of, 59; identity politics, 216–217; organizing, 12, 124
Interstitial spaces, 33

Jim Crow, 50, 62
Johnson, Boris, 76

Kaba, Mariame, abolitionist ideology of, 144
Kahoʻolawe, bombing of, 223, 226, 229; political motivations of, 226. *See also* Protect Kahoʻolawe ʻOhana
Kahoʻolawe Nine, 226. *See also under specific names*
Kanaka Maoli, practices of, 222–223, 231–232, 235
Kant, Immanuel, racial philosophy of, 72–74
Keraleeya Sugunabodhini, public statement of, 101
Khōra, as receptacle/in between, 24–26, 28
Kīhoʻihoʻi Kānāwai, 229
Kina Gchi Nishnaabeg-ogamig, 33, 36
King, Martin Luther, Jr., *Beyond Vietnam*, 202
Korean War, 201, 206; in media, 205–206, 208–209
Kūpuna, 223, 225, 233

Labor, issues in, 163; front-line workers, 88, 120–121, 126, 128; globalization, 110, 122; laws, 124; women and, 125, 173; worker exploitation, 121, 159, 161, 174
Labor shortages, 120, 125
Laclau, Ernesto, 46–47. Works: *Dislocation and Capitalism, Social Imaginary and Democratic Revolution*, 47
Latin Americanization, concern of, 113, 116
Law of Regeneration, 229
Lawrence, Stephen, murder of, 69–71
Liberalism: critique of, 44, 71, 147; and consumerism, 44, 47; racialized, 141–142; threats to, 44; Western, 44, 142
Liminal space, 38
Lorde, Audre, 35, 41
Lovecraft Country, 199–201, 205–209

Macpherson Report (1999), 71, 76
Mahila Mandiram, public statement of, 101
Malabar Marriage Act, 98–99. *See also* Matriliny: abolition of
Malatino, Hil, 5–7, 26–27, 59, 66, 180, 201
Man Who Lived Underground, The (Wright), 23–25
Mapping Abundance for a Planetary Future: Kanaka Maoli and Critical Settler

INDEX / 245

Cartographies in Hawai'i (Fujikane), 223–224
Martin, Trayvon, murder of, 176. *See also* Black Lives Matter (BLM): 2020 protests
Marxist dude-bro, 216
Masculinist, 50, 114, 205
Masculinity, Black, 66; hyper and toxic, 202–203
Materialism, 4, 6, 12, 81, 128, 172; and financial capital, 109, 159, 167; history of, 43, 52
Matriliny: abolition of, 97, 99, 102; colonial modernity, 98–99, 101; familial structure, 97–98, 100; sexual freedom, 98
McLuhan, Marshall. *See* Technology: and determinism
#MeToo Movement, 171, 176, 180
Michi Saagiig Nishnaabe. *See* Anishinaabe Nation
Milbern, Stacey Park, 88–89. *See also* Crip doula-ing
Misinterpellated Subject, The (Martel), 177
Mobile privatization, protest and praxis, 127
Monroe Doctrine, 107–109
Morrison, Toni, 63. Work: *Playing in the Dark: Whiteness and the Literary Imagination*, 63
Moten, Fred, 21, 25–26, 28–29, 87
Mouffe, Chantal, 46; and Ernesto Laclau, 46–47. Works: *Feminism, Citizenship, and Radical Democratic Politics*, 47; *Post-Marxism without Apologies*, 46
Movement for Black Lives, 85–86, 199–200, 203. *See also* Black Lives Matter (BLM)
Multiculturalism, 200–201; liberal, 147, 209; resistance of, 184; and secularism, 147, 149
My Life of Absurdity (Himes), 57–58

Nationalism: anti-imperialist, 51; Radical, 51; United States culture of, 109, 114, 116, 147. *See also* Ethnonationalism
Nation-state, 50, 102; features of, 147; postcolonial, 102, 116; radicalism, 116, 140–141
Natural order, theory of, 73
Negro Martyrs are Needed (Himes), 63–64
Neoliberalism, 161; crisis of, 124, 144, 157; labor and mobility, 121, 123–124, 167; progressive, 124, 172–173; and racial capitalism, 157, 160, 163, 166–167

Newsom, Gavin, COVID-19 response, 120
Nonintersectional. *See* Intersectional: failed attempts of

O. Henry (William Sydney Porter), 110, 112–113. *See also* Banana Republic: term, origin of

Pacific Century, 200
Palestine, 138, 202, 209
Pandemic. *See* COVID-19 pandemic
Patriarchalism, 25
Peoples Power Assemblies NYC, 85
periodicity, 10–12, 51, 82
Plan B (Himes), 58, 60–64, 66
Playing in the Dark: Whiteness and the Literary Imagination (Morrison), 63
Poiesis, 73
Police: British, 69–71; reform, 70–71, 77, 120, 149; response to racism, 70–71; use of technology, 188–189
Police violence, 23, 143; protest of, 76, 127, 143; visibility of, 200. *See also* Taylor, Breonna, murder of; Prude, David, murder of; Floyd, George, murder of
Political stratum, 110
Political struggle, 43
"Postcoloniality and the Artifice of History" (Chakrabarty), 48
Pride month, 82
Protect Kahoʻolawe ʻOhana (PKO), 223–227, 229–235. *See also* Kahoʻolawe, bombing of
Prude, David, murder of, 199
Putin, Vladimir, 189

QAnon, 141, 188, 190; and Capitol Riot, 190; religious affiliation, 141; rise of, 188
Quality of Hurt, The (Himes), 57–58
Queer temporality, 65

Racial capitalism. *See* Capitalism: racial
Racialized temporality, 70, 72; Black stasis, 70, 74, 77; and colonial modernity, 70–71, 75–77; progress, 71–72, 77
Racism: fears of, 175; institutional, 71, 76, 172. *See also* Anti-Black; Anti-Asian; Anti-Indigenous
Radical resurgence, 215
Religio-racialized, nationalism, 137–142, 149. *See also* Ethnonationalism

Reservation Dogs, 213–214
Resistance, political, 22, 184, 191
Ritchie, Andrea, 144

Salt Eaters, The (Bambara), 164–165, 168
Sandberg, Sheryl, 173
Sea Birds Are Still Alive, The (Bambara), 157–159, 162–164
September 11 terror attacks, 123; counterterrorism policy after, 138, 143–149
Settler colonialism, 142, 212; aftermath of, 218; ambitions of, 213, 222; and Indigenous resurgence, 213, 215, 218–219
Sewell Report, 76–77
Simpson, Betasamosake Leanne, 214–215. Work: *Islands of Decolonial Love*, 40, 42
Skepticism, 27, 52; misinformation from, 123, 126. *See also* under Social media: disinformation
Slavery: modern comparisons to, 69, 178–179; rationalizations for, 72–74, 142; U.S. Transatlantic, 70, 202
Social arrangement, of Nair households, 98
Socialism, political vision of, 25, 44
Social media: disinformation, 187–188; for political organizing, 123, 176, 189–191 (*see also* Technology, liberation); as social infrastructure, 90; sting operations, 188
Social reproduction theory, 173, 178
Sociohistorical, 102, 113
Sociopolitical reactionary practices, 97, 175, 209
Socio-structural, 81
Sovereign: new, order, 25, 158; via Khōra, 25–26; break of, Western state, 21, 144; biopolitical, issues/order, 22, 26–27, 140; conditions of, communities, 144, 159–160, 213
Spatiotemporality, 70, 96
Stasis: anti-Black violence, 71, 76–77; and fatalism, 77; progress, 71, 77
Stop WOKE Act, 175
Structural adjustment, 157–159, 162, 167; financialization, 158, 167
Surveillance: anti-Muslim, 138, 145, 149; capitalism, 187; as suppression, 127, 185, 189; technologies, 125–126, 189

Tang (Himes), 60, 64–66
Taylor, Breonna, murder of, 199; protest response, 127. *See also* Black Lives Matter (BLM): 2020 protests
Technology, 123–125, 128; Big Tech, 124; liberation, 183–186, 190–191; technological determinism, 128; techno-optimism, 185. *See also* Big Tech; Surveillance
Television, series, Indigenous themes, 213
Temporality, 4–6, 61, 81–86; as linear writing, 61; pace and speed, 85–86; queer temporality, 65; spatiotemporality, 70, 96; time, 81–84. *See also* Racialized temporality
Third World: historical perspectives of, 44; political behavior, 109, 158; relationship to West, 112, 116–117, 202
Trans activism, 59, 180
Transantagonism, 23
Transness, 24, 59, 174; anti-trans violence, 23, 26; disidentification, 26; liberation and rights, 23, 180
Trump, Donald: 2016 presidential campaign, 138, 172; 2020 presidential campaign, 20, 108, 112; Capitol Riot, 108–109, 112–113, 116, 140 (*see also* Capitol Riot); critique of, 20, 114; rise of ethno-nationalism, 108–109, 114, 116, 138, 141–142, 200; socio-political influence of, 112–113, 114, 116, 138
Tufekci, Zeynep, 184
Tulsa Massacre, 205

Undrowned: Black Feminist Lessons from Marine Mammals (Gumbs), 36
United States: capital advantages of, 108–109; empire building, 111, 114, 141–142; international opinions of, 109, 112; liberalism, 50, 122, 142; political culture within, 45, 109–111, 126, 187; social safety net/public goods, 161
United States Elections: 2016 Presidential, 138, 173; 2020 Presidential, 140, 209
Universalism: European, 44, 95–97, 100–101 (*see also* Eurocentric: universalism); Western, 43

Vietnam War, 201; films, 200, 202–204, 208

War on Terror, 145, 149; counterterrorism, 145. *See also* Counterterrorism; September 11 terror attacks; Surveillance: anti-Muslim

Weinstein, Harvey, 176

White supremacy, 139; extremism and rise of, 113–114, 116, 138, 146–147; ideology of, 199; language and ideology, 109, 199; organizations, 142. *See also* Capitol Riot; Extremism: Far Right groups; Racism

Williams, Raymond, 13; privatization/theory, 121, 125–128

Wokeness, 174–176

World Powers. *See* G7

World War I, 51

Wretched of the Earth (Fanon), 215

Wynter, Sylvia, 35

www.ingramcontent.com/pod-product-compliance
Lightning Source LLC
LaVergne TN
LVHW051930060925
820435LV00014B/92